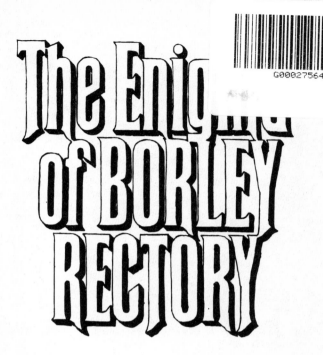

The Enigma of BORLEY RECTORY

•

IVAN BANKS

•

WITH AN INTRODUCTION BY

TOM PERROT

CHAIRMAN OF THE GHOST CLUB

•

foulsham

LONDON • NEW YORK • TORONTO • SYDNEY

foulsham
The Publishing House
Bennetts Close, Cippenham, Berks SL1 5AP, England

ISBN 0–572–02162–3

Typeset in Great Britain by Typesetting Solutions, Slough, Berks.
Printed in Great Britain by St Edmundsbury Press Ltd.,
Bury St Edmunds, Suffolk

CONTENTS

FOREWORD

BY TOM PERROTT

CHAIRMAN OF THE GHOST CLUB (FOUNDED 1862)

The alleged haunting of Borley Rectory has probably inspired more people to express their views on this highly controversial subject than upon any similar case in the long history of Psychical Research, and despite the fact that the rather ugly Victorian building was almost completely destroyed by a somewhat mysterious fire in 1939, the interest in this house of mysteries has continued over the years, unabated.

Unfortunately the site of the former rectory upon which new buildings have since been erected, is now rapidly beginning to resemble an impregnable fortress, as a result of the defences erected by its present occupants who feel such action is necessary to combat the depredations wreaked upon them by the legions of over-enthusiastic 'ghost hunters'.

But why has this intolerable situation been inflicted upon the honest inhabitants of this small Essex village?

In this fascinating re-examination of the case regarding the internationally known 'England's Most Haunted House', the author has been able to carry out exhaustive and thorough research over many years. He now offers some startling new thoughts on the history and causes of the phenomena and provides a controversial yet intriguing solution to the identity of the mysterious 'Nun of Borley'.

Many ghostly legends, some of which probably originated in the Middle Ages, contain certain recurring themes of jilted lovers, seduced chambermaids, eloping monks and nuns, headless figures and phantom coaches. A number of these tales may have some factual bases, in that religious establishments containing more than their quota of frustrated inmates, might have been found in the areas in question, and an array of coaches might have regularly been seen driving in a heedless manner into the darkness of the night, the night in which a myriad of unexpected dangers might have lurked and lain in wait for the hapless traveller.

A number of stories of this sort must have played a part in helping compound the Borley mythology and it is not difficult to imagine how persons visiting Borley for the first time, might have had previous knowledge of many of these legends, and could have pre-programmed themselves into believing that the house which they were to enter for the first time, was quite capable of manufacturing inexplicable phenomena in their presence.

These suppositions on my part, in an effort to rationalise upon the alleged Borley manifestations, are in no way meant to detract from the fact that many strange occurrences appear to have taken place there, which cannot simply be swept away in the light of sweet reason. It so often happens that over-zealous 'ghost hunters' are more likely to jump to supernatural conclusions which to the disciplined investigator are often more than useless.

This present volume, probably the most comprehensive of its kind so far produced, presents the whole Borley story in its entirety and it is for the reader to draw their own conclusions regarding this most enigmatic of sagas by drawing upon the information given, to form a balanced opinion.

In this book, the reader may examine the architecture of the famous building and its surroundings and perhaps discover for himself the possible areas from which the notorious nun might have manifested. He can also make the acquaintance of many of the leading personalities who played their varying roles there.

I am constantly receiving evidence of the fact that even in the very materialistic world in which we are living at the present time, the interest in ghosts, psychic investigations and the study of seemingly inexplicable phenomena is very much on the increase. I feel that this detailed and sometimes microscopic research can only provoke more serious interest into the whole field of psychical research, and it is hoped, create a new atmosphere of acceptance of aspects of the paranormal.

It is not difficult to imagine that in the conditions of this nature, the fascination of Borley rectory and its phantoms, will continue to stimulate the interests of genuine psychical researchers, inquisitive 'ghost busters' and the healthily curious for many years to come.

The author is to be congratulated on his remarkable achievement of being able, in such an excellent fashion, to re-assess the evidence and to offer such an unusual solution to be considered by all those intrigued by the enigma of Borley.

Tom Perrott
Chairman of The Ghost Club

ACKNOWLEDGEMENTS

It is an often levelled criticism that authors produce far too long a list of acknowledgements to those who have contributed to the production of some great tome or other, but it is most certainly the case that this book would have been unlikely to have ever seen completion but for the efforts and contributions of a great many people. Because of the exceptional nature of the assistance provided I would like to waive this rule and express my gratitude to all those who have played a part in the successful completion of this work. If there is anyone who has been omitted by oversight the writer offers his apologies.

First of all, thanks are due in no small way to Mr A. H. Wesencraft, the Curator of the Harry Price Library, London University, in whose care now rest the files and enormous collection of books gifted to the University by the late Harry Price. Thanks are also due to Dr. Kellaway, former head of the Institute of Historical Research, and who permitted the writer access to the archives of the Institute.

The writer also wishes to acknowledge the help given by Mr Peter Underwood, former President of the Ghost Club, and for his contribution of extracts from his own works on Borley Rectory.

I am also indebted to several people who have acted in their capacity as translators and transcribers to help sort out the often obscure contents in ancient documents held in archive departments far and wide. Among these essential helpers are Dr. Sylvia England, Dorothy Clarke, Miss Anne Oakeley of Canterbury Cathedral Library and Archives, and Mrs P. M. Winzar of Charing, Kent, who untangled documents relating to the arrest of Sir Edward Waldegrave.

Recognition must also be given to the many archivists both in this country and abroad who have provided material containing clues to some of the legends connected with Borley Rectory. They include Mr Victor Gray, Essex County Archives at Chelmsford, Mr J. A. Gordon of the Building Research Establishment, Mrs Alexandra Nicol and her colleagues of the Public Record Office, the Department of Manuscripts at the British Museum, also the British Library. Thanks are also due to the India Office Library and in particular to Mrs Amanda Arrowsmith of the Suffolk Record Office, Bury St. Edmunds.

The writer wishes to thank Mr Carr of the Shropshire County Library in Shrewsbury for his help in connection with the work and lifetime of Harry Price, and also Phyllida Melling of the Guildhall Library, City of London.

Thanks are due also to the archive departments of South Tyneside Metropolitan Borough Council, Durham County Council and to the Department of Paleography and Diplomatic at Durham University. Acknowledgement must be made to Dorothy Owen of the Cambridge University Archives for details relating to the late Rev. L. A. Foyster, Rector of Borley from 1930 to 1935.

Among those from abroad who have assisted the writer are M.. Alain Roquelet of Departement de la Seine Maritime in Rouen, Sylvie Barot of Mairie du Havre, M. de la Conte of Departement de L'Eure in Evreux, and Jean Favier of Archive du France in Paris. In Belgium, thanks are due to Andree Scufflaire of Belgian National Archives and Dr. W. Rombouts of Rijksarchief Te Antwerpen.

A great deal of valuable assistance has been forthcoming from members of the clergy and of the various Catholic convental orders now based in this country, and who include:- The Rev. Canon Niel Munt, AKC, of Ely, Richard Incledon, Parish Priest of Haselmere, Surrey, The Rev and Mrs Christopher Cook of Foxearth in Suffolk, and the Rev. Malcolm. T. Peach of South Shields. Among monastic orders, thanks are due to Sister Lucia, O.S.B., of Darlington Carmel, Dame Eanswythe Edward of Stanbrook Abbey, Worcs., Dom Boniface Hill of Downside Abbey, Bath, Sister Mildred Murray Sinclair O.S.B. of St. Scholastica's Abbey, Teignmouth, Dame Veronica O.S.B., Oulton Abbey, Staffs., Sister Benedict of Kylemore, Connemara, Eire, and to Sister Cecilia Thorpe O.S.B., of St Mary's, Colwich. The writer is also indebted to Susan O'Brien of the College of St Paul & St Mary, Cheltenham, Glos., and to members of English Catholic Ancestor.

A great many thanks are due to Professor Bernard Knight of Cardiff University Medical School and to a colleague of his, Dr. David Whittaker, especially for their views on aspects of the bone fragments found in the cellars of Borley Rectory after the fire, and the possible background to the death of Kate Boreham.

The writer also appreciates the contributions to his researches by several individuals including:- Mr W. H. Soundy, formerly resident in Borley, Mr Allen Neame of Faversham, Kent, Mrs Lucie Alice 'Cathy' Turner, wife of the late James Turner, writer and poet, Simon Welfare who co-edited *Arthur C. Clarke's 'World of Strange Powers'*, and also to the Countess Mary Waldegrave who, though disapproving of the Borley story, clarified important details relating to Arabella Waldegrave.

Thanks are due to Mr M. T. Baker, managing director of *East Anglian Magazine*, who permitted the use of their archive photograph of Captain Gregson kindly supplied by the British Library. The writer also wishes to acknowledge the views of Mr Roger Glanville of Henley on Thames concerning the 'Locked Book' compiled and bound by his father, the late Sidney Glanville.

One important part of this project, chapter 24, has been achieved through contributions kindly provided by various members of the Society for Psychical Research and others who have delved into the Borley story. Among these are items from Richard Lee van den Daele of Shipley, W. Yorks, from Guy Lyon Playfair, Dr Vernon Harrison and Andrew Mackenzie.

Finally, the author wishes to acknowledge the help of Mrs D. Davies of Shrewsbury Meole Brace for her valuable help in respect of Harry Price's boyhood years and his memory of Sequah, Mr William Schupbach of the Wellcome Foundation Library for his help on Sequah's visit to Shrewsbury, and to Mrs Corbett-Jones of Tibberton School.

All who have corresponded with the writer on the subject of Borley Rectory can, it is hoped, take pleasure from the knowledge that without their interest and their assistance, the making of this study would have been difficult if not impossible.

Ivan Banks
Maidstone, Kent. 1994

PREFACE

A little over forty years ago a book was published by Longman Green in which its author told a strange story that has since become both something of a legend and also an almost endless controversy. The book was entitled *The Most Haunted House In England*. Its author was the late and enigmatic Harry Price. In 1946, he completed a sequel, *The End of Borley Rectory*. Two years later, he was dead. Indeed, in his own very special way, whether one agrees or not with the results of his work, Harry Price was in many ways, as much an enigma as some of the curious things he explored during his long career.

Some eight years after his death, a trio of writers tried to consign the story of Borley Rectory to oblivion, but without much success. To this day, it is an episode that refuses to be buried, seeming to exercise a hold on all who delve into it, and in that respect the present writer is no exception.

In 1969 an extensive report by the late Robert J. Hastings took a fresh look at this extraordinary case and Harry Price's role in it and in 1973, the author and psychic researcher, Peter Underwood, in co-operation with the late Dr Paul Tabori, further supported the considerable numbers of firm believers in the story's authenticity.

Since then, a whole generation of the ordinary reading public has grown up to whom the story of Borley Rectory is little more than the occasional incomplete and often inaccurate article in some rather second rate periodical. It is for this generation in particular, that the writer has chosen to retell the story of Borley Rectory from existing records, and also to delve once again into what may be behind it from a historical point of view.

To disbelievers the haunting of Borley Rectory is like a millstone round their necks, and each fresh book in support of the case yet another blow to those who would seek to discredit the whole episode, people who seem to be unable to face the very real possibility that maybe Harry Price was right all along and that they have been looking in vain for misdeeds on his part that were never there. In writing anew about Borley Rectory, the present writer is well aware of the sometimes almost hostile reaction to both the story itself and the late Harry Price on the part of some fraternities. Against these protestors and their protestations, the writer is satisfied in his own mind that the essentials of the episode remain intact and that furthermore, the case has sufficient historical evidence to draw upon to suggest that the phenomena was more likely to be genuine than false.

In Harry Price's last days, he thought that the case was finished with, but time has shown that this was not to be, and there can be little doubt on the strength of past history, that people will still be arguing about the alleged haunting long after the present writer is dead and gone.

Burnt to a shell on a winters night in 1939, Borley Rectory itself is now but a memory. Amongst the tiny community it was built to serve, it has come to be viewed with a mixture of resignation, indifference, some disapproval and even some little amusement for the amount of attention it attracted during its decidedly curious history. To this day, Borley has to live with the backwash from the Rectory's controversial existence, and it says something for the people of this tiny village that, in spite of everything, they manage to remain at least tolerant of those who come with genuine interest to look and to ponder upon the site of this extraordinary episode in English psychic history.

If this book achieves nothing else, the writer can only hope that its contents will show that in historical terms at any rate, the people of Borley have been left with the legacy of the most haunted house in England for some good reason. If that aim is achieved, then it may perhaps be a little easier for the community to come to terms with the reputation of its famous Rectory, and accept its curiosities as part of Borley's history.

EDITOR'S NOTE

Harry Price, so often quoted by the author, stated on the last page of *The End of Borley Rectory*, published two years before his death:

> "... Some day I should like to visit Le Havre and study its conventual records in an effort to find out more about 'Mary Lairre' – if she ever existed."

Ivan Banks has, it seems, completed Price's quest and after ten years laborious investigation, achieved a result and conclusion that could not have been foreseen by anyone, even the man described as 'the world's greatest psychic researcher'.

To some, the author's ideas and his spiritual interpretations may not easily be acceptable, but for sheer tenacity, persistence and dedication, and for being able to produce so much fascinating new evidence in relation to the haunting at Borley and of the identity of the 'ghostly nun', the author, I feel, is to be congratulated.

This work will, surely, provoke further investigation, historical and otherwise, but few, I doubt will be able to achieve this high standard of research or its intriguing conclusions.

LIST OF ILLUSTRATIONS

INTRODUCTION

It would not be unreasonable to express the view that aside from politics, religion, economics or education, there is probably little in the field of the human experience that can have raised more eyebrows or caused more heated argument than that aspect of our world that has to do with the subject of ghosts and hauntings and the weird effects that they seem to produce.

For centuries, there have been reports of seemingly elusive forces that variously hurl belongings and pieces of furniture aimlessly about, lift or throw people out of their beds, or throw an odd assortment of missiles such as chunks of iron, bricks, doorknobs, slate, stones, crockery, books and much else, at hapless victims.

Other results of such odd goings-on include all sorts of peculiar visual effects such as horse-drawn vehicles, regiments of Roman or Civil War soldiers, nuns, monks, and various kinds of queer lights, also strange noises and curious smells. Such phenomena have long been the cause of many a drawing room row and heated, often acrimonious argument.

The whole country is more than handsomely endowed with reportedly haunted castles, churches, ruined abbeys, pubs, railway stations, cellars, garages, country lanes and all manner of seemingly troubled places. Some of them still remain to this day, possessed of their respective reputations or not, as the case may be. The catalogue of haunted locations is rather like a travelogue, with such places as York, Prestbury, Raynham Hall, Glamis Castle, Blue Bell Hill, Pluckley, and many others.

Among these reported hauntings of bygone years, one can recall such cases as Hinton Ampner, Epworth Rectory, Cock Lane, Berkeley Square, Tadworth, Ballechin House, Edge Hill and many others. Yet, in the annals of British ghosts and paranormal phenomena, one famous case above all others really steals the crown, so to speak, in spite of the controversy that surrounds it to this day. It is a story of the past, but also of the present, because quite apart from occasional reports which seem to indicate that a residue of its visual and audible effects continues to occur from time to time, there still remain the as yet unanswered queries concerning the historical side of this episode.

It cannot be denied, that much has been done in the field of psychical research to try to evaluate possible sources of energy that may be capable, under certain circumstances, of causing the eerie and nonsensical havoc that seems so often to be a hallmark of hauntings, sources of energy that still seem to defy the accepted laws of known science.

From a layman's point of view, it seems to me that what we have in these phenomena, is an ultimately traceable and measurable source of sometimes immense power, far from being of a mysterious or outlandish origin, though many folk still persist with the idea that this is something beyond human understanding, an outdated fallacy slowly being discarded by our more enlightened scientific investigators. It does seem, however, that we still struggle to equate these odd and often obscure phenomena to known scientific principles, when perhaps in this instance, these principles require changing to accommodate the phenomena, for which a specially devised system of quantification may be a key to a better understanding of the whole subject.

It should be understood at this point that the foregoing remarks are essentially a personal view on the part of the present writer, who cannot claim to have the benefit of a scientific education. Those readers who wish to delve into this most important aspect of phenomena should examine the work of those scientists and para-psychologists who are researching in this field.

What is surely of particular interest and value is the *historical* background to ghosts and hauntings, which so often, in the popular media seems to be passed by in the scramble to latch onto the spectacular, the horrific or the supposedly ghoulish aspects, thrilling enough one must suppose, in their way, but more often than not mostly imaginative rubbish. Old legends and popular theories aside, and there are quite a number that do bear relevance to the episode that is to be examined, very seldom does one discover just *why* a particular place should appear to be haunted, as opposed to how, and there really is quite a difference. Consider, for example, some of the great ghost stories from the past. Although the identity of the Brown Lady of Raynham Hall in Norfolk is known as Dorothy Walpole, sister of the Prime Minister Sir Robert Walpole, is she really the image photographed on the stairs, and if so, why?

All too often in the world of the layman, the everyday reader of books, or the average television viewer, the actual background to these happenings is either ignored or often misrecorded or left to little more than dubious legends or hearsay, hopelessly tangled up in the passage of time. It surely cannot be denied that in the world of the public at large, no less than in the sphere of the professional historical researcher, the possible historical reasons for these odd happenings deserve, at the very least, interest which is equal to that shown in the psychic field. This can most certainly be said to be true of the particular episode at Borley.

It would, however, be quite wrong to suggest that efforts to solve this particular mystery from a historical point of view have not already been made. Nothing could be further from the truth, for several dedicated men and women have, over the past fifty years or so, struggled to sort out this classic and most obscure and controversial of all British psychic episodes. Yet to this day, concrete proof of what lies at the root of it all still seems to elude all attempts to nail it down once and for all. The author ventures to suggest that the case in question is one of *the* most extraordinary of its kind in modern British history, a case about which a tremendous amount has already been written, mainly concerning the paranormal aspects, though by no means solely so, and varying from the detailed and informative to the mildly interesting, and through the speculative and dubious to the worst examples of sensationalised fiction.

Much, if not most, of the latter can be attributed to that somewhat wayward British institution, the newspaper business, almost inevitably it would seem, since sensational inaccuracy tends to be a hallmark of sections of the British popular press. In fact, it is sadly the case that on occasions, the way in which this particular story has been handled by some newspapers has varied from incompetent to atrocious, likewise some much publicised 'exposure' of the tale.

Never has there been such a prolonged episode, nor has the episode ever, in my opinion, been equalled for the amount of argument and controversy that it has inspired over the years, than that which was brought to the attention of one of Britain's most famous and, in many ways, most controversial ghosthunters by the editor of the *Daily Mirror* newspaper in June 1929, so bringing to the world at large the strange story of Borley Rectory. It would probably be fair to say that never before or since that first summer's day at what was to become 'The Most Haunted House In England' has so prolonged an investigation been expended by either one man or a team as was carried out by the late and often criticised Harry Price. He will forever remain an almost inseparable part of the story of that misfit country rectory with its strange and singular history. Whilst some might claim, with varying degrees of justification, that the case of Borley Rectory was possibly not quite the very pinnacle of his long career, at least from a scientific or historical view, it is most certainly true that without his efforts, irrespective of whether or not they were all capable of being completely vindicated, the whole peculiar story of Borley Rectory might very well have remained uninvestigated and totally unrecorded. But it should not be supposed that this last point lends any worthwhile weight at all to the idea popular among some doubting fraternities that Borley Rectory would not·have been a haunted house save for the intervention of Harry Price. In my view the balance of evidence seems to suggest that Borley Rectory's weird history did not, and still does not depend alone upon the work of Harry Price.

From the foregoing remarks, it is hoped that it has been made clear to the reader that the prolonged and often vociferous criticism of Price's work, both at Borley and elsewhere, has been duly noted and acknowledged. However, having looked at both sides of the coin, the writer feels that much of the criticism has been found wanting in so many ways, to the extent that really very little of it seems capable of standing up to really searching analysis. That successive attempts to discredit the story of the haunting have, by and large, failed to come up with any really hard evidence has been soundly demonstrated by the late Dr. Paul Tabori, Peter Underwood, and Robert J. Hastings in their own writings upon the subject.

In recognition of this long standing controversy about Price, particularly in respect of Borley Rectory, and also in recognition of the esteem in which he is still held to this day by a number of his fans, and more particularly for those of the younger generation, many of whom would not be conversant with his life and work, the writer sets out Price's contribution to the story of Borley Rectory in detail later on.

Aside from the important links between Harry Price and Borley, the main purpose of this book is to probe into the possible *historic* origins of the various ghost figures recorded as having been seen in or near the Rectory, together with some of the legends and stories attached to the Rectory and its occupants, both physical and spectral.

There can be little doubt, in this more enlightened scientific age that those whose work centres upon the scientific and psychic side of hauntings and poltergeist activity, will in due course be able to quantify once and for all the scientific causes of events at Borley.

To begin this account, I have attempted to bring together as much as possible of the relevant material dealing with the strange occurrences at Borley set out by Harry Price, his literary executor Dr. Paul Tabori and that of Peter Underwood. Reference has also been made to work by a number of other writers and researchers such as Dennis Bardens and David C. Knight together with the report by Professor Dingwall, Mrs K. Goldney and Trevor Hall who in 1956 produced what was felt by them to be evidence conflicting with the authenticity of the phenomena. It was this latter view that was itself destined to be subsequently called into question by the late Robert J. Hastings, whose own enquiry into Borley Rectory is also referred to at various points in this book. Detail has also been collated from the quantity of correspondence sent to Price and to Paul Tabori by several people, concerning not only Price's own work at Borley Rectory, but also curious events and experiences related by people who visited or stayed at the Rectory long before Harry Price became involved in its history.

It is recommended that any serious student of haunting of Borley Rectory really needs to study all this material, mainly because the correspondence in the files tells quite plainly, I believe, what actually happened and what was said.

Owing to much of the literature on the hauntings at Borley Rectory not always being available, even from libraries, and the details therefore being unknown to many young readers, information of the disturbances and the various investigations into them, have been set out from existing or previous accounts as a prelude to the writer's own research. Therefore the first part of this book is founded upon existing material since in my opinion this material has not had the accusations against it proved to *any* substantial degree.

The details that follow have been the source of prolonged and often acid controversy, especially since the death of Harry Price. The ranks of those who side for or against the hauntings are, it seems, fairly equal in number and almost equally vociferous. Whilst it should be quite clearly understood that the author openly sides more with the pros than the antis and consequently accepts the risk of being accused of bias as a result, wherever possible the views of those who are not satisfied with the story of Borley Rectory have been noted and where it seems to be appropriate, one will find my views of those opinions.

The writer has devoted the first part of this work to describing the Rectory and its surroundings and relating the strange things that happened there. The next section has been set aside for a look at the occupants of the Rectory over the years, in as much detail as surviving records would permit. The third section is given over to an examination of the truth or otherwise of many of the legends attached to the history of the Rectory and the site on which it was built. The reader will be able to share in questions about Sir Edward Waldegrave, the links with the monastic world, the still, (at this stage), unresolved mystery of the nun and much else besides about Borley Rectory, things that continue to bemuse the enthusiasts to this day.

But now, the famous and evergreen story, and mystery, of Borley Rectory and its ghosts awaits.

CHAPTER ONE

BORLEY AND ITS SURROUNDINGS

The tiny village of Borley lies on the Essex and Suffolk county boundary, roughly two and a half miles from Sudbury, one time home of the famous painter, Thomas Gainsborough. A little nearer to Borley lies Long Melford, with its splendid church, its maltings and the impressive timbered Bull Hotel.

Until a few years ago, the railway between Sudbury and Long Melford ran past the foot of the long shallow hill leading to Borley, passing Borley Hall, which until the end of the last century was the home of successive generations of the Waldegrave family, including the unfortunate Sir Edward Waldegrave, of whom more anon.

From about 1890 onwards, Borley Hall belonged to the Payne family, and until May of 1983, it was occupied by Patrick Payne, a man much liked in the village, but who has, unfortunately, since died.

The easiest way of approaching the village is by way of Rodbridge, once known as Rad Bridge, and where once stood Borley's gallows, a sobering thought!

The River Stour, having meandered its way across pleasant meadows, passes to one side of Borley Hall and its mill, last used as such in 1947, when the terrible winter of that year caused the wheel shaft to split.

On top of the rather windswept knoll which rises from the river valley is the belt of trees within which, from 1863 to 1944/5 stood Borley Rectory.

On the opposite side of the road, and set well back from the corner, stands the Parish Church, which is of unknown dedication and partly of 12th Century origin, with 15th Century additions. Among various interesting features, it possesses a rather unusual brick porch and perhaps best known, at least locally, an avenue of clipped and rather decorative yew trees which are most unusual in their visual effect.

However, by far the most extraordinary feature within this quite unique and delightful little church, which has become almost as famous as some or our great cathedrals though for the oddest reasons, is the Waldegrave tomb, with its hefty columns, family crest and the effigies of Sir Edward and Lady Frances Waldegrave laid upon the main plinth.

Alongside the church stands Borley Place, used by at least two rectors prior to the building of the new Rectory in 1863.

Across the road again, almost on the Rectory corner stands the only substantial surviving appendage of Borley Rectory, namely the stable cottage.

Behind this cottage stands the farm, also long associated with the Bull family and subsequently the Payne family. The former garden of Borley Rectory is now occupied by modern bungalows and is, as a consequence, somewhat fragmented.

The name of the village itself can be traced back into Anglo Saxon times and indeed, its name is a relatively modern development of the word Barlea, which variously translates as Boar pasture, or Place of the Pig.

At various times throughout its history, it has also been known as Borlee, Burley, and even Boreghley.

Part of Borley once belonged to Barking Monastery, an order of Benedictine nuns, whilst the Manor of Borley as such was the property of the Prior and Convent of Christchurch, Canterbury, from 1301 until it was requisitioned under the auspices of Henry VIII and, according to most records, handed over to Sir Edward Waldegrave of Bures.

Behind Borley Place lies another cottage and a large pond, a couple of big modern bungalows and then about a half mile of open fields, a turn off to Ballingdon and a farm road to Brook Hall.

Over the boundary in Suffolk, lies Borley Green with its ancient thatched cottages intermixed with some more modern houses.

Borley Rectory itself has now gone. The fire of February 1939 caused so much structural damage that the shell of the building became unsafe and in the end, there was little option but to pull down the remains, themselves in an advanced state of collapse.

Had the fire occurred some years earlier, or even after the war, then it is possible that the building might have been salvaged, but in wartime with no materials or spare labour available, there really wasn't a hope.

Visitors to Borley should therefore realise that the Rectory *no longer exists*.

There are still several items associated with the story of the Rectory which the visitor can look at but it should be borne in mind that, all remaining properties associated with the story, with the one exception of the church, are private to which the public do not have right of access and on which they must *not* go without the express permission of the owners.

Probably the main building of direct interest is the former stable cottage or coach house, which appears to be Victorian but is in fact rather older, for it appears on an old tithe map of 1841 in the Essex County Records Office at Chelmsford.

This cottage is the easiest relic to view as it stands right on the roadside. It now belongs to and is occupied by a Colonel Dorey.

Next to the church, there is Borley Place, which was used both by the late Rev. Herringham and by the Bull family for many years.

Down the hill towards Rodbridge, on what was once part of the Rectory garden, there are the remnants of two old stone gateways, now part of two separate properties.

At the foot of the hill, down by the River Stour, stands Borley Hall, for long the residence of various members of the Waldegrave family, whom many think were at the root of some of the Rectory's mysteries.

Away from Borley, two places of interest linked to the Borley story still exist. About two miles away, near Long Melford, stands the parish church of Liston, in the grounds of which lay buried remains, long believed to be those of Marie Lairre, the ghost nun of Borley Rectory, of which the reader will learn much in the pages that follow.

About four miles distant, and deep in rural surroundings, there still stands Pentlow Rectory, a massive and extraordinary looking place, in which Borley's then Rector to be, Henry Dawson Bull, was born in 1833.

Now called Pentlow Tower, it cannot be seen readily from the road, being well hidden by trees down a long curving driveway.

In the garden stands a tall and rather weird brick folly, from which the place takes its present name, and which was erected by Edward Bull, Rector of Pentlow, and from which it is said that some forty churches could be seen on a clear day.

CHAPTER TWO

THE BUILDING OF BORLEY RECTORY

From the details that follow, it is hoped to be able to make it apparent as to just why, what would in other circumstances have been merely a rather remote country rectory, has become over the years, a house with the most singular, and extraordinary history. In due course, it is also hoped to be able to show that much of the strange pageant of the haunting of Borley Rectory has, as its roots, something way back in the annals of history.

To begin with, it is perhaps best to enter upon the strange story of Borley Rectory during the middle years of the nineteenth century, a time when rural England and the English way of life still revealed some stark contrasts, displaying side by side in many instances, great wealth and appalling poverty, industrialisation cheek by jowl with unchanging rural remoteness.

It was still a time of rather rigid and set religious beliefs, and perhaps most significantly of all, in terms of this present study, a time of great spiritual interest in life after death and in ghosts and spirits in general.

But strangely enough, at a time when the world of scientific discovery was beginning to gather momentum, ideas that there might be a serious scientific background to ghosts and hauntings was often treated with a mixture of derision, contempt and even outrage, to the extent that some even considered such ideas as heresy, like many other theories which surfaced at that time.

Nowadays, we can look with some degree of amusement upon the storm that erupted over Darwin's theory of evolution, but to the Victorians, it was no laughing matter. Much the same tended to happen when people tried to link ghosts and hauntings with science. Nowadays, a much wider cross-section of society takes a far more open-minded view of these unusual events, though there are those who still seem to be guilty of blind ignorance and a myopic attitude to a serious questioning interest in this fascinating subject. This however, straying a little from the focal point.

In the countryside, life continued to centre upon the small village with its squire, blacksmith and the tenant farmers, and of course the long established routine of the parish church. Many of the smaller rural parishes were very isolated and some were to remain so until well after the Second World War.

It was in just such a quiet corner of rural England, that a rather peculiar story was soon to unfold, though few outside the district were to hear of it until many years later.

Upon the death of the Rev. John Phillip Herringham in 1862, the Rev. Henry Dawson Ellis Bull succeeded to the living of Borley. For some little while, Herringham had resided in the cosy little 17th century house called Borley Place, once thought to have been known as Borley Manor which survives to this day, together with its tithe barn on a plot beside the church.

To begin with, the Rev. Henry Bull followed suit and over the succeeding years, various members of the Bull family continued to make use of Borley Place.

Following his induction, however, Henry Bull decided to have built a new Rectory to house himself and his growing family. In due course, work commenced on the new house, and was completed during the following year, 1863. Oddly enough, there had already been a Rectory house on the chosen site, on the corner across the road opposite the church, and one might just ponder on the reasons

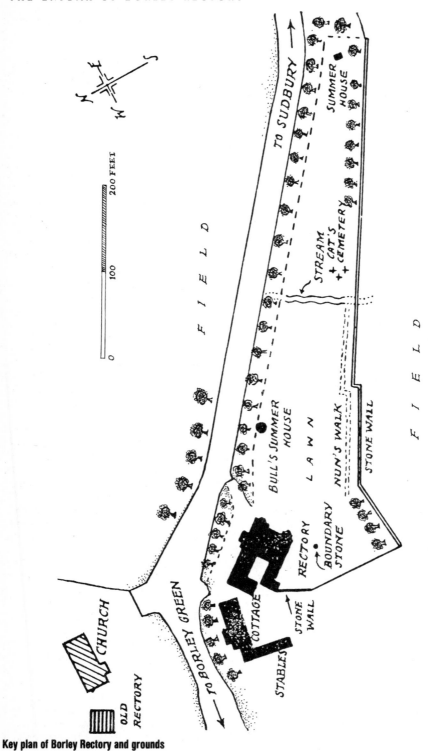

Key plan of Borley Rectory and grounds

why it was not used and adapted to suit the needs of the new Rector, especially as during Herringham's time it had been described as a fairly commodious place.

There are those who think that this old Rectory was a replacement for a much older one still, for such a building often figures in stories about past happenings on the site, possibly involving members of the Waldegrave family. As Herringham had been living at Borley Place for some time prior to his death, one cannot help wondering whether he simply preferred Borley Place, or whether he disliked the old house, or whether the old Rectory had fallen into state of dereliction, an idea that has some force in connection with theories that for a very long time, the old Rectory was locked and disused.

Is it just possible that the old Rectory was possessed of some of the very same features that were to make Henry Bull's new home a less than welcoming abode to so many people in later years?

Whatever the truth, the old Rectory was removed and was replaced by the new and impressive structure that was to become so familiar in later years. This was completed in 1863 and stood on the opposite corner to the church, in a huge garden hemmed in by the Cedars of Lebanon under which so many were later to watch and wait.

Until about this time, according to a tithe map of 1841 and a list of 1839, both now in the Essex County Archives at Chelmsford, the Rectory site had been divided off a little below the site of the former Rectory itself, with the latter house and some of the grounds belonging to Herringham. This surely indicates that he must have had a living and income independent of that gifted by the Walde-graves, for they were responsible for the appointment of Borley's rectors from the time of Henry VIII until the death of Henry Bull in 1892, after which the living and the gift passed respectively to his son Harry and the the Bull family.

The 1839 tithe list also tells us that the remainder of what later was to become the great rambling garden of Borley Rectory, belonged to John James Henry Waldegrave, a descendant of this large, rich and influential feudal family, whose connections with Borley seem to have finally come to an end at the close of the 1890s, when Borley Hall, the old Walde-grave home in Borley, passed to the Payne family, Mr Patrick Payne being its most recent owner. However it has now passed out of local hands.

By the time the new Rectory had been completed, the whole plot had been combined into a single very large garden, and it was to remain as such until the end of the Second World War.

Architectually, the new house could be said to have been something of a monstrosity. Like many Victorian rectories, it was large, exceptionally so in its final form, but it was very much in line with ideas of large houses then in fashion.

Notwithstanding this last point, Borley Rectory was in many ways an oddity in the context of Borley and its surroundings. For one thing, its particular style and appearance, whilst certainly contemporary Victorian, seemed to belong not to rural Essex but rather to such places as the developing wealthy areas of London or Manchester. In short, it was rather an architectural square peg in a round hole.

Its general appearance could perhaps best be described as massively sullen looking, with an air of impressive though somewhat clumsy grandeur. It was by no means a thing of beauty and in fact Sir William Crocker, who was to figure much later in its history, said in his memoirs, entitled 'Far From Humdrum – A Lawyers Life' that it was an example of the worst that the bad taste of 1863 could produce. In terms of weird and incongruous design, Pentlow Rectory where Henry Bull was born could show Borley a thing or two.

The Rectory at Borley cost some £3000 to build, which gives an idea of the state of well-being enjoyed by the Bull family, long established in the district and very comfortably off, to put it mildly.

The new building was of two storeys of red brick and in its initial form, was L-shaped. Entry to the grounds was by way of a carriage-drive from the lane outside, a drive which ran alongside the house behind trees and bushes that screened it

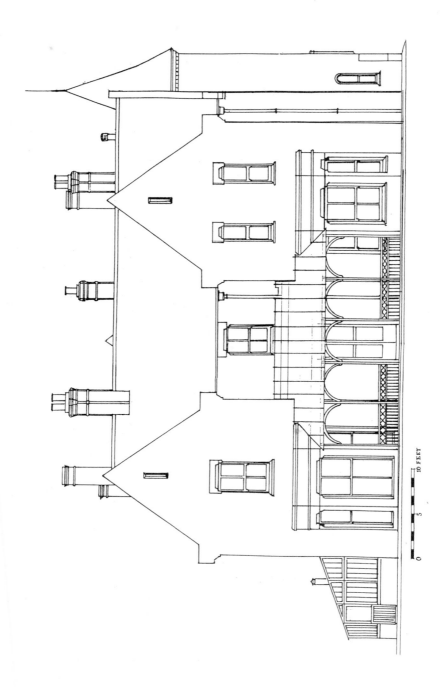

Borley Rectory – Garden Front (SE Elevation)

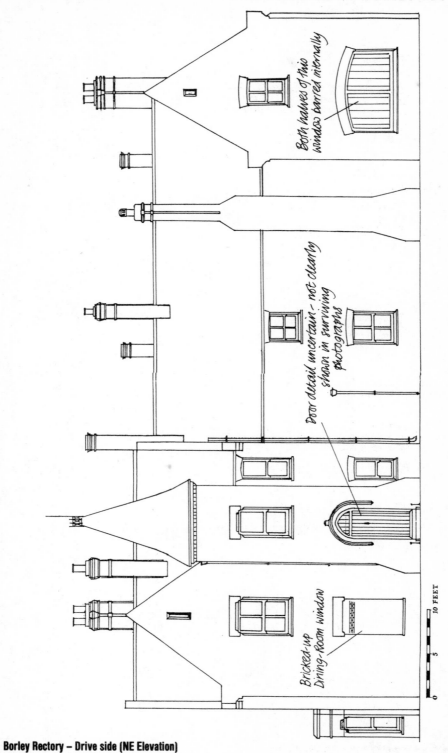

Both halves of this window barred internally

Door detail uncertain - not clearly shown in surviving photographs

Bricked-up Dining-Room window

Borley Rectory – Drive side (NE Elevation)

0   5   10 FEET

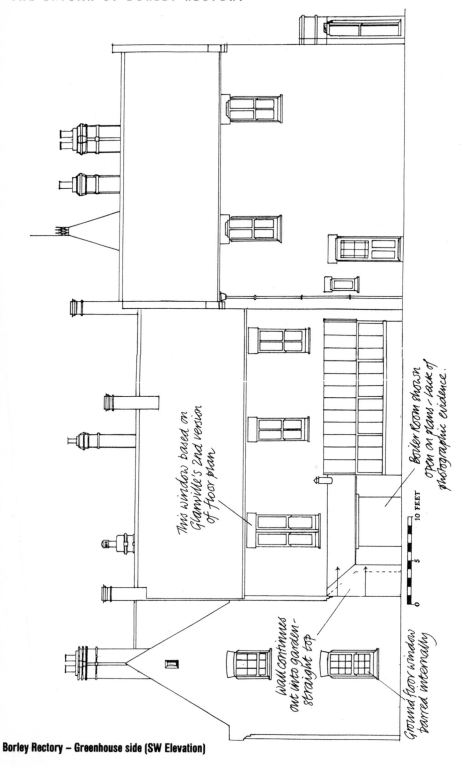

Borley Rectory – Greenhouse side (SW Elevation)

This window based on Glanville's 2nd version of floor plan

Wall continues out into garden – straight top

Ground floor window barred internally

Boiler Room shown open on plans – lack of photographic evidence.

10 FEET
5
0

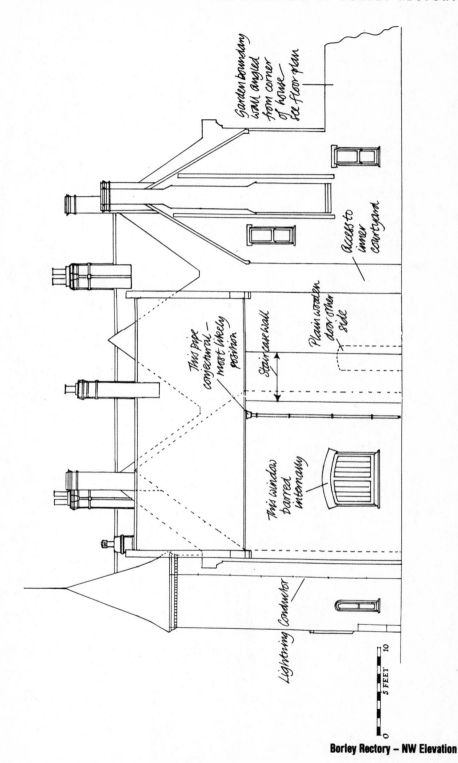

Garden boundary wall angled from corner of house — see floor plan

Access to inner courtyard

This pipe conjectural — most likely position

Staircase wall

Plain wooden door other side

This window barred internally

Lightning Conductor

0   5 FEET   10

Borley Rectory – NW Elevation

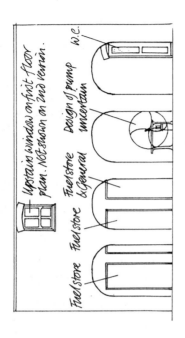

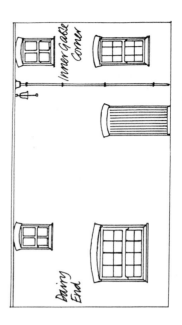

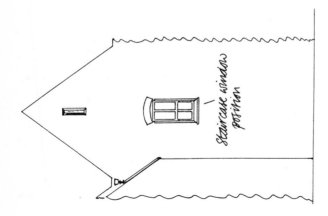

Internal courtyard elevations

almost completely, to emerge at an upper gateway between the Rectory and the associated stable-cum-coach house that stood behind it on the corner of the road. It is this building that remains today.

The main entrance to the Rectory itself was off this driveway into a porch which was topped, upon its upper floor, by one of those features so beloved of the Victorians, a sort of turret with fancy iron work on the top of it. This was an absurd looking appendage by which the Rectory came to be readily recognisable on old photographs.

The room of which the turret formed the roof, was once used as a bathroom, but many years later one of the subsequent rectors turned it into a tiny chapel, complete with altar rail and imitation stained glass window.

The front of the house, which was technically the back, faced East/South East onto the large lawn that merged into the enormously long garden, long since lost under modern bungalows.

This front-cum-back facade was of twin gable-end form with, on the ground floor, two large bay windowed rooms, of which the left hand one facing an onlooker had what appeared to be, full height French windows which were in fact false.

The windows and their bays were of typical flat-top Victorian design, and the French style windows of the left-handed facing bay illuminated a commodious drawing room. Between the two bays there stretched a glass roofed verandah from which a door gave access to and from another of those Victorian domestic features, a library. This and the room above it formed the centre span of the frontage.

Behind this massively gabled face of the house, its skyline was visibly dominated by several tall chimneys and on the far side, facing out over the fields towards Bulmer, following various extensions to the building to accommodate Henry Bull's growing family, there appeared a glasshouse and a boiler room. The glass house faced rather oddly into the shade of the trees.

As time passed, Henry Bull's family, especially the girls, grew considerably to the extent that the rector required his house to be enlarged, so the Rectory reached its final form between 1875 and 1892.

The result was a new wing on the far side of the house away from the road, in which the upper rooms were mostly given over to sleeping accommodation. Some of it no doubt was intended for some of the girls, whilst below on the ground floor of the extension were storerooms used for coal and lumber. At the back of the original wing, nearly enclosing the internal brick courtyard after the new wing was added, was a small domestic dairy.

In its final form, Borley Rectory had a room layout as follows:

GROUND FLOOR

Entering from the garden via the verandah into the library at centre-front and then turning right:

1. The main hall, with stairs up to the first floor, and containing a round iron stove. Off the hallway was the dining room.

2. The front exit via the porch.

3. The long corridor, with a pantry.

4. A secondary landing with another staircase to the first floor, and also stairs down to the huge cellars.

5. The sewing room.

6. A large kitchen.

7. A rear staircase up to the first floor.

8. To the right of these stairs, a larder.

9. The dairy.

10. To the left of the back stairs, a scullery.

Returning to the hall, and proceeding through the far side of the house, to:

11. The drawing room with its pseudo French windows.

12. A passageway with an exit to the garden.

13. Two large cupboards off this passageway.

From here, the remainder of the ground floor extension was walled off and was only accessible from the courtyard via an arched covered passage. To the left of this passage were the following:

15

14. A fuel storeroom.

15. Another storeroom.

16. A third storeroom, outside which was the cover of the main well, with a huge handwheel operated pump.

17. A lavatory.

18. On the far side of the lavatory, a woodstore with access from it to the boiler room and glasshouse.

The top floor of the Rectory was given over chiefly to bedrooms and the layout as follows:

19. Proceeding up the main staircase from the hall onto the landing, there was the Blue Room, the bedroom that directly overlooked the glass-roofed verandah.

Proceeding round the original wing of the house, there was:

20. A dressing room for the Blue Room, with a connecting door between the two.

21. Another bedroom.

22. Over the porch, a small bathroom, later turned into a small chapel.

23. The upstairs lavatory.

24. Stairs from a small landing down to the kitchen passage on the ground floor, and up to what passed for a loft, where in later years a water cistern was put in with better piping.

25. Originally a bedroom; this next room was later in use as a bathroom. The reader will recall that the old bathroom over the porch had been turned into a little chapel.

26/27. Two further bedrooms, the end one having an exit via a very small landing down the back stairs. These two rooms ran into the other without a corridor.

28. To the left, also just off the top of the back stairs was one other bedroom, directly over the scullery and overlooking the internal bricked courtyard.

One of these end rooms was later partly used for storing fruit and became known as the 'pear room'. Behind a curtain across one part of it, was a bed used by one of the maids who reported some curious happenings here.

Retracing our steps back to the staircase outside the Blue Room, the rooms in the top floor of the extension were arranged as follows:

29. A bedroom, at which point one entered to the right, the long corridor on this side of the house. A short way along it, the corridor slewed slightly to the left, with two steps down, leading to:

30/31. Two more bedrooms, served by doors off the corridor.

32. The last room in the wing, at the end of the corridor. From it both the back corner of the garden, part of the courtyard and the stable cottage would have been visible and the back of the farm which is still there today.

The courtyard just referred to was originally open to the garden, but the 1875 extension on the far side of the house, all but boxed it in, except for a narrow gap just wide enough to walk through. With the exception of one tiny sash, only the main stairs and those rooms in the original wing had any windows overlooking the courtyard. The inner wall of the extension, except for just that one tiny window indicated on the Glanville floor plans, seems to have been blank brick and in wet weather, the outlook in the courtyard must have been most dreary.

At both ends of the main landing at the front of the house, there were corridor archways of typical Victorian design, these being close to the Blue Room. Both the landing and the Blue Room featured extensively in the subsequent history of the building and these details will be enlarged upon later.

The large and irregularly shaped cellars of the Rectory were reached by a stairway from the ground floor between the pantry and the sewing room, but in no way did the cellars correspond to the layout of the building itself, but instead ran roughly diagonally across the house from beneath the kitchen corridor to a point beneath the library.

When, after the Second World War, the site was completely dug out, as distinct from the digging carried out in the ruins in 1943 under Harry Price's directions, the reason for the odd shape of the cellars seemed to reveal itself in the foundations of at least one if not two much older buildings. These findings will be described later.

Peter Underwood and Paul Tabori dwelt at length upon these post war excavations in their book 'The Ghosts of Borley' and owing to their obvious interest in relation to many aspects of the story of the Rectory, I have no hesitation in setting them out again later.

From these cellars ran a well, one of two in this part of the house. The other was more of a shallow tank than a well. The main well was the one in the courtyard and it was of considerable depth, some eighty feet in fact, and from it was taken the water for both the Rectory and the stable cottage, with a wheel-operated pump being used to effect supply. This appliance was hard work to operate and noisy in use.

The reader should be able to follow the foregoing description of the layout of Borley Rectory from the plans, one of each floor, drawn up during the late thirties by Harry Price's near neighbour and dedicated assistant Sidney Glanville and first published in Price's book 'The Most Haunted House In England'.

I feel it worthy of now turning to some of the oddities inside and outside the house.

The turretted porch has already been mentioned and it will suffice here merely to add that the outside corners of the porch were buttressed like a church tower. Close alongside the porch was another curiosity with very direct links to the story in hand. Butting onto the hallway and porch was the dining room, being the right hand room of the two bay-windowed rooms viewed from the lawn.

As well as the large bay window as originally built, the dining room also had a side window, and like most in the house a conventional sash type with stone lintel over the top. The Rectory had not been all the long occupied when, it is believed on the orders of the Rev. Henry Bull, that window was taken out and the opening bricked up. As Harry Price was later to comment, the blocked up window rather spoilt the balance of the building on that side.

This window looked out onto the driveway and as to why it was blocked up, the writer will elaborate in due course.

Another curious feature of the place was the heavy iron bars on several windows on the ground floor. This was apparently not as one might suppose to keep out burglars, for in a quiet area like Borley in those days, there would have been little need for such precautions, especially as the other ground floor rooms had substantial internal shutters. Rather, the iron bars were supposedly there for the purpose of preventing young maidservants from receiving the attentions of suitors or boyfriends, or slipping out for elicit rendezvous, when they should have been in bed asleep. The kitchen, kitchen passage, the scullery, larder and dairy windows were all barred in this fashion.

How much truth there was in the popular belief as to the barring of these windows is hard to say, but on the other hand, Victorian ideas on servants behaviour were often strict, despite the fact that the social behaviour of the employers sometimes left much to be desired.

From barred windows to bells!

Another interesting item, and one of very few relics of Borley Rectory to have survived the years since the fire, was the big rectory bell. This hung from a bracket high up on the wall overlooking the internal courtyard and was positioned roughly over the top of the kitchen passage doorway. Originally it had a long bellrope which would have reached nearly to the ground, but by the time Harry Price came upon the scene, that had gone, rendering the bell officially inoperative except that according to some reports, this did not prevent the bell from sounding of its own volition and under curious circumstances. Of these happenings, more later.

The exact purpose of the Rectory bell in that position could be said to be something of a mystery. There were, of course, stables at the rear of the Rectory, but a stable bell is more usually placed over the stable roof in a little cupola, or hung from a bracket under the eaves.

So why, if it was a stable bell, was that at Borley hung in the inner courtyard of the Rectory? Of course, if the bell was installed when the house was first built, then that courtyard could well have served as the family's carriage yard, with the bell being rung to inform the Bull's coach-

17

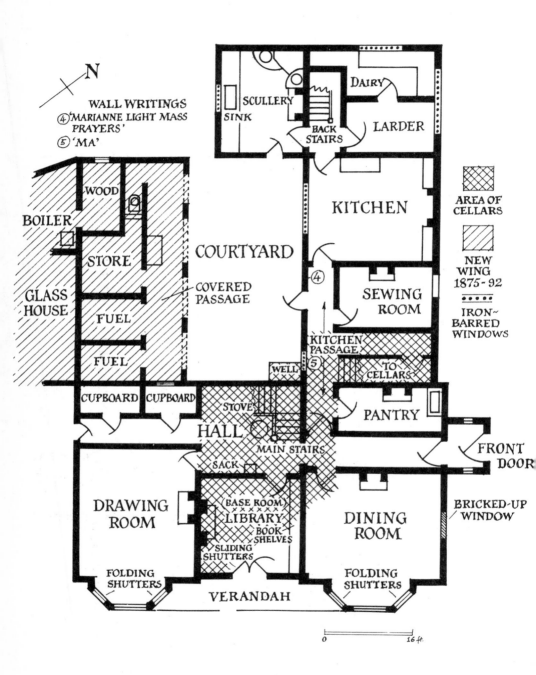

Ground floor plan

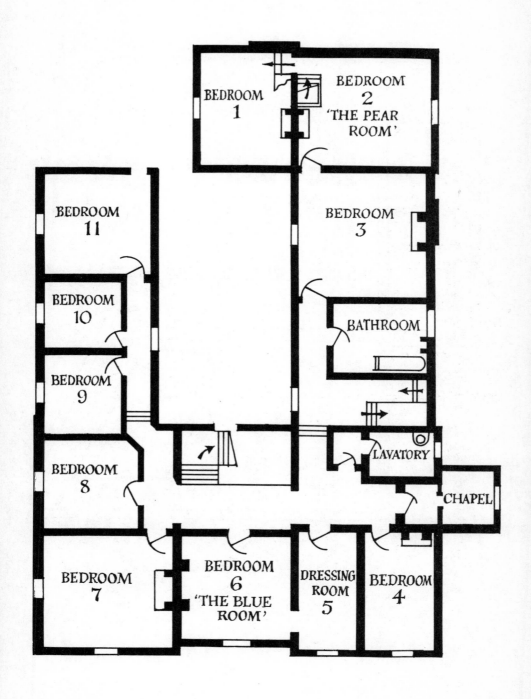

First Floor Plan

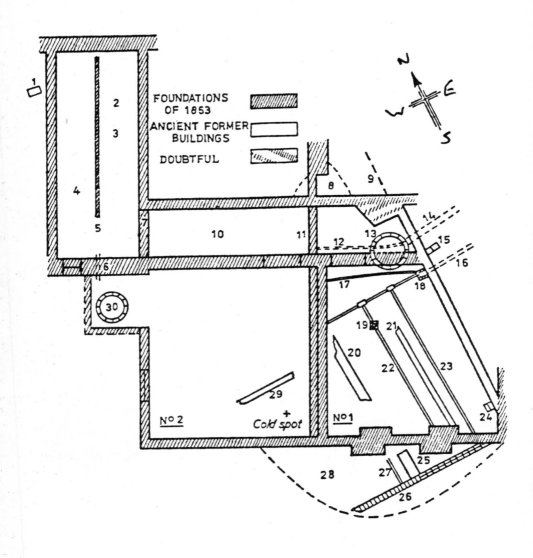

FOUNDATIONS
OF 1853

ANCIENT FORMER
BUILDINGS

DOUBTFUL

N
E
W
S

1
2
3
4
5
6
7
8
9
10
11
12
13
14
15
16
17
18
30
19
20
21
22
23
24
29
+
Cold spot
Nº 2
Nº 1
25
27
28
26

Plan of the cellars

Borley Rectory, Summer 1890, *opposite, above.*
The dining room, Borley Rectory, c 1890, *opposite below.*

man that the carriage was required. However, once the courtyard was, to all intents and purposes, blocked off by the later extension, one would think that the bell would have been moved accordingly.

Various other possibilities present themselves. It could, perhaps, have been used to summon the Rector from the church when he might have been pottering around therein just about mealtimes. Alternatively, it could have served as a meal bell within the Rectory grounds, to call in the various members of the family, especially in the summertime, when folks might be walking around in the far parts of the great garden. One wonders whether the blocked in nature of the courtyard might not have muffled the effect to some extent, although it has been more than once suggested that the shape of the Rectory caused sounds to be amplified and carried, though the writer will make some personal observations about this point later on.

So much, then for the Rectory bell and its purpose. After belonging to Harry Price for several years, having been given to him by Captain Gregson during the demolition, it now reposes at Peter Underwood's house in Bentley, Hampshire.

Inside the Rectory, the dining room and the drawing room both possessed features that were of more than passing interest. In the dining room was to be found perhaps the most prominent and unusual interior item. The bricked up window has already been referred to but the real eye stopper was the fireplace.

It was a heavily carved marble monstrosity, but what made it especially interesting was that on each of the side columns was carved a monks head, one hooded and one not. The significance of these lay in the once popular belief that Borley Rectory occupied a site on which had once stood a monastery. Arguments about this have rumbled on for years and the writer will deal with this controversy later on. Whatever the truth, behind the idea of a Borley monastery, the dining room fireplace at Borley Rectory certainly did reflect the idea in very solid form.

It is said to have come from the Great Exhibition of 1851, though if so, where it had had been in the intervening years was anybody's guess. It was of Italian origin, as was the one in the drawing room.

The drawing room fireplace was of similar peculiarity, but minus any carved monks heads, and was of coloured inlaid marble. It looked something like an arched portcullis in shape, and was entirely typical of some of the more preposterous bits of Victorian interior design.

Another notable room in the house was the now famous Blue Room, which was the upstairs front bedroom overlooking the glass roofed verandah. This room was interesting, not because of any structural feature, but rather because of the phenomena reportedly experienced in it, and seen in the remains of it after the fire. It also featured in one of the many stories connected with the Rectory, that of the 'Screaming Girl', which was briefly mentioned in passing by Harry Price in his first book about Borley Rectory. I will elaborate on that in due course.

We turn finally to the chapel. This oddity, the room over the porch with its steeple roof, was first used as a bathroom but some time after the end of the Bull era, a later rector, the Rev. Lionel Foyster, turned it into a tiny chapel. This curiosity in turn, created another, in that in order to provide a replacement bathroom, an adjoining bedroom was commandered for the purpose, resulting in the rather unusual combination of a bathroom with a fireplace. On a briefly lighthearted note, one is perhaps reminded here of a quip from that sadly departed humourist Gerard Hoffnung, 'Bedroom with bath I have'.

In the strange history of Borley Rectory the big garden was to play its own curious part, just as odd as events in the Rectory itself.

The top section from the Rectory itself to roughly the point where the second bungalow from the corner stands today, was the lawn. From there, the garden became a wooded copse, crossed about halfway down by a tiny pond-cum stream.

Aside from the upper and lower drive gateways, there appear to have been two

The drawing room, Borley Rectory c 1890, *opposite above.*
Borley Rectory in June 1929, *opposite below.*

other gateways into the grounds from the lane. These two gateways, with their curious stone wings, still survive, now somewhat broken up and on two different properties. It is this last fact that suggests that they were at one time part of the Rectory grounds. The gates that they sport are, however, not original or even very old.

On the side of the garden nearest the road, the lawn was screened by the Cedars of Lebanon, whilst on the other side was a low boundary wall, now gone, together with more trees, also now largely vanished.

Part of the garden has often been thought to occupy the site of an old plague pit, a burial ground for the victims of that awful pestilence that carried off a goodly proportion of the population of the Home Counties.

There were two rather interesting structures in the garden, together with one other curiosity. At the top of the lawn, fairly close to the lower drive gate, stood a large rustic octagonal summerhouse which faced out towards the far side of the garden, giving an unimpeded view. It was built around a solid centre pole of timber around which was fixed a table.

The inside perimeter of the summer house was supplied with stout wooden garden seats in which Henry Bull and his son Harry are said to have sat for many a long hour, smoking their pipes and watching, so it is said, for one of, if not *the* most odd and curious of the strange figures seen at Borley Rectory.

Further down, right at the foot of the copse, was another smaller summerhouse, an ornate and rather pleasing little Victorian Gothic structure, open at the sides and with a roof rather reminiscent of the lid of an old-fashioned tea caddy. In this, Harry Bull used to sit to commune with the spirits we are told, and often at all sorts of odd hours. Both these summer houses survived the fire of 1939, but during the following couple of years or so, some army personnel who tried to use the grounds as a billet, pulled down the small summer house. It would seem that the big summerhouse was demolished not long afterwards.

Now we turn to the curious oddity mentioned earlier. One of the most amusing aspects of Harry Bull's tenure at the Rectory was the huge entourage of pet cats that he kept, amounting to about thirty two of them in all. He is said to have known them all by name and it must have been more than a little comic to see them all follow him about the Rectory. It was Harry's cats that gave rise to the oddity mentioned earlier, because as they died, they were buried in a little pets cemetery, located in the copse. Each of the graves had its own little memorial board, inscribed with the name of the departed moggy. Rollo, Sandy and Gem were just three of this great brigade of cats. This cemetery was the scene of another of Borley Rectory's curious goings-on, as will be related later.

It should just be mentioned that when the Rectory was first built, the grounds also included the land that butted onto the far side of the garden, but this was all eventually turned over to farm land and orchard, and indeed it remains agricultural land to this day. A great pity has been the removal of many of the trees that used to surround both the Rectory itself and the lawn. These trees, the Cedars of Lebanon, under which Margaret Wilson was later to be buzzed by a curious flying insect as she sat painting a picture of the Rectory, gave the building its secluded atmosphere.

The writer has, it is hoped, sufficiently described the house and garden to enable the reader to relate the strange catalogue of events to the appropriate locations and draw as much atmosphere from these descriptions and the accompanying illustrations as can be portrayed in an account written long after the events occurred.

To make a complete description, it now remains to picture the stable cottage that stood behind the Rectory, and which had its share of rather strange happenings. It is this cottage which still stands today. This cottage does appear to be Victorian, and several folk over the years have assumed that it was built at the same time as the Rectory itself, but belying exterior appearances, the stable cottage is rather older. The 1841 tithe map and the 1839 tithe list tell us that this building was on that site before the big Rectory was built and some photographs of it show signs of its having been altered to blend into the new Bull rectory. One illustration of it in *The Ghosts of Borley* shows the garden side of the cottage, with its little porch, and immediately above this, there is visible evidence of a bricked up gateway. In its earlier form, the coach bay was in the bottom, with the living accommodation over the top. The Bull sisters are said to have related that the family carriage was stored in the ground floor, the stables being at the end of the cottage nearest the farm, and at right angles to the cottage itself. These buildings have also largely disappeared, leaving the cottage as the only solid surviving relic of the former Rectory establishment.

The stable cottage now boasts a large outward extension upon the garden side, which although a modern addition, blends well with the rest of the property. The same cannot be said, however, for the ugly blockhouse type dormer extension on the upper storey. The building now has double glazing and until relatively recently it was for most of the year empty, but has been bought by a Colonel Dorey, so once again the Rectory site houses a military gentleman.

The evidence in the Essex County Archives clearly indicates that the cottage is older than popularly supposed, or as described by estate agents. It certainly seems to be contemporary with the old Herringham rectory, which was demolished to make way for Henry Bull's massive pile.

CHAPTER THREE

THE HAUNTINGS ... 1863 TO 1927

If Borley Rectory itself was in many ways a curious great barn of a place, in architectual terms, then what is alleged to have happened in and around the building can, be described as little short of extraordinary. The long sequence is said to have culminated in the rectory becoming, at the height of the disturbances, almost uninhabitable. It would seem that little time elapsed after Henry Bull and his family moved into the rectory, before it became apparent to people who stayed there, that something about the house 'wasn't quite right'. That the Bull family lived there, apparently unconcerned, from 1863 to 1927 can perhaps be partly explained by the family's attitude to the strange events and by the fact that the Bull children came to accept them as just part of life in the house, though the various sisters were not above being caught by surprise on some occasions. In particular, two features about the Rectory that persisted throughout its existence were the stillness of the house, far more so than would normally be the case in such a large building filled with so many people, and its rather uncanny habit of appearing cold whatever the outside temperature might be. It should be mentioned in connection with this that admittedly, the Rectory was a pest of a house to heat properly in the winter months, partly because of its clumsy interior layout, but its chillness was often apparent in warm weather too. The stillness of the house was the more noticeable feature. In a place of such size one would expect, especially at night, to hear all sorts of creaks and groans, chiefly from contracting or expanding joists or floorboards and rafters, or from doors unwittingly left ajar so that they squeaked. At Borley Rectory however, the place seemed always to be dead still. However, many noises were heard in the house that seemed to have no physical cause.

Some items did produce regular noises of course, in particular the water pump which by all accounts was a very noisy contraption. There are those who suggest that the pump was responsible for many of the sounds reported as being paranormal, but, would not a person normally search for the source of such noise if they did not know where it was coming from?

We turn now to the specific incidents at the Rectory, beginning with some that occurred during the heyday of the house.

To begin with, a curious incident involving two of the Bull sisters is reported to have happened when they were young children. They were standing by one of the Rectory gates, with a family maid in attendance and as they stood looking out over the countryside, they saw a couple of their local friends walking across one of the fields. There would have been nothing very unusual about this, except that walking a little way in front of them was a young girl whom neither of the girls recognised as being local. We are told that later, the two sisters had occasion to meet their two friends and they ventured to ask who it was that had been out walking with them earlier. The response was that there had been nobody else in the field with them, nor had they met up with anyone else upon the way. The stranger in the field appeared to be dressed all in white.

Mention of this odd incident brings the author to another less certain occurrence, thought by some to be connected with the girl in the field. This episode, not in itself a psychic occurrence but rather the theoretical cause of one that happened very much later came to light when it was told to Harry Price by a Sudbury man, early on in his investigation. What is alleged to have happened is this. Not long after the Rectory was built, a girl was supposedly seen dangling perilously from the outside sill of the Blue Room window, screaming her head off. She is said to have then lost her hold, crashed through the glass roof of the verandah to the stone steps below and been killed. It was this incident that Harry Price himself seemed less than satisfied with as regards its feasibility, for no evidence to explain it had come to light by that time, 1929, nor it would seem, since. Harry Price himself recorded in his first book that he could find no evidence to substantiate this peculiar tale, and on that incomplete note, he left the incident. The idea behind this incident was that the girl, whoever she was, had been in some way assaulted by somebody in the Blue Room and in trying to evade her tormentor, fell out of the window, vainly trying to grab hold of the sill to save herself. Though the incident may appear rather far-fetched, we will take some time at a later stage to examine the possibilities and investigate the actual historical feasibility of the kind of incident described.

The supposed connections between this incident and the strange girl in the field, seen by the young Bull sisters, are twofold. The girl in the field is said to have been dressed in white, though some versions of the incident have it as being blue, and curiously enough, many long years later, after the fire at the Rectory, a girl dressed seemingly in either pale buff or pale blue was reported being seen standing at what had been the Blue Room window, but under the most bizarre circumstances.

Now other incidents. One of the most frequent and doubtless most annoying of the Rectory's odd phenomena was the persistent and seemingly pointless ringing of the servant bells when no member of the family had rung for a servant. It has been suggested, in the highly critical book called *The Haunting of Borley Rectory*, by E. J. Dingwall, K. M. Goldney and T. H. Hall, that mice were responsible for the incidents, getting among the rafters and bouncing on and off the bell wires, though this seems to have been fairly well disproved by the point that bells which had had their pull wires cut to stop the nuisance, continued to function from time to time.

One of the earliest of these incidents was when one of the Bull sisters, thought to have been Ethel, was alone in the house. For no apparent reason, every bell in the house started ringing at once. Following upon this, the sound of rushing water was heard inside the Rectory, again without any explanation. This was even more weird than the bell ringing, because the Rectory not only had no mains water supply, but no interior piping either, until after the end of the Bull family's days in the place, when a later Rector, the Rev. Guy Smith, spent a considerable sum of money having the archaic facilities improved. We must now turn to other curious happenings.

Cases of actual physical assault in poltergeist incidents or allegedly by ghosts, are extremely rare, though not entirely unknown, but one of the Bull sisters, whilst asleep in bed was woken up by having her face slapped. Nobody was in the room with her at that time, and again no-one could make any sense of the occurrence.

Other phenomena involved the same sister for some time. Each night as she was about to retire to bed, there would come a series of loud rapping noises on her bedroom door. After that, loud bangs and crashes would be heard in the house but as with much else at Borley Rectory, nobody could ever make any sense of these incidents.

The most persistent feature of all, was that of strange heavy footsteps which always seemed to occur at times when there was nobody in those parts of the house from which the sounds appeared to come. This phenomenon lasted from the time the Rectory was built until demolition men pulled down the remains of its gutted shell during the closing months of the Second World War. During the Bull sisters childhood years, perhaps about the period of the 'girl in white' incident, each night around half past ten the girls would hear steps passing their bedroom door, walking along the landing and stopping outside the night nursery. When the footsteps stopped, three taps would be heard and then all would be quiet, save for those nights when the loud crashing sounds could be heard.

Then there was the visit by a relative. He was put up in one of the bedrooms but afterwards, he flatly refused to sleep there again. As to why, regrettably he did not elaborate.

An often reported mystery was that of lights being seen in rooms that were locked or otherwise out of use. This was reported time and time again by numerous people, over many years. It should be remembered that throughout its existence, even up to 1939, the Rectory was illuminated entirely by oil lamps. It was never wired for electricity nor was there gas.

These, then were some of the early occurrences at the Rectory. We pass now to several strange happenings more precisely dated. The experiences of a one-time headmaster of the well known Colchester Grammar School illustrate the curiosities of Borley Rectory at that time.

During his time as a student at Wadham College, Oxford, young Harry Bull made the acquaintance of P. Shaw Jeffrey, who was later to become headmaster of Colchester Grammar School. As a result of their friendship, Shaw Jeffrey spent at least one summer vacation, possibly two, at Borley Rectory as a guest. When he later recounted his experiences many years after, as an old man of venerable years, although he was unable to recall the year or years of his visit, his memory of some curious incidents at the Rectory was fresh enough. Among other oddities, he recalled stones falling about inside the house. he also heard a horse drawn carriage more than once, and records a nun having been spotted by other members of the Bull family while he was at the Rectory. There had been about seventeen in the family at that time, though it seems that perhaps some of these might have been cousins from the Pentlow arm of the family, because there were reportedly only about fourteen Borley members as such. On one occasion, Shaw Jeffrey had removed his boots before retiring to bed, and left them near his bed, on the floor. The following morning he found them on top of a wardrobe. Also while he was at Borley Rectory, a French dictionary in his possession went missing. He was later disturbed in his sleep by a loud 'clump' and there on the floor lay his dictionary.

Another of the many people to recall strange events at Borley Rectory before 1900 was Elizabeth Byford, whose family served at the Bulls for a very long time. One of them had been the Bulls coachman at one time.

As a young girl, she was a maid at Borley Rectory for one brief month in 1886, and 43 years later in 1929, she related her experiences in a letter to Harry Price. During the year in question, Elizabeth was employed as an under nursemaid and was duly allotted a room in the Rectory, a room which, she was informed, was haunted. Knowing that a couple of the ladies of the house had been sleeping in that room only a little while before, she ignored the comments and went about her business. About a fortnight after starting work she was woken in the middle of the night, hearing what sounded distinctly like some person walking along the corridor towards her room, and making a noise as if wearing carpet slippers.

It was the routine for Elizabeth to be called by the Head Nursemaid at 6 a.m. and, no doubt still half doped with sleep, she thought that was who it was. But nobody knocked or entered her room and in spite of the other servants making light of her experience when she mentioned it next morning, she began to feel most unsettled and, not very long after, she gave up her post and left. As Harry Price commented in *The Most Haunted House in England,* were it not for the fact that the footsteps phenomenon was experienced and reported by countless numbers of people, Elizabeth Byford's experience could have been dismissed as the result of her own imagination arising from stories she had heard about the hauntings. Her report actually served to confirm and strengthen the evidence for the mystery of the strange footsteps. Among those who heard them over a period of very many years, one could mention several of the Bull sisters, Guy Smith and his wife, members of the Cambridge Commission who investigated Borley during the last war, and various other people including James Turner's wife, when they lived at Borley after the war.

Another fairly commonplace occurrence was that of the footsteps heard in the road outside the Rectory when there was nobody in sight. One of Harry Bull's brothers, Walter, was for much of his life away at sea, but at least on fifty occasions during visits to Borley, he had heard the sound of somebody following him along the road outside the Rectory, but there was never anyone in the area to account for the noise.

Ethel, one of the sisters, was also the victim of a number of rather disconcerting experiences. During one of these occasions, she was alone in an upstairs passageway, when she became aware of somebody standing by her side. She turned, somewhat surprised, to see a tall dark complexioned man, but before Ethel could collect her thoughts, the figure vanished completely. In another incident, something caused her sleep to be disturbed. She awoke to find standing by her bed, a strange looking man with a tall hat and dressed in very old-fashioned costume. It seems likely that Ethel was not the only person to see this curious figure. Some reports tell us that he was seen again later, sitting on the edge of the bed, whilst sometimes it is related that she felt the presence of somebody or something sitting on her bed. But it was Freda who was thought to have been one of the sisters involved in a most extraordinary incident in July 1900, when she was with her sister, Mabel. Details will be found in the special section relating to the appearances of the most famous of all Borley's ghosts.

We turn now however, to the numerous strange experiences of the Rev. Henry Bull's son, Harry, or Henry Foyster Bull to give him his proper name. It is the strange things that Harry Bull experienced and

talked openly about that received a lot of the often rather one-sided and rather pointless criticism in more recent years. There are those who have tried with great effort to dismiss Harry Bull as a teller of tall stories, a morbid dreamer and much else besides, yet his experiences were shared by so many others who visited or stayed at the Rectory. The writer has digressed as to Harry Bull's genuineness at this point because it is felt that he deserves at the very least the benefit of the doubt, a balanced view of him, as has, we hope, been properly applied to Price in the opening passages of this book. However, to proceed with Harry Bull's experiences:

He succeeded his father as Rector in 1892, and occupied that post until his own death in 1927. Although he did not live in the Rectory for the whole of his life, for he spent some time in Borley Place where he was born, during his years as Rector of Borley, he reported a number of strange events, perhaps the most visually unpleasant being that of a headless figure in the Rectory garden. This odd incident has been related many times in the various chronicles of Borley. In Price's first book, *The Most Haunted House in England,* we are told that Harry Bull had ventured out into his garden with a pet dog called 'Juvenal'.

Something is alleged to have disturbed the dog to the point that it began howling and cringing at something in the gloom ahead of them. Harry is said to have followed the dog's frightened stare and noticed the legs and feet of somebody standing among some shrubbery. The legs then moved into full view and, to Harry's consternation, the figure appeared headless! The figure then moved towards one of the garden gates, through which it passed even though the gate was closed and locked, and then disappeared from view in the vegetable garden. There have been arguments over the extent of this incident and Price's reporting of it, but the text of the notes from which Harry Price took his writings was revealed more recently by Robert J. Hastings in his own investigation of the story. The notes read as follows:

'Harry Bull in garden one day with the

retriever, Juvenal, who howled and cowered when Bull saw the legs of a man otherwise hidden by fruit trees, pass towards a small postern gate, which was kept locked, and pass through it. Someone chased the headless man through the garden who eventually disappeared in the veg. garden.'

An interesting sequel to this, some years later, was that in 1929, Guy Smith's maid, Mary Pearson, claimed to have chased a headless figure down the lawn until it vanished among the greenery, and in 1938/39, Captain Gregson lost two dogs, which yelped in terror at something that the Captain couldn't see in the rear courtyard, and tore off, never to be recovered. Of these events, more later.

Harry Bull also saw a little old man standing on the Rectory lawn, pointing up at the sky with one hand and down at the ground with the other. It is said that Harry Bull recognised this strange little man from stories passed down through generations of the Bull family, as an old family gardener called 'Amos'. One of the many theories about what might have happened on or near the site of Borley Rectory, years before, even suggests that old Amos had been employed at the supposed old Borley Rectory, a building that may have pre-dated even the Herringham rectory, not to be confused with Borley Place, which the late Rev. Herringham used in his later years and until his death. Going back over the numerous reports about a little old man seen several times near the place, one wonders whether he had any connection with the figure seen by Ethel Bull, or the man in her bedroom who so abruptly caused her to wake.

The old-fashioned coach, with its pair of brown horses, was another phenomenon that Harry Bull reportedly saw or heard on more than one occasion. He is said to have seen it once being driven by a headless driver. On another occasion, as he was returning to the Rectory, he heard the clatter of a horse-drawn vehicle approaching at some speed after dark. He stood into the side of the road, doubtless expecting to see a vehicle rattle past, but instead only the noise of it passed him. Of the vehicle and its horses or driver, there was nothing whatever to be seen!

One night, as is related in *Ghosts of Borley,* the servant bells all started ringing of their own accord and, puzzled by the sudden commotion, Harry Bull came downstairs, candle in hand and wrapped in a plum red dressing gown. The bells worried him greatly and he is said to have feared that they were an omen of some misfortune about to befall himself or his family. Oddly enough, it seems that almost anyone who stayed long at the Rectory suffered either from ill health or from a relatively short life. Henry Bull died in the Rectory at the age of 59, and Harry Bull died at 64 from cancer, both men passing away in the Blue Room. Guy Smith, Harry's successor at Borley, seemed to have escaped ill health but his wife Mabel was very ill for a time, just one factor that helped drive the Smiths out of the Rectory. Lionel Foyster, the next Rector, spent much of his tenure crippled with arthritis and his wife appeared to have suffered periodic bouts of collapsing, though these episodes had some curious aspects, not least being the fact that in spite of everything, Mrs Foyster outlasted them all, eventually dying in 1992, aged 93. A little baby she cared for at Borley died when only a few weeks old, and of course Harry Price, who spent 18 years working on the Borley case, eventually died from a heart attack in 1948 though not at Borley Rectory, but there is some evidence that he was taken ill once when actually in the Rectory one night in 1929.

CHAPTER FOUR

THE NUN MAKES HER APPEARANCE

I have reserved for this special section, the most spectacular of all the strange spectral figures of Borley Rectory, the curious Catholic Sister of Mercy, a title that presents some problems in the tracing of her identity.

Not long after the Rectory was completed, the Bull family began to be puzzled and to some extent pestered by the figure of a holy sister who took to staring in at the family through the side window of the dining room, with her face pressed close to the glass, when they were at their meals. In time, Henry Bull is said to have grown tired of this novelty and to have given instructions for the side window to be taken out and the opening bricked up. This window overlooked the outside driveway and it has been suggested that it was blocked up due to lack of privacy owing to people looking or trying to look through the window from the road. That sounds reasonable enough until one notices that not only was that window well back from the road but it was also partly obscured by shrubs and would, except in bright sunlight from the direction of the lawn, show only a rather fuzzed reflection to a casual passer-by.

It is sometimes suggested that there were times when bright light in the right quarter would shine on the strange marble fireplace in the dining room and there are those who have theorised that the nun was staring at that because of the monks heads carved on its side columns and not at the family. Whatever the truth of the matter, the side window was indeed bricked up and remained so for the rest of the Rectory's existence. One might initially think of the Window Tax, a long forgotten source of revenue to the Exchequer, but as Harry Price pointed out in *The Most Haunted House in England*, the window

tax went the way of most redundant statutes in 1851, twelve years before the Bull Rectory was built. The tax would have been in force during Herringham's time, so was that why he wouldn't use the old Rectory? It is conceivable that the old Herringham rectory (not to be confused with Borley Place) had more windows than Herringham was willing to pay for, moving him to abandon it as derelict.

There is some circumstantial evidence, admittedly based upon a secondhand account, of a nun being seen at Borley before the building of the Bull rectory in 1863. Of this, however, there is but the most scanty detail, but as to the coming of the nun upon the scene after 1863, that is a very different matter and indeed from the time of Henry Bull onwards, she has become the central character of the whole drama. Following upon the incidents of the figure at the window, the strange nun began to appear frequently upon the far side of the garden, the track that she seemed most often to follow, which ultimately acquired the name of 'The Nun's Walk'.

She usually seemed to appear in the top far corner of the garden and then would drift along that side of the garden before disappearing from view among the tangle of the copse below the lawn. In due course, there appeared at the top of the garden near the road, the now famous octagonal summerhouse and it is popularly supposed that Henry Bull had this built so that he and his son Harry could sit and watch for the nun to appear. Every so often, it would seem, she obliged and sometimes remained in view for several seconds. One might be inclined to smile indulgently now at the story of the summerhouse, since such structures were common in Victorian gardens, but that both men saw the nun, as did others at the Rectory, now seems to some, well accepted. In addition to her usual path by the far side of the lawn, she was sometimes seen in the road outside the Rectory and, as Edward Cooper of the stable cottage discovered during the First World War, she also drifted across the rear yard and out through the upper gate on to the road. As far as can be ascertained, however, she was never seen inside the Rectory or the stable cottage.

About 1900, Harry Bull claimed to have been followed by the nun from the church to the Rectory entrance. Having initially dithered as to whether to leave the porch door open, supposedly for her to enter, he decided against it. However, possibly the most spectacular happening of all, concerning the nun, came in the summer of 1900. On July 28th of that year, two of the Bull sisters were returning to the Rectory from a summer party. Reports as to which of the girls were involved seem to vary, Price stating Freda and Mabel Bull in his second book.

They entered the copse by one of the bottom gateways and proceeded up through the greenery towards the Rectory. They had barely cleared the trees at the foot fo the lawn when, there in front of them, over on the far side of the garden, stood the grey figure of a holy sister, sometimes stated to have been fumbling at a string of beads with her head bent down. The sight stopped the two girls in their tracks. There was something most odd about the look of the figure. Exactly what happened next has been argued over since, but the usually told version of events is that one of the girls gathered up her skirts and scuttled into the Rectory to fetch another sister. It is thought to have been Elizabeth, usually known in the family as 'Dodie', part of whose private diary is still in existence. She came out with her incredulous sister and snorted "A ghost – nonsense!" and promptly walked towards the figure. Harry Price tells us that the figure, which had been gliding slowly along the side of the lawn stopped, turned to face the girls and then promptly vanished. Price's reporting of the incident, which he based upon an interview

with the sisters at Chilton Lodge, Cornard in 1929, tells us that the figure displayed a facial expression of intense grief, but later the sisters are said to have recalled that only two of them saw the figure and not in perfect light, and also not closely enough to see its face, but they always maintained that the nun was there and after stopping where it was for a moment or two, turned to face the Rectory before vanishing from view. It is just worth mentioning that others since, have made remarks about the figure's apparently miserable facial expression, some claiming to have noticed traces of tears upon the spectre's face.

It was in the autumn of 1927 that the nun made another rather curious and spectacular appearance, this time unfortunately witnessed by only one person. At that time, the Rectory was empty, for Harry Bull had died in June, and presumably Mrs Bull had given up the place because there seems to be no mention of her after Harry's death. His sisters had been gone since 1920, having moved to Cornard and Harry Bull's successor, Guy Smith, had yet to come.

During this time, there came upon the scene a journeyman carpenter named Fred Cartwright, who at the time was lodging in Sudbury whilst engaged on repairing some farm buildings between Borley and Clare, which had and still has, an order of monks. To reach his place of work, Fred had to come through Borley early each morning and would normally pass the Rectory just as it was getting light. On his second day of walking to work by this route, Fred had walked up the hill from the direction of the railway as he had one on his first morning, but this time, as he approached the lower drive gate of the Rectory, he noticed standing at the gate, a holy sister dressed in what has often been stated to have been the habit of a Sister of Mercy, though there is a query attached to this description. Apart from wondering what she was doing there at such an early hour, Fred saw nothing particularly unusual about the figure, and walked on.

For the next three mornings, he saw no sign of the figure but on the fourth day there stood the nun, this time seemingly asleep where she stood, with her eyes tightly shut. Again, momentarily curious as to why she was standing there, Cartwright shrugged his shoulders and went on his way. A week went by and then there she was again, only this time as the carpenter passed, she appeared to be not only exhausted but also looked ill. Fred Cartwright was by now somewhat puzzled and, thinking that something was wrong with the nun, he made to turn back but the nun had disappeared. Thinking that she had gone inside the Rectory, he walked on. On the following Friday morning, he saw the nun again, for the last time. As he came up the lane towards the Rectory, there she was by the same gate and this time Fred decided to speak to her but before he reached the spot, she had vanished without a trace. One moment she was there, the next instant ... nothing! Thoroughly bemused, Fred pushed open the gate and walked up the whole length of the Rectory driveway looking for the nun, but she was nowhere to be seen.

CHAPTER FIVE

EDWARD COOPER AND THE STABLE COTTAGE

For a time during the First World War, and on various occasions in more recent times, the strange occurrences at the Rectory also affected the stable cottage, which survives today as virtually the last remnant of the Rectory establishment.

In April 1916, the Bull family enlisted the services of Edward Cooper and his wife and provided them with living accommodation in the stable cottage. For some time, the couple were pestered at night by the noise of what sounded like a large animal pattering about in a room adjoining their bedroom. This went on for quite a time, until one night things seemed to come to a head somewhat spectacularly. On the night in question, the Coopers were woken up by a terrific crash, sounding as though every piece of crockery in the place had been smashed in the same instant. Edward Cooper got up and went downstairs with a candle, expecting to come upon a scene of disaster, but only to find that not so much as a single teacup had been disturbed, but after that the noise of the padding animal was not hear again.

On more than one occasion, Cooper and his wife saw the nun figure and on one summer's evening, they saw the nun walk across the courtyard at the back of the Rectory and so through the gate and onto the road outside, crossing en-route one of those commonplace iron inspection covers which should have rattled if it was stepped on by any mortal being, but it didn't! None of these happenings could quite compare, however, with the sight that Edward Cooper saw on one very clear and brightly moonlit night. As he was getting ready for bed, he chanced to look out of the window and his eyes met with the most extraordinary spectacle. Crossing the road and clearly visible in the moonlight, was on old fashioned coach and horses, with its sidelamps lit. One, possibly two men were seated up on the driver's box, and everything including the horses' leathers and buckles were clearly visible. The coach tore across the road at a peculiar angle and went clean through everything in its path without making a sound. It followed a path completely at variance with the road itself, though over the years, the direction in which it was going has varied from one telling to the next. In the report by Harry Price, it was stated to have appeared in the field just alongside the church, crossed the road, passing clean through a hedge on the way, and to have vanished round the back of the farmyard behind the cottage. Some versions of events tell us that Cooper saw the coach appear *from* the farmyard and hurtle across in the opposite direction. Harry Price told his readers that he had interviewed the Coopers twice, in 1929 and again ten years later in their later home near Sudbury, and that their story did not alter in the slightest.

The Coopers were a hard-headed, no-nonsense couple and after leaving Borley in March 1920, having also seen a queer little man running round their bedroom early one morning, only to vanish before their eyes, they experienced nothing else.

CHAPTER SIX

THE STORY CONTINUES ...
1928 TO 1935

After the end of the Bull's years at Borley Rectory, and following on the experiences of Edward Cooper and his wife and Fred Cartwright's story, the strange story entered a new phase, probably the most argued-over period of its whole history.

The remaining members of the Borley branch of the Bull family now had some considerable difficulty in finding a new Rector to take up the living. Some ten or twelve hopefuls came to look and said "No!" The isolated location of the old Victorian rabbit warren that was Borley Rectory and its total lack of common domestic amenities put off one prospective tenant after another, until finally, a cultured and pleasant Eurasian gentleman, The Rev. Guy Eric Smith, accepted the living and in the autumn of 1928 he moved into the Rectory with his wife Mabel. The couple had no children. Their curious experiences began even before they had settled in, although it was not so much the phenomena that drove them out some nine months later, but rather the appalling state of the place, which they found depressing and very hard work to manage, in addition to which Mabel Smith was quite unwell for a time. They did however, seem to suffer more than their fair share of the Rectory's odd and often unwelcome curiosities, which only served to further their general dislike of the property. This point was made quite clear by Price in his book *The Most Haunted House in England*, and it is perhaps worth mentioning at this point that it has been other writers, and not Harry Price, who have recounted this aspect of the Smiths' tenure the wrong way round, by stating that the ghosts drove them out. If Price can be criticised at all over the Smiths' period at Borley, then it is in unwittingly causing the

extraordinary interest that arose when he did agree to investigate the case in the first place, which he would not have done, had not Guy Smith contacted a national newspaper, which passed details to Price, thereby resulting in the Rector having unwittingly destroyed his own privacy.

The bringing to the public notice of the Borley story did, of course, bring to the hapless village the inevitable sightseers and would-be ghost-hunting brigade, but it seems a mistake, on reflection, to blame Harry Price for that. Indeed, Price himself had little time for these folk, whom he referred to as 'rubbernecks', and when a party of youngsters later caused some trouble at the Rectory, he made some caustic remarks about them in his book. But to continue. Before they had properly moved all their own belongings into the Rectory, Mabel Smith was cleaning the house, which must have been in a pretty scruffy state, having been empty since the summer of 1927. In cleaning out a cupboard in the Rectory, she came upon a brown paper parcel which, when untied, was found to contain a somewhat unpleasant souvenir in the shape of a small human skull, thought upon closer inspection to be that of a young woman. Enquiries apparently failed to reveal how it came to be in the Rectory, though a local belief seemed to be that any attempt to remove it from the Rectory resulted in an increase in the disturbances therein. True or not, it could be said to have lived up to is supposed reputation in the light of the subsequent happenings in the house. Guy Smith, doubtless somewhat puzzled by the rather gruesome relic, reburied it in the churchyard and no doubt thought no more about it. One wonders what he would have thought about the skull had he had any inkling at the time of what lay in store.

Not long after they had moved in, Guy Smith was on his own in the house and on crossing the landing outside the Blue Room, he heard a gradually rising whispering culminating in a pleading voice crying "Don't Carlos, Don't", before the sound faded away. It was not the first time Smith had heard strange mutterings on the landing but only on this occasion did he hear some definite words. One suggestion made since, is that the Rectory had a habit of trapping sounds originating from people in the stable cottage behind the Rectory, which seems reasonable until one looks at the plans of the Rectory and realises that the Blue Room landing was at the front of the house, several feet from the stable cottage with numerous solid brick walls in between. The writer, having studied the Glanville plans, cannot accept that such sounds from the cottage would have carried that far within the solid and hefty structure of the Rectory.

The strange footsteps common in the Bull years were also heard by the Smiths, chiefly in locked and disused upstairs rooms, of which there were plenty, for apart from Mary Pearson and a part-time maid who left after only two days, they had no regular servants. Consequently they had little option but to limit themselves to a few essential rooms that Mabel Smith could manage to keep in order. According to some accounts, it was the footsteps that caused Guy Smith to think that there was somebody prowling about in the house uninvited and it is often told that he fetched a hockey stick, stationed himself in one of the upper corridors, where he thought the sounds were coming from, and lay in wait. The footsteps came in to earshot and when the Rector judged them to be level with where he was hiding, he sprang out with his hockey stick, doubtless hoping to land the would-be intruder a fourpenny one with it, but only to find that he was hitting out at thin air!

Turning now to the maids, it was reportedly Mary Pearson, the Smiths' only regular servant, who came scuttling indoors one morning saying that she had seen an old fashioned coach tearing silently across the lawn, only to vanish almost in front of her. Later questioning by Harry Price elicited the information that she had seen the vehicle twice, travelling first down the lawn and on the second occasion, up the lawn. It remained visible just long enough for Mary to notice the colour of the horses, which were brown, though sometimes, stories about the coach quote bay as the colour. It was, it seems, the same vehicle seen speeding across the Rectory corner late one night by Edward Cooper during the First World War, but whereas Cooper noticed one, possibly two, tall hatted figures seated upon the driver's box, Mary saw no men at all. The vehicle was apparently under no visible control when she saw it. It is also thought to have been Mary who saw a headless figure, standing beneath the trees, which she chased until it disappeared.

Out in the Rectory garden, Mabel Smith saw a greyish figure leaning rather wistfully on one of the gates, only to vanish when she approached it. At a time when the Smiths had been in the garden, and with nobody else in the Rectory, they returned to find a china vase lying at the foot of the main stairs, smashed to pieces. The Smiths also quite often experienced the servant bell phenomenon, most odd considering that on some of the bells the wiring had been ripped out or cut. A further curious incident was that of a light seen in an empty room. When first seen by Mrs Smith, she was alone, but on the second occasion, members of the choir were with her. On unlocking the empty room it was in total darkness.

The Rectory's weird reputation had been a talking point locally for many years, but by this time its reputation had become such that few people wanted to come near the place unless they had to, and Guy Smith, finding that many of his parishioners would not even come to parish meetings there, and tired of the way in which the Rectory and its atmosphere were disturbing the general order of things, sent an appeal to the press for someone to come and sort out the cause of the mysteries. The place was quite depressing enough with no gas or electricity and the drainage and water system in a poor state. The disturbances and their effect on the house were something that Smith was not prepared for and both he and his wife found them very puzzling. His appeal reached the editor of the *Daily Mirror* and a reporter, Mr V. C. Wall, was despatched to Borley to investigate. Poor Guy Smith! One wonders whether he would so readily have told the popular press about the strange events at the Rectory had he had any idea as to the extent of national interest that would follow. At one stage, after the story was printed in the *Mirror*, groups were even running charabanc trips from places such as Colchester, 'to see the ghost'. However, it is the visit of Mr Wall that concerns us now.

After a night spent in the grounds of the Rectory, during which time a light was again seen at the window of an unused upstairs room, Wall wrote a sensationalised article in the *Mirror*, which suddenly and irreversibly catapulted the Rectory and its phenomena into the public eye. It didn't really need Harry Price to achieve that. Any prominent psychic researcher, or a body such as the Society for Psychical Research (of which, in fact, Price was a member) could have been offered the challenge of Borley, but as we now know so well, the editor of the *Daily Mirror* telephoned Harry Price who accepted the suggestion that he should investigate Borley. Price and his secretary, Lucy Kaye, later Mrs Meeker, together with Wall, motored down to Borley Rectory on June 12th 1929, and arrived in time to take lunch with the Rector and his wife, to learn some of the legends about the Rectory, its past history and its current mysteries. For Harry, it was the start of what could well be described as the strangest and most controversial case that he was to undertake in the whole of his career.

With the onset of the evening of that first day at Borley Rectory, Price and Wall were in the garden when Wall, spotting a moving shadow looking like a figure, close to the far side of the garden, called out "There she is!", thinking that he had sighted the nun. Price turned to look just

too late and was never certain that he had spotted the figure. That was the beginning of an extraordinary first experience of the Rectory's phenomena for Price. As the two men went to re-enter the house by the verandah entrance, something dropped through the glass roof with a crash and landed close by, showering the pair with slivers of broken glass. The object was found to be a piece of brick.

Having previously sealed all those rooms that could not readily be watched, the two men hurried into the house and checked, in particular, the upper floor to see whether someone had thrown the brick down from there, but all of Price's seals were untouched and still in place. In one room that they unsealed and re-entered, a pair of red glass candlesticks stood on the mantle piece, and both were still in place when the couple left, locked the room and resealed it. As they descended the stairs however, one of these candlesticks hurtled over their heads down the stairwell, struck the stove in the hall below and smashed.

Standing with the Rector, surveying the sad remains, the party was then showered with a crazy assortment of pebbles, bits of slate, mothballs and other sundry junk of seemingly inexplicable origin. This prompted another extensive search of the Rectory, with no tangible result to provide an answer to the hail of debris. The next curious phenomena was for the library and drawing-room door locks to eject their keys on to the floor for no visible reason, though some folk have since tried to suggest air pressure as the cause, ideas that certainly do not sound at all convincing. Much later that night all assembled in the Blue Room where, under Price's supervision, a seance was conducted. The chief contact reported to have been made during this session was, we are told, with the late Rev. Harry Bull about whom various bits of information came to light, mostly never to be published as some of the people involved, such as the Bull sisters, were still alive. Consequently, the recorded details of the results of this seance had, of necessity, to be, at least partly, held in confidence. Because of an obvious responsibility to those still living, there was little, if anything, that Price could do about this at the time and though the details of the seance would probably be harmless now, various papers have been lost over the years and, regrettably, some of the details pertinent to Borley have been lost for good. However, one incident that was recorded during the seance is still on record.

Some feet away from where the party was sitting was a wash-stand with a water jug beneath. During the proceedings, there came a loud 'clunk' from the direction of the wash-stand and upon investigation it was found that a cake of soap had leapt from it and struck the top of the water jug with such force that the soap was deeply dented. Also heard during the seance was a persistent knocking sound which was found to be coming from the back of an old wooden framed mirror.

The seance was wound up at about 4 a.m., after which, as Price tells us, he retired to bed in the Blue Room, in which nothing further untoward was to occur that night.

Harry Price was to make numerous visits to Borley Rectory over the next few years but in the meantime, the atmosphere and the lack of home comforts were telling on Guy Smith and his wife who had been quite ill for a time. By the summer of 1929, not very long after Price started his own investigation, they had had enough and whilst continuing to carry out his duties as Rector, Guy Smith with his wife moved into lodgings in Long Melford. During this period, with the Rectory once again unoccupied, things continued to occur that were odd to say the least. Local villagers continued to report seeing the light in the locked upstairs room, and on return visits to the Rectory, a previously closed and locked window was found gaping wide open. On paying a further return visit to the Rectory in February 1930, the Smiths were surprised to find that some of their furniture, which they left in store there as a temporary measure, had been hurled about the room, also part of a stone fireplace had been dumped on one of the staircases. Writing to Price later, the Smiths recounted that on approaching the house on or about the 18th of March 1930, they heard 'the most horrible sounds coming from the house'. In April 1930, the Smiths finally left the area altogether, moving to Sheringham.

The building was once again without a tenant and, for a while, it looked as though Borley would have difficulty in finding a new Rector, but finally the surviving members of the Bull family managed to persuade a cousin to return from Canada to take up the post as Rector, and on the 16th of October 1930, Borley Rectory saw the arrival of the Rev. Lionel Algernon Foyster M.A., together with his much younger wife Marianne, and a little adopted baby daughter, Adelaide. Their arrival signified the start of five of the most stormy years in the whole of the Rectory's history over which controversy has continued ever since. In the face of the recorded happenings that follow, there have been varying accounts by many people of what did or did not happen between 1930 and 1935, when the Foysters finally packed and left. Marianne's side of the story, as she recounted it in more recent years, far from resolving the controversy, just added to it, providing yet another slant on the efforts of Harry Price and others such as Trevor Hall, to respectively prove or disprove the whole episode.

One of the most fascinating aspects of the Foysters' tenancy at Borley was a diary kept by the Rector, telling of some of the most extraordinary phenomena in the house. There have been suggestions made that the diary, though inspired by things that happened in the Rectory, was compiled with a view to it being published and was, as a consequence, somewhat embroidered. This idea cannot be entirely discounted of course, but one wonders whether such ideas were entirely in keeping with the diary writer's position as a man of the cloth. It is now, generally believed however, that it was the intention of Lionel Foyster to circularise the diary among members of his family, of which there were several, dotted about in various places. Like their relations the Bulls, the Foysters were quite a clan, Lionel's side of the family having provided successive Rectors for the parish church of All Saints' in Hastings, Sussex, where Lionel himself was born. There were, in all, four versions of this diary, including a hand written one and a typed manuscript in which Foyster concealed the location of the house, called it 'Cromley Hall'. He also altered the names of the people involved, though it still ran pretty true to what other people witnessed at the Rectory during those five years, the diary itself dealing with about eighteen months of that period.

Regarding the criticisms about the diary, there have been statements to the effect that items that went missing in the Rectory, apparently without any logical explanation, were in fact mislaid by the Rector due to supposed absentmindedness on his part, but again, though that is possible it is an answer to the phenomena that seems to me to be too convenient, and in many instances, it is a solution that is not good enough. The characters of Lionel Foyster and his rather curious young wife will be looked at in greater detail in a chapter set aside for their tenure as residents of the Rectory. For the present though, we are here concerned with the phenomena that are said to have occurred while they were at the Rectory and so to continue.

We are told that on their first full day in the house, Marianne was alone in the building at one point and heard curious disembodied voices calling out her name. Referring to the Rector's diary, we learn the following, that:

Footsteps were heard by the Rector, his wife, Adelaide and a helper. Marianne reported seeing the figure of Harry Bull more than once, clad in a dressing gown that local folk recalled him having worn often when he was alive. In addition to the appearance of Harry Bull, other more annoying things happened. Assorted utensils, such as jugs and other crockery would go missing and then reappear elsewhere in the house. On one occasion, the Foysters noticed a strange, rather enchanting smell like cologne and lavender mixed, the smell being most pronounced in the Blue Room, which they used as their bedroom. The familiar bellringing incidents continued to take place, some-

times for long periods at a time. One day, Marianne, having taken off her wristwatch to wash her hands, turned to put it back on, only to find that the bracelet strap had vanished. It was never recovered. There then followed the appearance of a lavender bag, not seen before, first on the mantlepiece in the sewing room, then in the Rector's coat pocket a day or so later. In the typed 'concealed location' version of the diary there appears a remark that Marianne supposedly made about the lavender bag; "Don't throw it away. If you don't want it, I'll put it in with the washing".

Then there occurred the strange incident of some old books found in the toilet upstairs, next to the chapel. A book was found on the window sill. When removed, it was found later to have been replaced with another and another and so on until, on the last occasion, a book was found lying on the floor with its cover torn off. This last episode is reported as having occurred during February 1931.

On the 25th of that month, a number of missing items of crockery, lost some time before, were found piled in the kitchen. At Lionel's suggestion, Marianne asked whoever or whatever was responsible for these capers to return a missing teapot. The teapot reappeared. The lost watch-strap was also asked for, but sadly with no success. Upon waking the following morning, February 26th, they found some old books thrown under their bed. Later the same day, a stack of Durham Mission hymn books was found on a shelf over the kitchen range. A popular version of this incident has it that the church was rather short of hymn books at that time.

On the evening of the same day, is said to have occurred the nastiest of all incidents during the Foysters' tenancy. Marianne was outside the Blue Room, carrying a candle in her hand, with nobody else near, when she was struck in the face with sufficient force to cause a cut beneath her eye and to blacken the eye itself. The following evening, February 27th, 1931, shortly after retiring to bed, the couple were buzzed by a cotton reel and then by a hammerhead on a snapped-off handle, both of which skimmed across their bed, the hammerhead landing on the floor with a clatter and the cotton reel striking the wall before dropping to the floor. When the Rector lit a lamp, the strange antics stopped.

A day later, when Foyster had been in his study writing, and had left the room for a few minutes, he returned to find pins sticking point-upwards in two of the chairs. Following this incident, the Rector tripped over an old oil lamp and a saucepan lying on the floor outside his room, and later he came across a floor polisher handle in one of the passageways. The lamp and saucepan he did not even recognise as belonging to the household. On the night of March 5th, Foyster was hit on the head by his own hair brush and later on, Marianne had a doorknob thrown at her from behind whilst traversing the passage from the bathroom. On the two days following, more things were thrown and articles were dumped on the floor. In one case, pictures from the wall on the stairs were found lying on the floor, books on a shelf in the sewing room were hurled on to the floor, and stones were thrown.

On March 9th, working men arrived at the Rectory to thaw out frozen pipes which had been installed earlier. While the men were working there, stones were heard and seen tumbling down the back stairs. Foyster was apparently satisfied that when Marianne entered the building, having been outside, she was not responsible for the incident. Later, in walking from the kitchen to the sewing room, Marianne was pursued by a large chunk of iron which came scudding along the corridor after her and landed inside the sewing room as she tried to shut the door against it. Then Marianne was in the process of making up the fire in the kitchen range, when a stone flew over the room and struck the door just as the Rector passed behind it. On the 10th of March, in the morning, Marianne woke to find small stones behind her pillow.

Following this came further disturbances including the breaking of the window on the stairs by something thrown through it from *inside*, while all the occupants of the house were downstairs near the hall

stove. Not long after this, various odds and ends were found in the house, such as a tin travelling trunk, not seen before, a powder box and, most odd, a wedding ring which had disappeared by the following morning. An odd sequel to the ring was that a few years later, on the last day of Harry Price's own tenancy of the Rectory, when he and a colleague Mr Geoffrey Motion were checking, prior to locking up for the last time, they found a gold ring, possibly the same ring, on the floor in one of the rooms.

Returning to the Foysters' experiences, the next dubious treat in store was for Marianne to trip over a brick lying by the bathroom door. The following day saw the arrival of two priests who, accompanied by the Rector and Marianne, covered the whole house, reciting prayers and using incense and holy water in an attempt to put an end to the disturbances. Though nothing further happened for a while, their efforts proved ineffective, like all such attempts to clear the Rectory of its phenomena. Later, a small boy passing by outside had a stone thrown at him and when the Rector returned from having been out during the latter part of that day, he had another stone thrown at him. Shortly after, another stone fell near the hall stove, narrowly missing the Rector's head.

The next incident recorded by the Rector occurred on March 12th, when some clean linen, which had been put away in a cupboard in the kitchen, was found to have been turned out and strewn all over the floor. The following day, Marianne was again injured, this time by a piece of metal hurled down the back stairs. At supper that evening, a piece of brick dropped by the Rector's plate, but without breaking anything. On a later occasion, Marianne was not so lucky when a potsherd hit her causing a cut on the forehead. Two days later, the Rector was sitting at his desk using a typewriter and, for comfort, had taken off his dog collar. This was suddenly thrown at him. Next, his walking stick was flung across the room, shortly followed by a piece of coke. Early the next morning, March 16th, Marianne came down to the kitchen to find the contents of one of the cupboards hurled about and the kitchen table lying upside down. During that day, the Foysters had left open their bedroom window. That evening, it was found to have been closed the wrong way round, i.e. top sash at the bottom, bottom sash at the top. On March 23rd, the Rector was ill in bed and whilst climbing the stairs with a plate of food for him, and carrying in her other hand an oil lamp, Marianne had part of a flat iron thrown at her from behind, and which knocked the glass chimney off the lamp. The following day, various small bits and pieces were thrown at Marianne while she was house cleaning. During the next few days she again reported seeing Harry Bull on his usual beat on the stairs and this time, he might just have been seen by a tenant of the stable cottage although, as stated in *The End of Borley Rectory,* the possibility that the ghost of Harry Bull was subjective to Marianne alone should not be ignored.

Another more unpleasant experience came when Marianne, whilst near the kitchen, was tapped on the shoulder by what she described as a 'monstrosity that had a touch like iron'. Little baby Adelaide was also alleged to have been struck on the face by a similar apparition when sent to lie down in one of the rooms. This incident seems rather casually reported by the Rector, for surely, the three-year-old would have screamed out if struck in this way? However, according to the Rector, when asked how she came to have a bruise on her face, she merely replied, "A nasty thing by the curtains gave it to me". Little has ever been recorded as to how baby Adelaide reacted to the various incidents in the Rectory, though there is the possibility that she constituted no psychic focus worth the name and was thus largely unaffected by the phenomena. There was, however, just one other occasion when she seemed to be disturbed, when visitors to the Rectory found objects hurtling about, and Adelaide with Francois d'Arles' small son, cowering by the dining room door in obvious discomfort. One of the two tots is reported to have said, "We don't like so many 'fings falling about."

April brought a fresh crop of incidents to the hapless Foysters, with various objects being thrown at them both. One tea time, a full jug of milk had been placed upon the table, but when the Rector went to pour from it, it was empty. He made a sarcastic remark about not wanting to drink from the same jug as ghosts. Foyster recalled in his diary counting about a dozen times that he had objects thrown at him in various parts of the house between six and eleven o'clock at night. One evening in May, the Foysters had a nasty time in the kitchen for among other things, Marianne had pepper thrown in her face. The Rector procured some creosote and used it as an incense or fumigant to try to halt the disturbances, which worked for a time but only after he himself was struck by a piece of cement. Coming downstairs with the creosote, he was buzzed by a metal spanner! The following evening, Marianne tried fumigating the place but didn't use enough creosote it would seem, because there followed bell-ringing, stone throwing, and a near miss from a jam jar which struck the kitchen door and smashed, just as Marianne was returning to the kitchen.

At 9 p.m. one Monday evening, Sir George and Lady Whitehouse, from Arthur Hall, near Sudbury, arrived to see what was happening. Plenty, it would seem, for whilst they were at the Rectory, a smell of burning became very noticeable. A hurried search was made of the upstairs rooms, where, in one room not normally in use, a part of the wainscotting was found to be alight. It was put out, but the would-be fireman was rewarded by being struck by a stone. Notwithstanding what we now know about Captain W. H. Gregson who later bought the Rectory, and the many allegations surrounding its destruction, the burning skirting board was, in a way a precursor of what was eventually to befall the building. Over the next few days, Marianne visited the Rectory on and off, and found among other things pieces of paper floating about with her name written on them in a childish hand.

On June 6th, there was another spate of stone throwing and the following evening, while Marianne was in bed, unwell, a chair in her room twice overturned by itself. During that night, there was a bout of the usual bangs and crashes that seemed to have been commonplace during the earlier Bull years.

On Monday, June 8th, the Foysters had a morning of chaotic disturbance, including books, dirty linen, a suitcase and a linen basket hurled down the main stairwell, the linen basket twice hurtling to the ground floor. Following this, Marianne was roused from bed by a great racket coming from the Blue Room. Upon entering the room, she was confronted with the aftermath of a noisesome disturbance, with the bed moved and other pieces of furniture overturned and flung about, though the noise ceased the moment she entered the room. According to the Rector's diary for that day, as was recorded in Price's book, a doctor who called at the Rectory also saw some throwing of objects.

Lady Whitehouse's nephew Richard, who later was to become Dom Richard Whitehouse, O.S.B., also visited on that day, and what he saw and experienced is worth relating in some detail. The following details are drawn from his report as it was later set out in *The Most Haunted House in England,* over which Harry Price was subsequently to be heavily criticised by Messrs Dingwall, Goldney and Hall. He was however, later partly exonerated, not only by Robert J. Hastings, but also by Dom Richard's further testimony, in which the only thing he queried as not being correct was Price's reporting of the incident concerning paranormally precipitated bottles, one of which Price described as having appeared in mid air, changed its shape, then crashed to the floor. Bottles did crash to bits in the kitchen on the occasion in question, but more of that shortly.

Taking a summary from Richard Whitehouse's report, we learn that he was met by the sight of contents of the Blue Room that had been hurled down the main stairs, the dropping at his feet of a watchcase and a metal bookrest (both whilst standing talking to the Rector near the stairs), the precipitation of a brass stiletto

normally kept in the study, and the ejection from her bed of Mrs Foyster. At the moment that this happened, the second time that morning, Whitehouse was just going downstairs after speaking to Mrs Foyster who was in bed, unwell yet again, when he heard her cry out in alarm and returned to find her face-down on the floor with mattress and bedding on top of her. Marianne was again thrown out of bed once more after Richard had departed. To Whitehouse, she related that she had felt the bed tip, and something punch her and push her out. The results of what Richard saw led him to ask Lady Whitehouse to come to the Foysters' aid by sheltering them away from the Rectory for a time and in response, the Whitehouses packed them all into a car and took them to Arthur Hall, Sudbury. Marianne in fact stayed away until July and the Rectory was not occupied at night for the rest of that June except when the Rector could find someone to stay with him at the house. One night when Francois d'Arles was asleep there, hearing a noise that seemed to come from his room, the Rector went to look. d'Arles was asleep but pushed up against the inside of his door was a paint pot. d'Arles said he knew nothing about this paint pot, but the incident does seem rather insignificant when compared with other phenomena.

At one point during August, two investigators came to Borley and held a seance at which, initially, the contact was thought to be the spirit of a certain 'Joe Miles', who supposedly admitted to being the cause of all the trouble at the Rectory. Subsequently, however, this was discarded as being inaccurate.

Early in September, according to a letter in the Harry Price Library, the Rector was called over from the church by Marianne to find his study in a state of confusion with the desk thrown over, chairs overturned, books out of their shelves and a general mess. Pondering briefly upon this last incident, it seems that whilst anybody could have easily have thrown chairs and books about, only someone fairly brawny could have turned over a traditional heavy desk such as one normally finds in Rectories. This would therefore seem to eliminate Marianne, whom one could perhaps initially suspect. The writer has paused to dwell on this point because of statements often made that Marianne perpetrated some of these incidents herself. More will be said about these allegations later.

Returning to the phenomena, we learn that it was also in September that the Foysters were locked out of their bedroom, whilst little Adelaide was locked in hers. A relic of Vianney, Curé d'Ars, carried by the Rector, when used in conjunction with a prayer, usually but not always resulted in locks being released. It is sometimes suggested that occurrences like that, involving religious relics, often revolve around a strong faith in the results, which of course one might expect from a devoted churchman. Whilst some may disagree, the writer feels that this may be one of those grey areas where religious faith, psychic power and mind over matter merge at the edges. It is to be hoped that in due time, the scientists whill finally be able to enlighten us all on this subject.

Yet another annoying incident, experienced by Marianne and the first resident maid to work there since the Foysters arrived, involved a saucepan of potatoes. This had been left on the stove in the kitchen, which was left empty for a few minutes. Upon returning to the kitchen, the two women found the saucepan completely empty. Other things went missing in the house, including some typewritten papers that the Rector had been working on.

On October 13th, 1931 came the incident that caused the rift between Harry Price and Lionel Foyster. Together with others of his Council for Psychic Research, one of whom was a later critic, Mrs K. M. Goldney, Price visited the Rectory where the party witnessed a flying bottle and other incidents of throwing objects, and another instance of somebody being locked in a bedroom, in this case Mrs Foyster. During this visit, there also occurred a wine into ink incident, which Price thought for some time to be a trick. The party had brought with them two bottles of wine to contribute to the refreshments supplied by Mrs Foyster. When the bottle

of red wine was uncorked and some was poured into a glass, it reportedly turned into ink and a glass of white wine was found to smell of Eau de Cologne. The wine remaining in the bottles was apparently quite normal. Another bell ringing episode also took place during this visit.

A further incident reportedly manifested itself to the party's driver, Mr James Ballantyne, who not being much interested in ghosts sat downstairs and read a newspaper whilst Price and his colleagues carried out their investigation. As Ballantyne sat there, a hand appeared round the door, moving slowly up and down. He was rather surprised, and a little curious but didn't attach any real importance to the incident, doubtless having heard in advance of the Rectory's story on the way down from London, and he continued to read his newspaper.

Upon returning to the Bull Hotel, Long Melford, the party discussed what they had seen and experienced, and Harry Price in particular came to the conclusion that embarrassing though it might be, a lot of what had occurred happened while Marianne Foyster was out of sight and, therefore, there seemed to be a strong possibility that she had been responsible for at least some of the phenomena. Upon returning to Borley Rectory to tell the Rector of their doubts, the party incurred strong protest on the part of Marianne, whose part was also taken up on the spot by one of Price's own party, Mrs Goldney, and the Rector was said to have been furious. Poor Harry Price found himself barred from the Rectory and to crown it all, as the group made their way back to London, their car driven by James Ballantyne, developed clutch failure and they arrived home tired, cold and fed up.

This unfortunate state of affairs between Price and the Rector was, fortunately, salvaged after a period of time with the help of Sidney Glanville, when Harry Price began to feel that incidents he previously thought to be fraud were perhaps not so.

Phenomena continued during October 1931, the Rector being awakened early one morning by having a water jug

Reproduction of a pencilled wall-message that appeared near 'The Blue Room' in Borley Rectory, in the presence of Mrs. Foyster and Dom Richard Whitehouse, O.S.B., on June 16, 1931, and which appears on page 197 of *The End of Borley Rectory*.

Marianne Please help get ~

One of a number of pencilled wall 'Appeals' to Marianne (taken from illustration facing page 180 in *The End of Borley Rectory*).

dropped on his head. He put it down on the floor, but it was then dropped on Marianne's head. It was also during that autumn that the incident involving Adelaide and the 'monstrosity' occurred, an incident detailed earlier, and similar to the assault on Marianne outside the Blue Room. Marianne is said to have told a visitor to the Rectory, Mr G. P. L'Estrange, that the assault on her was like a blow from a man's fist.

There was further trouble on November 13th, a Friday just to add to the weirdness of the whole episode. The Rector, having to go up to London on business, asked Richard Whitehouse to come up from Sudbury to give an eye to the folks at the Rectory. He arrived at about tea time, to be greeted by a peal of servant bell ringing. The two children were put to bed and the rest of the household then withdrew to the kitchen, including young Katie, the maid (not Katie Boreham of later planchette origin). As Marianne sat in a chair in one corner of the kitchen, there came a loud crash from beneath the chair. A bottle, which had appeared from heaven knows where, had exploded and there was glass all over the place. A little later as Richard Whitehouse went to sit down to some supper, the same thing happened again, beneath his chair . . . Bang! . . . and another mess of broken glass, which a mystified Kate proceeded to sweep up. Yet another bottle dashed itself to pieces on the floor . . . Crash! . . . more sweeping

up for Katie. Then there followed the sound of footsteps on the back stairs, culminating in another bottle rolling in through the door, this time without breaking. Interestingly, the cellars had once been used for storing bottles of wine, the brick bins remaining in situ to the very end. It was thought that the bottles that showered themselves all over the kitchen might well have come from the cellar.

Then the bells started up again, and this time the yard bell, outside on its bracket high up on the Rectory wall, also began to join in, perhaps in sympathy.

Later that evening, with the Rector long overdue from London because of his train being delayed by fog, Mrs Foyster decided to retire to bed. As she and Whitehouse began to climb the main stairs, Marianne collapsed in a heap, and Richard was fortunate to grab the lamp she was carrying just in time, though it guttered and went out. Feeling his way up the stairs in the gloom, he carried Marianne up and placed her on the floor by one of the bedrooms. To his relief, the Rector came in at that point and was able to take over. It was with some relief that Dom Richard was able to depart for Sudbury, and his own bed. He had had quite enough of that house for one day.

These bouts of collapsing by Marianne were rather curious and will be mentioned in greater detail later.

On December 14th, Richard White-

45

house again called at the Rectory prior to going to Sheringham, Norfolk, to talk to Guy and Mabel Smith, the previous inhabitants, who had moved there after spending a short time at Long Melford. Later, the couple moved to Ashford, Kent, when Smith was appointed Rector of Sevington, and they were there in 1939 when their former home went up in flames. On the day of this further visit by Dom Richard, Lionel Foyster was in bed ill, with arthritis, and Marianne was with him in his room. Whilst all were present, a thin glass tumbler dropped at Whitehouse's feet and rolled round to stop intact. Dom Richard later expressed the view that nobody could have thrown the tumbler without breaking it.

Also during this period, the bottle smashing continued at intervals, but on another occasion, Lionel Foyster's bottle of pills disappeared. Later the same day, Dom Richard, who had visited the Foysters was on his way back to Sudbury and near Rodbridge level crossing, he started to put on his overcoat and must have been mystified to find Lionel's bottle of pills was in one of the pockets.

During January 1932, members of The Marks Tey Spiritualist Circle visited the Rectory and were greeted with pandemonium. A shower of bottles hurled down the back stairs, left a pile of broken glass and then the bellringing started again. Following the departure of the Spiritualists, however, Foyster recalled that the place seemed quite diffrerent, though minor incidents continued to occur right up until October of 1935, when the Foysters packed and left, chiefly because of the Rector's ill health. In fact, he was in such poor shape that he carried out no further clerical duties from then on.

Whether or not the Marks Tey group thought they had finally cleared the Rectory of its tricks is hard to say, but in the light of subsequent happenings, we can see now that they might as well have squirted water at an elephant for the lasting effect it had.

The authors of *The Haunting of Borley Rectory* viewed the advent of the Marks Tey Circle as significant, and came to the conclusion that the change of atmos-

phere afterwards was due to Marianne having been rumbled, so to speak, thus leaving her with no worthwhile reason to continue with the supposedly fraudulent phenomena. However, like so much else in that publication, this all sounds like dramatically impressive evidence against Marianne and the Rectory in general, until one realises that again, this proposition seeks to deny testimony about the Rectory's phenomena from Dom Richard and many others. The writer points out, as did Robert J. Hastings, the nonsense in the suggestion that Whitehouse was suffering from the effects of a nervous breakdown *while at Borley,* which, had it been true, might well have impaired his judgement. He had at one time suffered from a nervous illness, but that was well before his interest in Borley Rectory, and he had completely recovered from it.

Two other visitors to the Rectory during the Foysters' tenancy, Sir John and Lady Braithwaite, thought that there was hysteria on Marianne's part, and more than one person since has described her as neurotic. If she was, we may never be able to prove it. Comments on the possibilities of psychic capabilities viz-a-viz Marianne, a possible answer to her bouts of collapsing, appear further on in this book. As to hysteria, Lionel Foyster argued against it as a total answer to the situation. If Marianne was hysterical at Borley, she might just as well have been so elsewhere. There is no evidence known to the writer that such events occurred elsewhere in her life and that being the case, it does not seem possible to *prove* with any absolute certainty, that hysteria was to blame for the Foyster phenomena. Once again, we come back to a central point about almost all the periods of tenancy at Borley Rectory, where psychic phenomena are concerned.

With the exception of the most violent disturbances and wall writings, whatever occurred during one tenancy had already happened to a considerable extent during the previous period and re-occurred during the time of the next occupancy. Certain types of phenomena, particularly the smashing of objects such as glass and china, were commonplace from the Smiths' time on. They, in turn, experienced some of the curious visual effects common during the years of the Bull family's occupancy. The stone throwing, frequent during the Foysters' tenancy, spilled over into the war years as witness the experiences of the two Polish officers at Borley during 1943. The physical assaults had various parallels in all but the Smith period. A Bull sister had her face slapped, while Marianne was clouted in the face with some violence and a later visitor was pushed into a puddle by unseen hands. The idea that successive sets of tenants at Borley Rectory inherited from one another the supposed idea of continuing to produce fraudulent psychic phenomena, becomes ridiculous when one realises just how long a period was involved. The Rectory was completed in 1863 and its burned out shell was not completely cleared until early 1945. From when it was first occupied, there were disturbances logged in the place, right up until the time of its final ending, a period of just about 82 years, possibly one of the longest hauntings in British history. The disturbances saw out three families, Harry Price and his team, Gregson, and the war years of dereliction.

For that reason, if for no other, the coming upon the scene of Harry Price made little if any difference to the total picture of phenomena. The result of Price's interest in them was that, what had for many years been a fairly common topic of interest in Borley, became a talking point throughout the country. In other words, the Rectory's oddities were already there, and all Price did was to tell the world about them.

There were other witnesses to the weird and often annoying phenomena at Borley Rectory, among whom was Mr G. P. J. L'Estrange, who in 1932 was living at Bungay in Suffolk. He visited the Rectory in January 1932, having motored over from Colchester on the day in question. Even as he got out of his car, he noticed a dim figure standing stock still in the angle of the porch wall. As soon as he tried to approach it, the figure disappeared. L'Estrange went inside and joined the Foysters for a cup of tea, but in the midst of

that came a loud crash! The two men, going out into the corridor to see what caused the noise, found smashed crockery all over the floor. According to the Rector, the wreckage belonged to china from the kitchen dresser at the rear of the house, whereas all the smashed bits lay in the hallway. No sooner had the men returned to their tea when there came an absolute pandemonium of smashing glass. When the two men again got up and went to the door, it was in time to see bottles hurtling and crashing in every direction.

During a tour round the house a little later, with the Rector, L'Estrange learned of the blow to the face suffered by another guest (d'Arles, who is said to have reported being struck in the face by a ghostly form in his room when he tried to grab hold of it) an assault similar to that on Marianne. During his stay L'Estrange himself was faced with a similar sight in his room, and though he tried to approach the curious shape, and talk to it, he felt as though something was pushing him back. He also related having to summon all his concentration to get the unpleasant phantom to disperse. It did, slowly dissolving into nothing. Other disconcerting happenings during his visit included the sound of footsteps passing right behind a settee in which he was sitting, only to fade through an adjacent wall. The fuller report of Mr L'Estrange's visit can be found in Price's second book, *The End of Borley Rectory.* Again, before jumping to the sort of erroneous conclusions about this that many of Price's critics would have us believe, it should be remembered by the reader that all this sort of harrassing uproar had occurred before in front of other witnesses.

Among other incidents at this time, a bowl narrowly missed the Rector before smashing on the floor, and items from their best tea set were broken, one of the cups hurtling *up* the staircase. On another occasion, Mrs Foyster was in bed unwell and claimed to have woken to find the oil lamp in her room lit, though it wasn't when she dozed off, and the rest of the household were out. The Rector upon returning home went upstairs to light his wife's lamp, only to find that it was already alight. The reader would be forgiven for thinking that only Mrs Foyster could have lit the lamp, but the Rector at the time believed that his wife was not in a fit state to get out of bed. It is worth mentioning in passing that Mrs Foyster seemed to either collapse or be taken unwell on numerous occasions at Borley, an interesting point that will be dealt with more fully later.

We turn now to the wall writings, the one major set of reported occurrences not recorded before the Foysters came, but which continued *in partial form* after the Foysters left, though later mainly in the form of squiggles and scrawls and not as complete or semi-complete messages.

Readers will recall that many strange incidents in the history of the site have been recorded, amongst which was that of the Rev. Guy Smith who heard a pleading voice calling out "No Carlos, Don't!" while his wife found a skull in a cupboard. Both of which, if accepted as genuine happenings, could be taken as indicators of something rather untoward in former years – but what?

Leaving aside for the time being the claim often made that they were faked, the wall writings were unique, in that they supposedly related to one entity throughout, namely the nun or 'Marie Lairre' as she always been called since, and of whom there will be much to relate later.

The wall writings were preceded by pathetic little messages on pieces of paper that appeared about the house, all pleading for 'Marianne', supposedly wanting help in some way. One suggestion often made was that these were the work of the nun, who allegedly died a young girl and now sought assistance from a person who was also young and female, a status that applied in both ways to Mrs Marianne Foyster. One of the earliest full messages appeared on the wall of the kitchen passage on the ground floor. It read: 'Marianne Light Mass Prayers'. Nearby were also found scrawled the letters 'Ma'. On the first floor, the name 'Marianne' appeared. Then, outside the bathroom was discovered: 'Marianne, Please Help Get', since thought to have

been, not broken English written by a French entity, but more likely an incomplete message in English viz 'Please help. Get . . .'.

However, possibly the most curious of all, also found by the bathroom was 'Marianne At Get Help-Entant Bottom Me' which was subsequently redefined as perhaps being intended as: 'Well Tank Bottom Me', at first sight looking like incoherent nonsense, until one learns of some of the later theories about the nun and the well in the grounds.

Mrs Foyster, noticing this message, wrote beneath it 'I cannot understand. Please tell me more'. The entity replied but in such tangled form that only the following could be deciphered with any accuracy: 'Light In–Write Prayer and O'.

Another message, again outside the bathroom, simply said: 'Edwin'. Reported by Harry Price as being a friend of the Foysters, 'Edwin' was in fact Richard, later Dom Richard Whitehouse, Edwin being his middle name.

The next major message read: 'Get light Mass and Prayers–Here-Tibil', or possibly 'Sibil', 'Mas by Boy'. This message curiously enough also seemed to relate to Dom Richard because the expression 'Boy' was a nickname bestowed upon him by older relatives when he was a small child. There were many interpretations of the wall writings sent to Price after the publication of his first book. For example, one person thought that 'Mas by Boy' might have been intended as 'Mass by Abbey', but if the whole business of the nun was connected with France, then that could just have easily have meant 'Mass by Abbe' or 'Abbot'. Canon Pythian Adams took a fresh look at one previously seemingly unreadable scribble and dissected it into 'Trompee', which means 'betrayal' or 'to mislead', and the phrase 'Repond Ici'.

During the tenancy of Harry Price, there appeared on a wall in front of watching observers, a set of upward curving lines resembling the Prince of Wales' feathers. One suggestion made was that this was intended to represent the Waldegrave crest, whilst another theory was that it was a Fleur de Lis, which in some people's eyes strengthened aspects of the French nun story.

A good many people have since maintained that Marianne Foyster wrote these wall messages herself, and in fact Peter Underwood, in a letter to the *Journal of the Society for Psychical Research,* confirmed that when he submitted samples of the messages to a graphologist the opinion was that, except for one word, they all seemed to have originated from Mrs Foyster. The present writer raises this point later and suggests that as these wall markings also appeared in the absence of both Marianne and Harry Price, who is also accused of having written some of the messages, there is no clear proof that Marianne produced them, unless she was being used as a channel for psychic activity by entities with which Borley Rectory was supposedly soaked.

Another curious twist to the claims that Marianne Foyster wrote the wall messages was that in the Owen and Mitchell report in the *S.P.R. Journal* for 1979, she stated that the wall writings puzzled her and that, furthermore, she was cross when she first discovered them, because the wall on which they first appeared had only just been redecorated and that it took her ages to clean the marks off. It is obvious now that she could not have cleaned all these off because some of them at least were still there when Sidney Glanville photographed the interior of the Rectory during Harry Price's tenancy of 1937/38. We do know that Marianne did in fact write messages on the walls quite deliberately, because she replied to one of the messages that 'appeared' by asking the originator of it to tell her more.

However, so far as the other messages are concerned, as Marianne has so often flatly contradicted her own evidence, we still have no real proof one way or the other.

The wall writings caused another row after Price's death, when his critics tried to claim that he had told Sidney Glanville to pencil the messages in so that they could be photographed, thus supposedly proving that Price was on mischief-bent yet again! The truth of this has since turned out to be rather different. Glanville undertook the photographing of samples of the wall writings as part of his extremely thorough and dedicated work at Borley Rectory and it was he who asked Price whether it might be advisable to carefully bring the writings out more clearly so that they could be photographed. One should not forget that many of these markings had appeared during the Foyster tenancy, and that they had departed in October 1935. Sidney Glanville did not undertake his investigations until 1937 to 1938, by which time any pencil markings would have been well faded unless in total shadow. The writer would go so far as to defy anyone with an ordinary camera to get satisfactory results from pencil on plaster after such a period of time *without* having to go over the marks again, especially in a building without any adequate lighting. The very bright flashbulb outfits, then in use by most photographers, might even tend to 'blind out' such faint marks on plaster. Remember also that at Borley Rectory, there was no mains electricity supply that could be used for studio lighting equipment and that consequently, Glanville would have had to use flash for most of the interior scenes and time exposures for the wall writings.

Whether or not we can totally accept the wall writings at Borley Rectory as evidence of paranormal activity is, and probably always will be, arguable. If they were of psychic origin, possibly through the medium of a living contact in the form of Mrs Foyster, then it is by no means certain that they referred, as has always been supposed, to the nun. If they signified anything at all, it could just as easily be something that occurred during the existence of the Rectory rather than before it was built. Whichever ultimately proves to be the truth of the matter, the wall writings, like so much else in this strange tale, could fairly be said to be one of the enigmas of Borley Rectory. On that note, we must leave the Foyster phenomena and pass on to events that occurred over the next four years.

CHAPTER SEVEN

THE FINAL PRE-WAR YEARS
1936 TO 1939

With the departure of the Foysters in 1935, the use of Borley Rectory for its intended purpose was finished for good and when the next incumbent, the Rev. Alfred Clifford Henning, arrived in the district in 1936, he took up residence at Liston Rectory, the two parishes by now having been combined. The Rector was instructed to make arrangements for the old Rectory to be sold, but for a time, it was available for renting by a lay person. It was under these conditions that Harry Price became its tenant for a year in 1937. His preparations for extensive investigation have been recorded in a separate chapter, so we will concentrate here on some of the events that took place during the period that Price's observer team were carrying out their work.

The first to carry out a tour of duty at Rectory was Sidney Glanville, with his son Roger, on June 19th, 1937, and they stayed until the following morning. It was during this visit that Glanville took the measurements from which floor plans were later prepared. He also installed a corundum (crystallized alumina) powder tracing device, which if moved, normally or paranormally, would leave a clear trail, but it was apparently not touched or moved. Sidney Glanville commented as have many others, upon the coldness and the stillness of the Rectory. During his first visit, late in the evening of that day, they heard a sharp click and later two soft taps, the origin of which they could not locate.

On August 14th, 1937, Glanville again visited the Rectory with Captain H. G. Harrison, his brother-in-law, and during a period in which they were taking photographs of some of the wall markings, they discovered fresh marks on one section of a wall that they had left only shortly

before. The only noises that were heard on this occasion were a sharp crack and some scrabbling noises, but much more curious on this occasion was the discovery that somebody had turned over part of the cats cemetery, but for what reason, heaven only knows!

On Saturday, August 28th, 1937, Sidney and Roger Glanville, with Captain Harrison and Squadron Leader Horniman visited the Rectory and stayed overnight. They reported hearing bumps and thuds which they could not locate. Also during this visit, 'light tripping footsteps' were reported to have been heard, and this was later to cause trouble when the Borley Rectory story came under the scrutiny of Messrs Dingwall, Goldney and Hall.

When the Glanvilles, father and son, went down to Borley on September 18th, 1937, they heard two taps that seemed to come from the dining room wall.

A curious occurrence befell a friend of Sq. Ldr. Horniman during a visit to the Rectory at this time, in that when he passed across the first floor landing outside the Blue Room, he became bitterly cold. Mark Kerr-Pearse, who was on duty at the Rectory at the same time, felt the man's hands and confirmed that they were abnormally cold. It was this spot on the landing at which Guy Smith had heard whispering voices and it was also here that Marianne had been struck in the face.

Realising the significance of this spot, Glanville drew a miniscule pencilled cross upon the floor. He, with his son and Doctor H. F. Bellamy, then left the building, but before doing so, they placed a tobacco tin on one of the downstairs mantelpieces as a control object. When they returned, the tin was found right on top of Glanville's little pencilled cross on the floor of the upstairs landing, yet there had been nobody in the Rectory in the interim period.

On October 28th, 1937, the Glanvilles and Mr Alan Cuthbert stayed overnight in the Rectory, and during that time, whilst Cuthbert was asleep in the library, the Glanvilles and Mark Kerr-Pearse, who was again on duty, all heard some heavy muffled footsteps crossing the hall. It was not Alan Cuthbert, because he was still fast asleep in the library.

Another incident to cause a row in later years occurred on November 20th, 1937, in the presence of Messrs Glanville and son, Harrison and Dr. H. F. Bellamy. At about 8.25 p.m. that evening, whilst in the library, used as a base room, all noticed that the window blind was moving at the sides, as though a draught was moving it. Both the doors on to the verandah and the hall doors were shut. To try to find out what was moving the blind, they resorted to puffing cigarette smoke into the narrow gap between the blind and the window, to see if it would disperse in any draught that might be present. The smoke did not disperse, indicating that, firstly there wasn't a draught, and that secondly the blind had apparently moved inexplicably.

About this time, the exterior of the Rectory was repainted and among the men engaged on this work was a foreman painter, Mr Hardy. He had often carried out work at the Rectory and on one occasion, was puzzled to see rising from the lawn, a coil of smoke, for which there appeared to be no sensible reason. Some doubting Thomases have since scornfully dismissed the occurrence as the sighting of a cloud of gnats, but the idea that a country-born man like Hardy (who lived in Borley all his life) couldn't tell the difference between gnats and smoke is somewhat incongruous. Hardy had a son, aged about 19 at the time of the Glanville visits to the Rectory, and he reported that on passing the church one evening after work, he heard chanting coming from within, at a time when the church was locked up for the night. He did not feel inclined to stop and take a look.

On March 12th, 1938, occurrences were limited to the discovery of an odd, sticky sort of substance on the floor of the chapel in between rounds of inspection, and a sound like that of a chair being dragged across the floor.

Having given some dated specific examples of what was experienced by various observers, we will now take a look at a resume of the happenings during the period of Price's tenancy, with the exception of the seances, which will be looked at separately.

An occurrence that has been related many times before was that of the movement, under odd circumstances, of a 50 lb bag of coal for a distance of about a foot and a half. Its movement was apparent from the stain left upon the floor from where the bag had originally been placed.

Pencil marks continued to appear though they were not of the same quality or quantity as before. However, the fact that this continued to happen after the departure of the Foysters and in the absence of Harry Price, tends to considerably weaken the accusations that Price was responsible for them. After Price's death, one investigator claimed that during a summertime inspection of the Rectory, with Harry Price present, marks kept appearing as they made their rounds, but that on the last tour of inspection, he got behind Price and kept him in his sight in the lamplight and, to quote: 'we never found another mark'. Unfortunately for the critics, as Robert J. Hastings was later to point out, at the time of this last round of inspection, in the early hours of a summer morning, it would in fact have been daylight, making nonsense of the claim about moving into a position with the lamp in such a way as to put Price under visual control. Under conditions of broad daylight, Harry Price would have had little or no chance to play games of that sort without being caught.

Reports from the various members of Price's team, now in the files at the Harry Price Library, indicate a number of points about this period in the Rectory's history which are worth looking at against the background of the often hostile criticism of Price's handling of the Borley case.

Opinions varied considerably among

the investigators, some expressing the view that there was nothing of significance about the Rectory, others reporting numerous happenings that did indeed show every sign of being most peculiar.

There were other contradictions. Mr Mark Kerr-Pearse, for example, mentioned finding many traces of mice in the Rectory, whilst others stated just the opposite, saying that they had particularly noted *no* traces of mice, the very presence of which could, of course, lead to a good many scrabbling and scratching noises. When considering this point, the reader should remember particularly the one comment about the Rectory that was common to virtually *everybody* who stayed in it, that it was an extremely still and soundless house, unnaturally so, the more so in an empty building with such a large area of wooden flooring and joists.

On the question of mice, Price himself stated that he had found no trace of mice in the Rectory, which is quite possible *at the particular times at which he was present.* The fact that others did find traces of mice does *not* prove the contention popular among the critics that mice were responsible for many of the noises heard in the Rectory.

Investigators also mentioned the apparent fact, as did Price himself, that access to the cellars was feasible, if risky and dangerous, via one of the well covers in the courtyard, and though lockable, the cellar door could be jemmied open from the inside. However, forcing open that door, especially in a house that was largely empty, would in itself cause noise, and consequently an intruder would have had little or no security against being discovered by any investigators that might be present. Interestingly, some investigators, having experienced curious occurrences, also stated that in their opinion, nobody could have got into the Rectory during their turns of duty without their knowing about it, and furthermore, if somebody wished to fake phenomena, then to break in when nobody was in the Rectory (except to plant phenomena, something for which there is *no* proven evidence) would be, to some extent, a

pointless waste of time, since phenomena in the presence of other people would be far more telling than to play to an empty house.

Another problem that occasionally came to light was that when some investigations were in progress, especially in the Rectory garden, the cottage tenant Mr Arbon, was inclined to appear on the scene to see what was happening, thereby causing problems for those watching the Nun's Walk.

One investigator went as far as to ask Price to get Mr Arbon to desist from entering the property when investigators were at hand. Strictly speaking, Arbon's only function was to act as a keyholder and to check the credentials of members of Price's investigating team arriving at Borley for their turns of duty. Apart from these people, and of course Price himself from time to time, the only other persons allowed in the place were the Rector and occasionally the odd parishoner attending parish meetings with the Rector.

When members of the BBC arrived, discursive comments made by Gordon Glover about the state of Mrs Foyster's mind during her time at the Rectory, and the capabilities of Price's team of investigators misfired in one of those unfortunate but generally inconclusive misunderstandings that occurred from time to time throughout Price's career. Price unfortunately took offence at Glover's remarks, and the latter had to go to some lengths to explain what he had meant. The writer is of the opinion that too many critics have allowed these occasional heated disputes to get in the way of a clear assessment of reported phenomena, which after all, were the focal point of the investigation.

The big mistake made by so many people since, has been that of taking too much notice of Price's sometimes volatile temper and overt sensitivity, and not enough of the Rectory itself and what was occurring in it. Price's somewhat argumentative disposition often caused others to take a dislike to him, thus forming a far from ideal background to a fair assessment of his work. There is quite a lot of evidence to suggest that several incidents at the Rectory during the Investigation

Team period 1937/38 were attacked by later critics from a position of prejudice, and that therefore, these criticisms can not really be taken at face value. As Robert Hastings demonstrates in his work on the case, the records of supposed evidence against Harry Price and his handling of the investigation team at Borley Rectory are littered with misquotes and misleading accusations and rather too much tactical withholding of verbatim material by people who have sought to accuse Price of that 'offence'.

The 1937/38 period of investigations into the mysteries at Borley Rectory, which Price genuinely wished to be the most extensive, really turned out in some ways to be the most disappointing but I am certainly not satisfied that the critics have proved this to be the result of Price's handling of the period. There seems, for one thing, to be another no less interesting point that has been rather ignored, and this concerns the nature of the disturbances and in particular the level thereof, in relation to the periods of occupancy of the Rectory and the numbers of people living in it at any one time. This aspect of of the disturbances will be looked at in more detail shortly, but for the present, we will continue with happenings that were reported during the investigation team period.

On one occasion, the Rev. Henning and his wife, and Mark Kerr-Pearse conducted a seance in the Rectory and in response, there came from the direction of the kitchen a series of thumping noises which proceeded along the passageway towards the Base Room (library), where the seance sitters were, but as they stood up to see what might be causing the noise, it stopped.

During Kerr-Pearse's sojourn at the Rectory, he found a piece of rotten timber in one of the fireplaces, the odd thing being that whereas the chimney was badly in need of sweeping, there was no trace of soot on the piece of wood.

Mark Kerr-Pearse was also, once, locked in the library. He was alone in the house but fortunately, the key was on the inside, otherwise he would have had to decamp via the French windows.

About this time, there was a repetition of the noise heard by the Coopers in the stable cottage during the First World War, namely a tremendous crash, as of pots and pans or crockery being thrown around or smashed.

Another odd occurrence concerned the installation of an electrical contact breaker which had been made by Doctor H. F. Bellamy. It was placed on the dining room mantlepiece, beneath some books and was so designed that if anything on it was moved, a bell would ring. The operation of this gadget was carefully checked and the books put in place, after which it was left untouched while Dr. Bellamy and those accompanying him moved off to examine the rest of the Rectory. At about ten to one in the early morning, they were disturbed from resting in the Blue Room, by the response unit's bell ringing. The sound stopped suddenly before they could reach the dining room, but when they entered they found that the books had all been moved, one of them right off the contact. What was even more odd was that with the contact upset by the moving of the books the bell should have kept ringing. Instead, it stopped quite suddenly.

It may interest readers to learn that there had been more than one occasion on which there has been odd interference with electrical equipment during investigations at Borley.

I have learned of two such incidents that occurred long after all trace of the Rectory itself had vanished, and were it not for this fact, the reader could well be forgiven for thinking that Dr. Bellamy's contact breaker was malfunctioning. In 1961, during an investigation at Borley, both battery torches and car headlamps all failed without obvious cause. More recently, during an investigation involving the adjacent church, a tape recorder cut out of its own acord. On one occasion just after the war, a motorbike rider passing the Rectory corner, had his engine cut out. Upon checking to see the reason, he found that something had turned off the ignition.

During a visit by Mr W. S. Hammond to the Rectory with some colleagues, they heard a door being closed somewhere in the house, three times in one night. Investigation failed to reveal a cause for these noises. Even more mysterious is the fact that visitors to the shell of the Rectory after the fire, also heard doors closing, on one occasion with a loud crash as of someone slamming a door in a fit of temper!

The unusual pencil marks continued to appear and it was during this period that the marks resembling the Prince of Wales' feathers appeared.

Another investigator, Mr Burden, heard dragging sounds that seemed to be coming from one of the upstairs corridors and Dr. C. M. Joad, later of *Brains Trust* fame, witnessed the appearance of fresh pencil marks.

The investigators also experienced curious odours in the house, under circumstances or conditions for which no explanation could be found. Mr Hammond, mentioned earlier, noticed a nasty odour like that from a lavatory, whilst two R.A.F. officers, Mr Carter-Jonas and Mr Caunter, noticed a smell as of incense whilst standing outside the Rectory, this particular occasion being after Price's own tenancy had ended and the Rectory was closed and locked.

There were other small incidents no less interesting, such as the moving of a little pin box, originally found by Colonel Westland who left it where it was found, in one of the two little room-cupboards off the passageway leading to the garden from the hall.

Loud thumps were heard coming from the empty Blue Room, and there were other sundry knocks and taps. On one occasion, a penetrating wailing noise was heard.

Mark Kerr-Pearse, during a turn of duty at the Rectory, heard the safety-gate at the top of the stairs open, in spite of the fact that it had been properly fastened. He also found a dried out frog outside the drawing room, which was definitely not there a short while before. All doors and windows in the house were shut at the time.

Further pencil marks were found about this time, including the letters 'MA'. It is rather interesting to note this, in conjunction with the later graphological opinion of the wall writing.

More bumps and thuds, bangs and metallic sounds were also heard by various members of Price's observation team during this period.

Colonel Westland discovered a tatty, blue serge lady's coat in the Rectory and the little pin-box that he found in the hall cupboard was found later to have moved from its marked position on two occasions. It was Col. Westland who, in conjunction with Sidney Glanville, took several of the interior pictures of the Rectory, including some photograhs of the wall markings.

S. G. Welles, from University College, spent some time in the Blue Room and saw a luminous patch appear on the ceiling near the window ... *and watched it move!* The other observers tried to duplicate the phenomenon with torches, but nothing that they could shine into the room from outside, produced anything like the curious light that Welles saw. For one thing, all attempts to reproduce it resulted in clearly defined shadows, whilst the luminous appearance witnessed by Welles produced no shadow at all.

In December 1937, Messrs Burden and Stainton, from Christchurch College, Oxford, visited the Rectory and Burden recalled that the chapel (the former bathroom) had 'an evil feel to it'. He also reported a feeling of being watched whilst in one of the rooms, certainly not the first time that this had been noticed by observers. The chapel and its 'evil' sensation he queried as being possibly the result of imagination. Another of Price's observers, Dr. Joseph, mentioned finding the house 'repellent'.

Another very interesting re-occurrence of an old phenomenon was reported to Harry Price by the Rev. Henning in November 1937, in a letter which is reproduced here from Price's first book, *The Most Haunted House in England*.

"Dear Mr Price,
I thought you might be interested to know that a light has been appearing in the Rectory, and so far we cannot account for it. It was seen (a *bright* light) by Mr and Mrs Payne and

The octagonal summer-house, *opposite above.*
The dining-room fireplace: note the carved monks' heads, *opposite below.*

they say it was from the window on the wing looking south (i.e. Room 11).

It looks out towards the fields and is at the corner close to the garage covered way.

The light was also seen by our man Herbert Mayes on the same night at a different window, the large one on the stairs. This can only be seen at one point on the road opposite the Tithe Barn at Borley Place.

I have seen the Arbons and they say the place was all locked up on Monday night and no-one there ... Our maid also saw the light on Thursday night, but is rather vague about its position.

Yours sincerely
A. C. Henning"

In October 1938, Miss Ethel Bull, writing to Sidney Glanville, related that a friend of hers, another parson, had 'nosed around outside the Rectory and heard a terrific crash like furniture being thrown about'. This was another interesting throwback to earlier years. Readers will recall that during the period that Guy Smith and his wife were lodging in Long Melford, they visited the Rectory on one occasion and heard a frightful racket coming from within.

At the time that Ethel Bull's friend reported a sound like furniture being hurled around, there was none in the Rectory, but at the time the Smiths heard the same noise, there was ... theirs! When they opened up the Rectory later and checked inside, they found their stored furniture had been thrown about all over the place!

On May 9th, 1938, Harry Price ended his occupancy of Borley Rectory, and he and Geoffrey Motion cleaned the place out before locking it up and returning the keys to the Rev. Henning. It was on this occasion that they found the gold wedding ring.

The final chapter of disturbances at Borley Rectory befor the fire and the start of World War II was destined to be very short indeed!

The Rectory was sold, out of Church use, to Captain William Hart Gregson in the autumn of 1938, and in December he and his two sons, Anthony and Allan, took possession of it. They moved into the stable cottage, storing most of their belongings in the Rectory, which the present writer is convinced was to have a direct bearing on what was soon to happen.

In the light of what I have discovered about the Captain, and particularly the information unearthed by young Richard Lee van den Daele of Shipley, it will soon become apparent that what the Captain reported over the short period that he was in residence, comes under question as to its validity. There is evidence to suggest that he bought the Rectory with the intention of capitalising on its reputation, and not really to use it as a home. Greater details appear later.

It has to be admitted though, that the phenomena reported by Gregson merely seems to suggest a continuation of the disturbances that had been taking place in the Rectory virtually since it was built. Viewed in that light, there is really little alternative but to give Gregson the benefit of the doubt.

During that winter of late 1938 and early 1939, following a fall of snow, footprints were found in the grounds under seemingly curious circumstances. Even more peculiar was the discovery of carriage wheel tracks across the lawn leading from a place in the hedge that you could have hardly have squeezed a wheelbarrow through, let alone a carriage!

Then came the broken glass incident. The Captain and one of his boys had been sorting their belongings in the Rectory hall. The lad, becoming thirsty, obtained a glass of water, drank some of it and left the glass on a bracket table in the hall, where it was then forgotten about. The following day, the glass was found broken in pieces and with no traces of water to be seen!

During his residency, Gregson became concerned at the dangerous state of the small well in the Rectory cellar and an old heavy wooden door was found and placed over the well to seal it off. A day or so later, this was found to have been thrown off and was lying several feet away.

The Rectory as seen from the tower of Borley Church, *opposite above*.
The elements steadily claimed the ruined Rectory, *opposite below*.

Then came the often reported incident of the two dogs. Gregson had bought a dog, and on the first occasion, was coming into the rear of the Rectory with his dog when it yelped in terror at something not visible to the Captain, wrenched free and tore off, never to be recovered.

Gregson replaced it with a second dog, but a short while later, the same thing happened again! The outcome of this is rarely recorded in print, but it is alleged that one of these dogs was later found wandering about in a crazed state and was promptly shot, whilst the other was apparently run over by a car and was found lying dead by the roadside.

On the night of February 27th and 28th, 1939, the end of Borley Rectory as an intact structure came suddenly, for the infamous pile caught fire. In spite of the efforts of Sudbury Fire Brigade, the place was ruined beyond repair. During the blaze, a local constable insisted that two figures were standing watching the Rectory burn, whilst Gregson was certain that only he and the firemen were there. Villagers watching from the road also claimed to have seen two figures, but one of them just a blurred form, standing in one of the windows of the burning Rectory.

By dawn on the morning of February 28th, the Rectory, scene of so many weird and outlandish happenings, was a roofless smouldering mess, a tragic burned out ruin!

But in spite of the fire, which one might well expect to have put an end to the disturbances, this was to be far from the end of Borley Rectory's extraordinary history.

It is perhaps worth spending a moment or two looking at the relative levels of allegedly paranormal phenomena in relation to the numbers of people present in the Rectory at any one period in its curious history.

Although the writer makes no claim that this analysis has any scientific basis, he is of the opinion that the hauntings at Borley Rectory reflect a commonly held view that paranormal phenomena feeds on the presence of people. It does appear in many cases of haunting that such curious events are more frequent in their occurrence the more people there are in the location.

Looking at the hauntings at Borley Rectory, one notices that the 'golden age' of this particular episode, was not as critics might like to think, during the involvement of Harry Price, but during the heyday of the Bull family. Allowing for the obvious and usual doubts as to the veracity of all the reports of happenings during that time, it is noticeable that there was a greater concentration of combined phenomena during the years from 1863 to 1927. During the young years of the Bull sisters, there was almost every kind of psychic phenomena from visual phantasms to isolated noises.

Among these phenomena, one can list the nun, the figures of an old man, a strange man in a tall hat, a coach and horses, sounds of rushing water, bell ringing, bangs and crashes with no obvious cause, strange odours and much else besides.

From the time of the Smiths, things seemed to change quite noticeably, although there is some evidence that there was a degree of overlap in the nature of phenomena from one period to the next.

With the coming of the Foysters, things altered again. Most of the visual phenomena during this time, seem to have petered out, to be replaced by a lot more physical disturbance, some of it of considerable violence. At the same time, there is the feeling that some of this may have been provoked, possibly without her realising it, by Marianne, and whilst it is an often expounded view that she faked much of the phenomena of that period, the writer inclines more to the belief that she was acting as a focus, and that by her nature, Marianne Foyster was something of a target channel for the disturbances.

It is rather telling in Harry Price's favour, rather than to his detriment, that the phenomena seemed to have been *less* marked during the time when his investigation team was on the premises, and less spectacular in many ways, and it is interesting to consider why this might be so!

To the writer's way of thinking, a great

deal hinges on the fact that during the time of the Bull family's incumbency, there was the highest concentration of people in the house of any period in its history. Remember that during those years especially, there was a high concentration of adolescent girls present, and their apparent propensity for attracting psychic activity is of old lineage in the study of this controversial subject.

It seems relevant that in spite of Harry Price assembling his team to mount a long term watch on the Rectory and its surroundings, the time each of them could give to this task on any given ocasion was to some extent limited. Thus, there were lengthy periods between visits by members of the team when the Rectory was devoid of occupants altogether, in stark contrast to the Bull era when the house was a hive of little groups of twos and threes almost all the time. Ghosts prefer not to play to empty houses it seems.

These comments are not intended to be a scientific analysis of the nature of the phenomena. What they suggest however is that the distribution of the different kinds of phenomena and levels thereof, throughout the Rectory's history, rather overturns some popular views as to the validity or otherwise of the case of the Borley Rectory hauntings, and strengthens, in my opinion, the view that there was and is a lot more to this story than any mere commercial or publicity orientated journalistic exercise!

CHAPTER EIGHT

GHOSTS AMONG THE RUINS.
THE SITE FROM 1939 TO 1945

The destruction of the Rectory on February 27th, 1939, far from putting an end to the strange disturbances as one might have expected, seemed instead to make not the slightest difference. It would be fair to say that never again was the old building to be the scene of quite so high a level of phenomena as had once been the case, but on the other hand, it now seems clear that the phenomena did not by any means cease. Among numerous occurrences reported during the war, there were lights seen in the smashed and burned out openings that had once been windows, to the extent that A.R.P. wardens were called to deal with what they assumed to be somebody breaking the air-raid blackout regulations, only to find of course that there were no lights showing there at all. Army officers who tried to billet themselves in the grounds had stones thrown at them and found the atmosphere of the site such that they felt disinclined to remain there. One particularly unwarranted act on their part was to pull down the little Gothic summer house and dig a large hole upon its former site, for no obvious reason.

Among other curiosities at the site after the fire, was the experience of a group of young people who stood on the lawn, watching the burned out Rectory by the light of the moon. As they looked, one of the party saw the figure of a girl or young woman appear in the opening of what had been the Blue Room window. As far as could be seen by moonlight, the figure appeared to be clothed in either pale blue or buff. After some seconds, the figure vanished. Among the group of watchers, opnions as to how the figure disappeared were divided. One thought it had, seemingly, fallen backwards into the dark of the ruined building, whilst another thought that the figure turned and faded *through* one of the walls. Either way, the incident was very curious, because the damage to the Blue Room was such that nobody could have been standing at the window opening, the floor having been burnt away. When the reader comes to the details of the visits by the Cambridge Commission, there may appear to be a contradiction insofar as members were able to get into the Blue Room and others upstairs, albeit with some difficulty. During a visit by two Polish Army officers, some temporary planking was laid across some of the upstairs floor joists and when the Poles departed, the planks remained.

Concerning both the figure at the Blue Room window and the light in the window, the writer feels moved to rule out of order suggestions often made that the Rectory reflected lights from trains on the Sudbury to Long Melford section of the Stour Valley railway line. As lights seen there during the last war were concerned, firstly the glass of the Blue Room window had gone and secondly, even when defoliated by winter, the trees in the grounds were dense enough to block any light from a train passing at least half a mile away, if not rather more. Furthermore, the burnt walls of the ruin would not reflect the lights of a train, well obscured by trees, at that distance. There is another technical argument against the train light claims. The writer, amongst other interests, is a railway enthusiast and so the following remarks are made in the context of some knowledge of the working of the London & North Eastern Railway, who as successors to the Great Eastern, operated the Stour Valley line. Even as late as the war years, local trains such as those used between Marks Tey and either Cambridge or Bury St Edmunds and would pass close by Borley Hall when approaching or just leaving Long Melford, were more usually the preserve of elderly coaches with gas lighting, which is rather yellowish and *not* bright enough to be seen through woodland at that distance. Furthermore, once the blitz was under way, when trains of stock from other lines might well have come through there carrying troops, trains at night on the Stour Valley line as everywhere else would be required to run with blinds down and very dim lighting. Those lights would *not* be visible at Borley.

Yet another curious occurrence was reported by Herbert Mayes, a chauffeur, who was returning home by bicycle one night after dark. As he approached the burnt out shell of the Rectory, he heard the sound of horses stampeding. He dismounted from his bike and pulled in against the hedge to let the horses pass, but no animals came into view. The sounds passed him, gradually fading away as they did so, but of the horses themselves, there was nothing whatever to be seen. Mayes shone his bicycle lamp both up and down the lane but there was nothing there. The reader will recall how, many long years before, Harry Bull heard a horse drawn vehicle approach and pass him without anything being visible.

In *Haunted East Anglia,* by Joan Forman, there appears another record of a visit to the burnt out Rectory not long after the fire, by a group of young people. Among this group was apparently a young girl named 'Violet Sorfleet'. In her account of the incident, she recalled that the group had walked to the ruined Rectory on a very cold night and, having arrived, stood leaning on the drive gate looking at the burnt out building. The night was clear and a frost was forming. They had stood there for some minutes, wondering, since the place didn't look particularly unusual, why it had been the focus of so much attention, when without warning the party was blotted out from each other's sight by a thick and clammy fog that seemed to drop on them from nowhere. 'Violet Sorfleet' told later of feeling that there was something unnatural

and unpleasant about the fog. The group were all young, impressionable and scared! They scarpered and as they ran back down the hill, towards the cottages at the bottom, it felt as though whatever had frightened them off was laughing at them.

This incident did not appear in Harry Price's accounts of the Borley story, and seems to have been recalled only to Joan Forman by Miss Sorfleet. But was the fog incident a genuine experience or did Miss Sorfleet rehash one of many already recorded happenings at Borley Rectory? So far as the writer is aware, no other fog phenomena cropped up concerned with Borley, and this incident is therefore mentioned here only as an alleged experience. A couple of points about it are worth noting.

In view of the weird history of Borley Rectory, one ought not to be surprised at the possibility of fog phenomenon. However, it has to be said that this oddity doesn't fit the general pattern, which consisted largely of noises, lights, smells and visual effects such as the nun, the headless man, the coach and horses and the various figures seen inside the Rectory, together with poltergeist activity such as the throwing of objects.

Now, however, to other incidents. On Easter Monday, April 10th, 1939, Mr W. Davey, from Ipswich, tried to take a photograph of the shell of the building. No sooner had he pressed the shutter on his camera than it opened again immediately of its own accord, spoiling the negative. He tried again, but with the same result. He then gave it up as a bad job. His camera, then five years old, had never malfunctioned in such a fashion before.

The visits to the site by two Polish Army officers also proved to be rather odd as regards phenomena, but before detailing their experiences, the story of Mr H. F. Russell's strange experience should be told.

He visited the remains of Borley Rectory on November 12th, 1941 and, as far as can be ascertained,he was near the gateway between the back of the Rectory and the stable cottage, when an unseen something seized him from behind and threw him face down in a puddle of dirty water.

Now we turn to the Polish officers. On June 28th and 29th, 1943, two Polish Army officers visited the ruin. They were Lieutenant Kujawa and Lieutenant Nawrocki. On the evening of the 28th, Kujawa was in the remains of the kitchen passage when he was struck on the shoulder by a stone and his colleague had stones thrown at him also. That same evening, a moving shadow was seen near the Nun's Walk but it disappeared. Early on the morning of the 29th, Lt. Nawrocki heard whisperings in the kitchen passage but couldn't distinguish anything definite. The couple paid another visit on the same days of the following month, July 28th and 29th, the supposedly appointed day of the phantom nun's appearance each year and once again, a shadowy figure was seen near the Nun's Walk.

The major part of the wartime watches on the ruined building were carried out by the University of Cambridge undergraduates who formed themselves into the 'Cambridge Commission' under the leadership of Andrew J. B. Robertson, MA, of St. John's College, Cambridge. Members visited the Rectory on repeated occasions between 1939 and the final removal of the Rectory's remains in 1944. Harry Price detailed their findings at some length in Chapter 9 of his second book, *The End of Borley Rectory*, and the commission's original reports are currently in the Harry Price Library. From these details, the writer gives the following precis.

The group's first visit to the Rectory proved unproductive but on the second visit on October 31st, 1941, by Mr Robertson and Mr I. P. Williams, during which some temperature readings were taken on the site, a luminous patch appeared on the wall between the sewing room and the remains of the corridor. This happened at about 12.45 a.m., and lasted about a second or so, but the watchers were not impressed by it. At about 2.10 a.m., some heavy noises like footsteps were heard on the back stairs and a moving dark outline was spotted flitting rapidly from a moonlit spot into complete darkness.

On December 20th, 1941, Messrs Robertson and Angelbeck were at the Rectory and in response to experimental knocking on one of the walls with a torch, heard a repeated knocking at fixed intervals, seeming to emanate from somewhere near the ruins of the drawing room.

On February 27th, 1942, three years to the day from the time of the fire, Robertson and another colleague, J. P. Grantham, visited the Rectory and again they experimented with knocking signals. In response, they heard a click, and then a few minutes later, three heavy knocks from the direction of the front door, *not* as a result of any visitor to the Rectory. Shortly after this, a luminous patch was again seen on the sewing room wall. Various objects were placed around the house to see if they were paranormally moved, but nothing happened. The observers did however hear very clearly at about 11.31 p.m. and then again at 11.34 p.m., a noise as of heavy furniture being moved. The sound seemed to come from the ruined upper floor. Further sounds amounted to a single knock, a rustling noise from outside, and the sound of a door closing somewhere inside the ruin. Throughout this time, a thermometer was in use as on the first and second visits. On earlier visits, changes in temperature were noticed but on the February 27th occasion there were no changes recorded.

July 28th, 1942, brought Messrs Armstrong, Robertson, White and Williams to the Rectory, but nothing worthy of comment occurred, but during a visit by three members of the Commission on September 22nd, 1942, some interesting things did occur. Following some cracking sounds at about 11.00 p.m., the sound of heavy and measured footsteps was heard, coming it seemed, from one of the upstairs rooms. The observers walked across the room they had based themselves in, and the footsteps followed them, only to end abruptly. Although the observers felt that they couldn't be sure as to whether or not the sounds could have been produced by normal means, access to the upper floor was by now barred, due to the nailing up of one of the passage doorways. At one stage during the war, however, some observers did get into the upper floor by climbing up over the roof of the boiler house on the far side of the Rectory, but even then, save for the planks left by the two Poles, the upper floor was difficult to traverse. But to return to the earlier visit, throughout the night, one of the team, Mr Lankester, heard a clock ticking though there wasn't one in earshot. The church tower opposite did not, and still does not, possess a clock. Oddly enough, Mr Lankester's mother, in Ipswich, woke at about midnight on that same night, hearing a clock ticking in her room, though there was no clock there.

It was not until March 21st, 1943, that a visit produced further phenomena:

1. Two occurrences of a sound resembling that of a horse stamping its hooves, though no horse was anywhere near.

2. At 10.30 p.m. – the sound of someone in the garden near the pond-cum-stream.

3. At 12.38 a.m. – the sound of someone shuffling about in the kitchen passage.

The next group from Cambridge, Messrs Cook, Hay and Wadsworth, visited the Rectory on the night of April 30th, 1943 and during this visit there occurred:

1. The sound of five footsteps from near the back stairs.

2. Thuds heard in intermittent twos and threes.

3. Three occurrences of a noise like moving furniture.

4. A sound like a packing case being dragged over the floor.

5. Four taps sound like a mallet striking a wooden surface.

6. A very loud noise, as of a slamming door.

7. A noise like a falling brick.

This last sound could have been a brick, as the shell of the Rectory was in a pretty sorry state by this time and was collapsing bit by bit. The noise happened after a request by the watchers for the door slamming noise to repeat itself.

The next group at the Rectory, on June 8th, 1943, noticed only a curious halting of what had been a steady drop in temperature. The slowly changing temperature stopped its course for about an hour,

before the drop continued. The following night, two visitors, Mr I. G. Gordon and Mr J. R. Palmer, recorded the sighting by one of them of what he thought was a whitish object moving across the lawn and into the trees near the boundary stone. During the night there were various squeaks and cracks and assorted other noises, but Mr Gordon noticed that whenever any attempt was made to 'contact' the late Rev. Harry Bull, noises of one sort or another followed shortly afterwards. Whatever the reader might make of these occurrences, they make a rather interesting sideline to Harry Bull's comments to J. Harley in 1922, about making himself known to the future occupants of the house by causing 'mechanical disturbances'.

Mr Gordon returned to the Rectory on June 16th, 1943, with Mr J. V. Owen and Miss J. Camock, but nothing of interest was recorded. Three days later, Messrs Heap and Longmuir spent a night at the ruined Rectory and reported the following:

1. The sound of falling rubble in the cellar.

2. A white shape by one of the trees close to the greenhouse, but this was not a trick of the moon light, because the moon was well down, though it could possibly have been an instance of bark-fluorescence on a tree. The shape had gone only a short time later.

3. Various noises like chirping, dismissed as mice.

4. A smell as of fruit, an odour that moved slowly from the upstairs bedroom next to the large end room of the 1875 extension, to a point near the two steps in the corridor linking those rooms.

Temperature changes were again noticed, this time between an encased and an uncased thermometer.

Visits on June 22nd, 1943, and on the 16th and 17th of July were totally unproductive. The next group to visit the site, where two other groups were already present, arrived on the night of September 25th, 1943. Messrs Low, Mills, Snushall and Wilden-Hart teamed up with those already there. About 1.30 a.m., half a dozen footsteps were heard by Wilden-Hart and by Mr Leeman, the noise coming from the courtyard. Investigation revealed no obvious cause for the sounds.

On December 3rd, 1943, a group consisting of V. J. Cattrell, J. L. Howarth, V. J. Smith and G. L. Squires heard four whistles, like somebody trying to attract attention, each a little more forceful than the last. Various possibilities were put forward in the group's subsequent report on this visit but without any conclusions being drawn.

During a visit on December 6th, only the moving of a sheet of paper from a nail seemed in any way odd. A party who went down to Borley on March 20th, 1944, noticed the advanced state of demolition then in evidence, but little else worthy of comment.

On April 5th, 1944, however, Harry Price made one of his few wartime visits to Borley, accompanied by an American magazine photographer Mr David Schermann, and by Miss Cynthia Ledsham. The visit led, after Price's death, to quite a row and the cause of it was an occurrence that might arguably be said to be the one Borley phenomenon caught on film. Standing viewing the sad remains of the Rectory, Price felt sure that he had seen a brick rise by itself from a pile of rubble in the remains of the kitchen passage. Mr David Schermann took a photograph of the ruin, with a little camera having a very fast shutter speed, and when the negative was printed, there in mid air against the darkness of the passage was a brick. After the war, Miss Cynthia Ledsham protested about Price's account of this incident, stating that he had in effect claimed it to be paranormal when the incident was of natural origin.

In Price's defence, as noted many years later by Robert J. Hastings, it was made plain that Price had made no such assertion about the brick, and had only commented upon the occurrence itself. A popular assertion by some of Price's critics, including Dingwall, Goldney and Hall, was that the brick had been tossed up by workmen busy pulling down the Rectory. In fact there was *one* workman there upon the day in question, and the writer now asks his readers to study David Schermann's photograph, which is reproduced here from *The End of Borley Rectory*. A lone workman is indeed visible on the far left-hand side of the picture. The brick caught in mid-flight is over on the other side of the picture. The workman could have had no justifiable reason for throwing a discarded brick so far, when he could have just dumped a yard or so away any debris that he wished to throw to one side. In addition to this point, observers will note that the workman is facing the wrong way in relation to where the brick is visible. Also, look carefully at the area around the brick itself. There are bricks lying on the ground to the right and below the 'floating' specimen. There are also loose bricks in the partly demolished wall above and to the left of the 'flying' brick. If one of these fell it would drop straight down and not fly out at a tangent. Lastly, on the remains of the wooden floor above the spot, there is some debris. Close examination of this will reveal what is almost certainly plaster rubbish, but no bricks. At the far right hand end of that bit of derelict floor there *is* a piece of brick, but it is nowhere near the falling point for the brick which concerns us here.

Having studied this photograph and examined the Hastings report, the writer is of the view that Harry Price cannot be blamed for any so-called misrepresentation of the incident. In terms of the Rectory and its curiosities, the photograph certainly deserves the benefit of the doubt and the author suggests that Schermann may well have been just lucky to catch one of the Rectory's tricks on film.

From flying bricks however, we must now move on. On April 30th, 1944, more investigators, complete with various bits of test apparatus, witnessed another reoccurrence of the light in the window phenomenon. The writer would remind readers of the comments earlier, concerning lights from trains penetrating the Rectory site. Torches were also dismissed as a cause on this particular visit. The party had two, neither being where the light appeared.

Visits on June 5th, 1944 and on June 9th produced nothing worthy of note.

The last visit by members of the Cambridge Commission was on the night of July 22nd, 1944 by two parties. One group consisted of P. Brennan, P. Brown, C. J. Lethbridge, R. J. Watkinson and D. Williams. The other group was made up of E. R. Broome, P. J. Farr, L. B. Hunt and P. H. Lord and the two groups, rather oddly, were unaware of each other's presence. The second group, rather foolishly, indulged in some fake phenomena.

This, then, was the end of the Cambridge Commission investigation, which apart from the last little bit of nonsense on July 22nd, had been an extensive and interesting project, conducted under considerable difficulties due to the various participant's over-riding academic commitments.

I would again remind readers that in order to fit the Cambridge Commission project into this chapter, it has been necessary to condense it slightly. For the full picture, students should consult Price's second book, *The End of Borley Rectory,* and also, by application to the Harry Price Library, the original Cambridge reports themselves.

One of the oddest reports sent to Harry Price during the war as that from a lady who claimed to have seen the carriage in full daylight, though as there was no clue given as to whether this occurred while the Rectory was still intact or after its destruction, Harry Price merely recorded it for what it was worth.

According to the lady's story, she had been out for a walk, and was walking towards the Rectory during daylight. She was munching at some chocolate as she walked, when she saw a coach and horses turn into the Rectory drive. She thought that either there was film-making going on, or that there was some sort of fete or party, for which the carriage had been hired, but what happened next allegedly stopped her in her tracks. The coach stopped, and two men in tall hats got down drom the driver's box and went inside the Rectory. After an interval, they reappeared, remounted the coach and drove out through the drive gates. Then without warning, the whole thing just shot straight up in the air and disintegrated . . . wheels, shafts, horses all scattering in every direction! There was no corroboration for the story, but it is suggested that the reader carefully studies the chapter on the mystery of Katie Boreham, later in this book.

And with that, we must close the chapter on the disturbances recorded during and just after the war. The period during which the stable cottage was occupied by the writer James Turner, from 1947 to 1950 is covered by a chapter set aside for his time at Borley.

What happened after 1950, on and near the site, has been reported by Peter Underwood and the late Dr. Paul Tabori in their book *The Ghosts of Borley.* The next chapter turns the clock back, to look at the various characters who lived in the Rectory from 1863 to 1939.

CHAPTER NINE

THE REVEREND HENRY DAWSON BULL

It was Henry Dawson Bull who was the first occupant of this, Britain's most infamous Rectory. The Bull family had a long history of residency in the district and it is even suggested that there was a link between the Bull family and the detested Queen of Henry VIII, Anne Boleyn, or Bullen, the mother of Queen Elizabeth I. At one time she kept a house at Bulmer, not far from Borley, and with her brother, and several associates and favourites were beheaded on Henry's orders. It is suggested, in order to escape further persecution, that surviving members of the Boleyn and Bullen family altered the name to Bull. Many accounts of the Borley story imply that Henry Bull was also in some way related to the Waldegrave family, in whose hands the gift of the living had been from the time of Henry VIII, finally passing to the Bull family themselves upon the death of Henry Bull in 1892. Both these ideas will be investigated shortly, but for now let me turn attention to the man and the family for whom Borley Rectory was built.

Henry Dawson Ellis Bull was born at Pentlow in 1833, the son of Edward Bull, Rector of Pentlow. The Bull family home, known now as Pentlow Tower, was, and still is, one of the most extraordinary looking buildings in the district. Like Borley Rectory, it was built of red brick and still possesses two curious features. It has enormous stained glass windows, making it look like something from Elizabethan times, and in the rambling great garden there still stands the folly from which the place gets its present name. In later years, it passed to Harry Bull's brother Felix, and in his time, Harry recalled one of the maids there having the ability to make objects move by themselves. On one particular afternoon, Harry Bull had gone to Pentlow Rectory with a friend and the maid, upon being asked to show them her apparent powers, said nothing and went on with her chores, but as she did so, the fire irons flew out across the drawing room floor with a clatter. This, then, was the peculiar household in which the young Henry Dawson Ellis Bull was to grow up.

From his Pentlow birthplace, Henry went on to take up the career that was ultimately to bring him to Borley and the building of its haunted Rectory. Henry graduated from Wadham College, Oxford, subsequently becoming a curate at Holy Trinity Church in Ely in 1858, a post that he held until 1860. Enquiries made of the archives of Holy Trinity in Ely did not reveal very much about him as a curate at Ely, but one or two basic items came to light through the help of Canon Niel Munt.

As curate, Henry Bull conducted his first baptism at Holy Trinity on May 1st of 1858, and his last such service in May of the following year. At these functions, he signed himself Henry D. E. Bull, and stuck to that form for the rest of his life. The first burial service at which he officiated was on June 17th of 1858 and his last was on 6th November, 1859, the day after Guy Fawkes' Night. On November 7th, Henry Bull took the only wedding service at which he officiated whilst at Ely, a point which moved Canon Munt to comment that Henry's vicar must have liked doing weddings, as apart from that one occasion, young Henry didn't get a chance to deal with any other duties.

By the time he came to Borley in 1862, following the passing of John Philip Herringham, he had become something that was very much an English speciality, a wealthy Squire-Parson, not least because he was able to avail himself of the considerable wealth that the Bull family enjoyed. This was readily apparent when he ordered the building of his new Rectory in 1862/3, but let us take a look at the character of the first Bull of Borley Rectory.

Devoid of a moustache, but sporting mutton-chop side-whiskers, he was an immensely strong, tall and broad-shouldered man and among his many pleasures during his off-duty hours was that of hunting, in which he took part with great zeal. He was also a proficient boxer and no mean shot with a fowling piece. One of the many memories of him often related is that he could sometimes be found sprawled upon the floor of the library at Borley Rectory, potting at rabbits on the lawn through the open French windows.

It is believed to have been at Henry's instigation that the big octagonal summer-house was built at the top of the lawn. It was also Henry who had the side window of the dining room bricked up, supposedly because of the habitual staring by the nun when the family were at their meals.

There is contained in Sidney Glanville's Locked Book a suggestion that among those who knew him intimately, and among members of his family, he was known by the nickname 'Carlos'. However, when some of the surviving Bull sisters were interviewed many years later, they were said to have claimed that he had no nickname. Oddly enough, when one comes to examine the results of the various seance experiments carried out at Borley Rectory during 1937, there does arise the suggestion that Henry Dawson Bull *was* referred to as Carlos!

The exact number of children born to Henry Bull has varied from one account to another, and aspects of this bear on some of the strange stories attached to the history of the Rectory. It is often stated that Henry Dawson Bull fathered 14 children, of which 12 survived, but the record of baptisms for Borley Parish Church, checked by the Rev. Christopher Cook, show only 13, as follows:

DATES OF BAPTISMS, NOT BIRTHS

1. Henry Foyster Bull, March 25th, 1863.
2. Caroline Sarah Elizabeth Bull (Dodie), April 17th, 1864.
3. Winifred Margaret Bull, March 17th, 1865.
4. Alfred Richard Graham Bull, February 23rd, 1866.
5. Basil Walter Bull, January 11th, 1867.
6. Ethel Mary Bull, January 20th, 1868.
7. Adelaide Mabel Bull, Christmas Day, 1868.
8. Edward Gerald Bull, December 18th, 1870.
9. Constance StClere Bull, January 14th, 1872.
10. Hubert Ellis Bull, January 12th, 1873.
11. Emily Poundrow Bull, February 13th, 1876.
12. Cyril Garwood Bull, January 21st, 1877.
13. Alice Kathleen Bull, January 26th, 1879.

There are some points about these records that deserve attention. The first concerns Henry Foyster Bull, or 'Harry' as he was always called. Though usually recorded as having been born at Borley Place, the 1871 and 1881 Borley census returns state his birthplace as Guestingthorpe!

Caroline Sarah Bull eventually married the Rev. William Hayden, and died in 1937. Her mother was also Caroline Sarah Bull.

Cyril Garwood Bull is the one who died after only a few weeks, and is buried in Borley churchyard.

Oddly enough, there is no mention in this list of Freda, unless this was an additional christian name either not used by one of the above listed daughters, or adopted unofficially by one of the girls. Similarly, there is no mention here of Harry Bull's brother Felix, who apparently became Rector of Pentlow, unless he was neither born nor baptised at Borley.

For years, there were stories in the district that Henry Dawson Bull fathered three illegitimate children, and that he died from a sexually transmitted disease. For the moment it will suffice to record that Henry Dawson Ellis Bull died on May 2nd, 1892, from *Locomotor Ataxia*, which is listed in *Balliers Nursing Dictionary* as 'a manifestation of tertiary syphilis'. He was 59 years of age. The background to this has proved to be almost certainly connected with the history of Borley Rectory, but details of what this means must wait until later.

also seen by others, and not always by people who knew him.

Not for nothing was Harry Bull the best remembered of Borley's rectors, though of course the Foyster tenancy attracted much attention in later years. That he held an interest in the after life we now know well enough and it is some aspects of this side of Harry Bull that has, rather unfairly, earned him the reputation of being a morbid dreamer, a reputation that he doesn't really deserve.

There was more to Harry Bull than any supposed morbidness or just his interest in the spiritual world, but before continuing with detail, it is worthwhile mentioning one episode connected with his spiritual interests.

In 1929, on June 15th, Mr J. Harley wrote to Harry Price and his letter tells us that during a visit by Harley to Borley Rectory in 1922, the two men (he and Harry Bull) had discussed the subject of spirits. Harry Bull held the view that a spirit attempting to attract the attention of those living could only do so by causing some mechanical disturbance, such as breaking glass or some other element. He also stated that following his own death, he would, if discontented, adopt this method of communicating with the later inhabitants of the house. It is odd indeed, irrespective of one's individual views, that the Rectory was the scene of much physical disturbance in the years following Harry Bull's death, disturbances that included stones being thrown, china and glassware smashed, some furniture hurled about, and more besides. It is a curious coincidence also, that, Marianne Foyster, wife of a later Rector, who was himself a relative of the Bull family, should report on more than one occasion having seen the ghost of Harry Bull inside the building. One must, of course, follow one's own beliefs about the subject of ghosts and the meanings that may be put forward for their appearance aside from historical considerations, but one cannot help but wonder, in view of Harry's remarks to Mr Harley in 1922, whether the outwardly cheerful and rather ebullient countenance of the Rev. Henry Foyster Bull did in fact conceal some inner sense of disillusionment? Certainly nothing of such showed itself to his contemporaries, but it is quite likely that not even his closest friends in the community, or members of his family would have necessarily known of his innermost thoughts. Indeed, he was known in the district for his rather bouncing, jovial and often humorous approach to things, even to his clerical duties. He was in the habit of running across to the church to take the services and apparently he would return from such duties to the Rectory, very out of breath and exclaim, according to a report in *The Ghosts of Borley,* "Oh! Very puff! Never missed a word, and beat my own record."

A sort of cameo of life at Borley Rectory during Harry Bull's time can be gained from the memories of a frail but grand old maiden lady, aged 93 when the author interviewed her.

Though she chose to deny it, she was a maid to the Bull household about the time of the Great War. It could, with some degree of justification, be said that to rely on the frail memories of a ninety-year-old lady for historical details, is more than a little dubious, but in this instance, there is photographic evidence to support at least some of her recollections.

The following are, verbatim, notes made at the time of my conversation with the lady.

'Details about the lifestyle and interests of the Reverends H. D. E. and H. F. Bull are hard to come by after so many years, virtually all those who might have remembered those days during the heyday of the Rectory's existence having long since passed away ... the identity of the lady will not be revealed, in deference to her wishes and those of her relatives. As a young girl at Borley School, she recalls the Sunday School lessons, for which the children walked to the Rectory (Presumably after church ... IB) The Rev. Harry Bull instructed the boys, whilst the girls were in the charge of Mrs Bull. When she died, her duties were carried on by the eldest Miss Bull, Freda.'

At this point, a couple of items call for explanation. The eldest Miss Bull was in fact Caroline Sarah Elizabeth, sometimes mistakenly referred to as 'Elsie', and known in the family as 'Dodie'. Another point concerns the Sunday School lessons. In some parishes they would be held in the church. At Borley, however, the Rectory offered a school room, the room in which a light was twice seen from outside by Mabel Smith, when in fact it was locked and in darkness. In practical terms, especially in the winter months, this room in the Rectory would have been warmer than the church by many degrees.

There may arise also, some confusion as to whether the Mrs Bull referred to by the old lady was Harry's mother, or his wife. This old maid was born in 1890, so that at least until 1910, it would have been Harry's mother who took the girls for Sunday School. Between 1910 and 1914, it could have been either, but in 1914, Mrs H. D. E. Bull died. Harry did not marry Ivy Brackenbury until 1911, and in spite of Price's note that Harry's mother died in the Rectory, in fact she died in Borley Place. Both Henry and Harry Bull nevertheless did die in the Rectory. To continue with the old maidservant's memories:

'The Bull sisters also took their turn in instructing the village girls at needlework lessons.

'From the old lady's memories, Harry Bull was tall and thin in stature, and dark haired, Mrs Bull by comparison being rather on the plump side. By all accounts, the Rector and his sisters took part in almost all that went on in Borley, being popular with the local people.'

It may be desirable to remind readers that after 1920, the Bull sisters were no longer at Borley, having moved out of the Rectory to Chilton Lodge, at Cornard, near Sudbury. But to continue:

'In common with many houses of that size in those days, Borley Rectory had a staff of maids ranging from cook through parlourmaid, to housemaid. There was also a gardener but he apparently did not reside in the Rectory, but in the village.

'One feature of the Rectory was the annual Easter treat for the school children, whereupon, having attended service in the church, they were marched over to the Rectory in a column of twos, and in through the rear door, to be given hot cross buns and an orange apiece. In fine weather, these events took place on the Rectory lawn.

'Another popular pastime there during the summer months, was the holding of tennis parties on the lawn. This can be seen in an old photograph of Borley Rectory, the earliest known to have been taken, wherein can be seen Mrs H. D. E. Bull and seven of the girls, and a tennis net placed across the lawn close to the house and just visible against the dark background of the trees.

'The old lady's memories also encompassed the existence of the little "Bower" or Summer-house which stood on the Rectory lawn, close to the road, built for the two men, Henry and Harry. The garden at that time ran down almost the whole length of the hill to the edge of Borley "wood", this being long before much of the ground was sold off for building.'

One can glean something from these notes of the lifestyle of the Bull family in those days before the Great War. The reader will not doubt also recall the memories of the family, related by Mr P. Shaw Jeffrey, who stayed at the Rectory as a guest of Harry Bull during his university days.

T. H. Hall's view of Harry's life was that there was nothing to suggest that his marriage to Ivy Brackenbury was unhappy but it seems that in some respects, this may not necessarily have been the case. I have earlier pointed out R. J. Hasting's comments about relations between Harry Bull and his stepdaughter, and certainly it is not unusual for relations between step-parents and step-children to be strained.

But there are other points about that marriage which I feel Hall has misunderstood. In *New Lights on Old Ghosts*, he deals with Harry's marriage to Ivy, and some of his views are worthy of note.

Firstly, consider the occasion of the couple's moving from Borley Place into Borley Rectory, and, as Hall put it in his book 'removing his sisters'. The move back into the Rectory was apparently at the wish of Harry's wife, Ivy. But did Mrs Harry Bull not actually *demand* the move? Could she perhaps have been a rather

Mrs Smith claimed, in a letter written many years after their time at Borley, that she and Guy had lived there for over three years but factually it was, as I said earlier, only a mere nine months, from October 1928 to July 1929. For the rest of that period, they lived in lodgings in Long Melford, from where Guy Smith carried out his parish duties. Many reports suggest that they were driven out solely by the ghosts, but taking a cross-section of evidence, it seems that there was no single factor responsible for abandoning the Rectory, but more a mixture of problems, which can best be described by itemising them as follows:

1. The Rectory was in a very poor structural state, difficult to heat properly with no gas or electricity. The sanitary arrangements were, for a house of such size, appalling, with broken drains adding to the problems.

2. Mabel Smith was quite ill whilst at Borley, due to a combination of the state of the place and the likely probability that she *was* scared of being in the Rectory, as some locals remember her being.

3. Whether the Smiths believed the Rectory to be haunted or not, it was a fact that no maid would remain in the place, Mary Pearson being the only one who seemed to have stayed for any time at all.

4. Following the publication of V. C. Wall's article in the *Daily Mirror* in June 1929, the Smiths were harrassed by sightseers, Smith having to summon the police on one occasion to remove uninvited visitors from his garden.

5. It is apparent, more particularly from Guy Smith's testimony than from his wife's, that the couple *were* subjected to poltergeist disturbances and some visual phenomena, the latter chiefly reported by Mrs Smith, e.g. the figure leaning over the gate etc.

It is when one adds up these individual problems and allies them to Guy Smith's death in 1940 and the way in which that affected his widow one begins to understand what was probably behind most of Mrs Smith's denials and erratic memory about Borley in her later years. The tone of her letters to Harry Price about the time

of Guy' death tells us a great deal about her own feelings. She was quite plainly very attached to her husband and his death was a shattering blow to her. I would suggest that this may well have compounded a generally distasteful memory of Borley, and subconsciously, Mrs Smith was trying to block out the episode by sheltering behind a smoke-screen. But assuming that to be so, the results could be odd, as evidence shows. Her lapse of memory upon the subject of Borley was not total but selective.

For example, though she could remember Charles Sutton's visit to Borley Rectory, the more remarkable for the fact that the Smiths were not at the Rectory at that time, she had no recollection of either Dom Richard Whitehouse's nor Sidney Glanville's visits at, Sheringham and Sevington, Kent, after the Smiths had left the Sudbury area in 1930. On those occasions, the couple's comments clearly seemed to indicate that they were quite prepared to accept that, as far as they were concerned, the place was haunted. In addition, Guy Smith's comments in a letter to Lord Charles Hope in November 1929 are interesting. In the letter were the words:

"You and the others know the place is haunted, and I am sure you will agree it was no place for my wife to reside in, seeing that no maid would stay there."

From this, it can be seen that Guy Smith believed the Rectory to be haunted during his tenancy, and whilst his wife's views made a complete U-turn in later years, *his* views show no evidence of changing from then until his death.

Then again, there was the wine-into-ink episode during Price's visit to the Foysters. Mrs Smith's version of this was that it had occurred during her husband's time at Borley. What seems to have happened is that Mabel Smith may well have mistaken an event from the Foyster period, very possibly because Price made reference to it in a letter to Guy Smith, who would very probably have shown the letter to his wife.

Another example of Mrs Smith's contrariness concerns Price's first book, *The*

Most Haunted House In England. When it was published and Mrs Smith received a copy, she was most enthusiastic about it and indeed congratulated Price on his work, wishing her husband was still alive to read it, yet after the war she stated that she had burned the book without reading it.

This echoed further contrariness, in that during the heyday of Price's investigation of the Borley Rectory occurrences, the Smiths thought very highly of Harry Price, indeed the tone of correspondence between Guy Smith and Harry Price suggests that they were on the most amicable of terms.

After the war, however, Mabel Smith was wont to blame Price for much of the Borley episode, unfortunately giving his enemies some very misleading ammunition for their attacks upon his integrity.

Guy Smith himself died in August 1940 and unfortunately, a balanced latter-day view of the Borley story, from the Smith's side of the fence, died with him. Harry Price's recording of the Smith period was of course mainly, though not solely, con-cerned with events rather than people and indeed, most of his accounts have related very little about the Smiths themselves. It could be stated that apart from the details in Underwood and Tabori's *The Ghosts of Borley*, the information in R. J. Hastings' report gives just about the only extensive portrayal of the Smiths.

After leaving their lodgings in Long Melford in April 1930, Guy and Mabel Smith moved to Sheringham in Norfolk, where they were visited by Dom Richard Whitehouse, following one of his visits to the Foysters, during the height of the disturbances. By the time Sidney Glanville called upon them in 1937, they had moved again, to Ashford in Kent, where Guy Smith was Rector of Sevington for a while and would really have been close to a community more concerned with railway engines than ghosts. They were still there in 1939 when Borley Rectory caught fire and are said to have claimed that on the night of the blaze there, some live coals fell out onto their hearth and nearly caused a conflagration there as well.

CHAPTER TWELVE

THE REVEREND LIONEL FOYSTER AND MARIANNE

The story of Guy Smith's successor at the Rectory, and perhaps more particularly of his rather strange young wife, is in some ways a sad one. It is hardly to be wondered at that Mrs Marianne Foyster, widow of the Rev. Lionel Foyster, ended her days in distant North America, fearful of any further attention to herself in relation to the story of Borley Rectory.

Lionel Algernon Foyster, a cousin to the Bull family, was born in Hastings on January 7th, 1878, the son of George Alfred Foyster, then the Rector of the local church of All Saints'. Lionel was educated at Bilton Grange and at Haileybury, and was admitted to Pembroke College, Cambridge, in October 1897. He gained a B.A. in 1900 and his M.A. seven years later. Like so many sons of churchmen in those days, Lionel followed his father into the priesthood just as other lads might follow their fathers to sea or down the mines. He was ordained as a deacon at Wakefield in 1903, and as a priest in 1904. It was in 1903 that he took up his first post as a cleric, when he became a curate at Heptonstall in Yorkshire, which position he held until 1905. For the following five years he was a curate at Oughtrington in Cheshire. At the end of that period, he travelled to Canada and from 1910 until the end of the First World War, Foyster was Rector of Hardwick in New Brunswick, prior to taking up general missionary work in the province until 1927, the year in which his relative Harry Bull died in Borley Rectory. In that year, Lionel Foyster became Rector of Sackville, Nova Scotia, and remained so for two years.

About the end of 1929 or early in 1930, he was persuaded to return home by member of the Bull family, and take up the living of Borley, where the huge, cold and lifeless Rectory had lain empty since the departure of the Smiths.

It was in October 1930 that Lionel and his wife Marianne actually arrived at Borley with their possessions and accompanied by a little adopted daughter, Adelaide Tower, of whom more later. Lionel Foyster was a rather slightly built, cultured and good-natured man, and like Harry Bull, he became well liked in the district. Many years later, however, Marianne claimed the he wasn't popular. In fact, it is more likely that it was Marianne that the Borley folk didn't take to, for reasons that will be stated a little later. One of the sad aspects of his time at Borley, especially when one considers that he was only 52, was that for much of the time he was stricken with illness, worst of all being rheumatic arthritis, the curse of a country with a wet climate, and indeed it was ill health as much as anything that forced him to quit the living in 1935. At one time, he was crippled enough to require a wheelchair, but sometimes used only a walking stick. This latter accoutrement seems to have incurred the displeasure of something in the Rectory, for on one occasion it was hurled across the room as he sat typing. Lionel Foyster was absolutely committed to his young wife, in spite of her alleged wayward background, and she in turn by her own recent admission was also devoted to him. It comes as no surprise, therefore, to learn that Foyster would brook no criticism of his wife and when Harry Price and members of his visiting party tried to explain that some of the phenomena seemed to originate with Marianne, the Rector was furious.

Comments by various people who knew and met Lionel Foyster all seem to indicate that he was utterly straight and honest, and most important, a man unlikely to be fooled or misled by fraudulent imitation of phenomena, either by his wife or anyone else.

The record of happenings at Borley that he kept for about a year and a half was the result of conscientious documenting of events that he viewed as genuine. The writer has already expressed the opinion that Foyster would not have compiled such a record with the deliberate intention of publishing it. He did circulate reports about Borley among his family, a very different, private matter, and who can criticise him for that?

One aspect of Foyster's time at Borley is that like a number of people closely associated with the Rectory, especially those who lived within its walls, the place and its atmosphere seemed to seriously damage his health. His arthritis has already been mentioned and during his last sermon at Borley, he collapsed at the pulpit. When the Foysters moved to Ipswich, Marianne having 'married' a Mr Fisher, though still Lionel's legal wife, he lay almost totally crippled and confined to bed in the same house, and was often mistaken for Marianne's father because of his appearance. Strangely enough, Marianne herself though she also lived in the Rectory for a goodly part of five years, outlived most of the former tenants.

The Reverend Lionel Algernon Foyster died at Dairy Cottages, Rendlesham, Suffolk, on April 26th, 1945, aged 67 years and was buried in the parish churchyard of Campsey Ashe, beneath a headstone simply inscribed 'Lionel Foyster, Priest, 1878–1945'.

We must now turn to the next player upon the strange stage of Borley Rectory. To relate the story of Borley Rectory and its curiosities without telling something of Marianne Foyster would be like Conan Doyle writing of Sherlock Holmes whilst forgetting Dr. Watson. Harry Price was an integral part of the story of Borley Rectory and was, inseparable from it! Much the same could be said of Marianne Foyster.

It is not that easy to point to hard evidence to substantiate the accusations sometimes made that Marianne used Borley Rectory's reputation to fraudulen-

tly maintain its haunted background for her own ends. On the other hand, it could be fairly said, without any disrespect, that she was in many ways a curious woman who didn't quite fit into any established slot in society but rather seemed to have functioned in a fascinating world of her own.

This enigmatic lady was born on January 26, 1899, in Romiley, Cheshire, the daughter of William Shaw and Anne Woodyatt. Their little daughter was christened 'Emily Rebecca Marianne' but throughout the years she has simply been referred to as Marianne. Even at the time, her later role as Lionel Foyster's wife was almost foretold, because the Foysters and the Shaws were even then acquainted, and it is said that Lionel as a young curate, in fact, baptised Marianne. There was to be a curious sequel to this later.

Marianne began her rather curious married life at the age of fifteen, when she was wedded to an Irishman, H. G. Greenwood, giving her age as seventeen. That was to be the first of many occasions on which she lied about her age, something that is said to be a woman's privilege, though Marianne did rather exploit this. The couple had a child during 1915, later to travel to Canada with his mother, where Lionel Foyster paid for the child's education. By about 1920 this, her first marriage, seems to have dissolved into limbo, though there appears to be no record of a divorce or annullment. After this, Marianne departed these shores for Canada, the beginning of a long association with North America that she was to renew some years later, and it was there in the town of Salmonhurst, New Brunswick, that she married Lionel Algernon Foyster on August 22nd, 1922. Lionel is said to have boasted to the man who married them, about having baptised Marianne as a child, and he is said to have been shocked when the other priest told him that the marriage was not right in the eyes of God, because in effect, Foyster was Marianne's spiritual father. The point is perhaps arguable.

Marianne's marriage to Greenwood was allegedly terminated at the whim of her parents by a legal separation, which considering that Marianne was only fifteen when first she married, is not impossible. Greenwood later died in Australia, but during their brief marriage the couple had a son named Ian. It is interesting to note, however, that Greenwood was apparently dead by the time Marianne married Lionel Foyster, and if that is so, it renders invalid at least one accusation of bigamy against Marianne.

Two years after their marriage, the Foysters came to Borley for a short holiday in 1924. It was during this time that Marianne became acquainted with Harry Bull and one does rather wonder what might have passed between them, given Marianne's tendency to waywardness with various men. She and Lionel returned to Canada and did not see Borley again for six years. They lived in Canada until 1930, when in response to appeals by the Bull family, Lionel came home to England with Marianne and their adopted daughter, Adelaide. Adelaide Barbara Alice Tower was born on March 20th, 1928, her mother dying in childbirth and her father dying shortly afterwards as a result of fatal injuries suffered in a farming accident. It was following this tragedy that she was adopted by Lionel and Marianne Foyster, but her ultimate destiny was not to be a very happy one. In 1940, she was put into an orphanage, the reason given by critics of Marianne was that she had grown tired of looking after the girl. It has to be said that the combination of her adopted father's ill health and her adopted mother's liking for relationships with other men was perhaps not a viable situation in which to bring up an orphan. After 1940, there seems to be little or no record of what became of Adelaide, and there seems to have been little heard of her since, though it is believed she was reunited with Ian in the 1990s.

Much the same appears to have happened to Ivy Brackenbury after Harry Bull died. From 1927 onwards, there is almost no trace of her in the Borley annals.

Marianne's marriage to Lionel, whom she referred to as 'Lion', lasted in spite of her would-be marriage to a Mr Fisher, until Lionel Foyster died in 1945. Marianne's next and last husband was Mr O'Neil,

with whom, not long after the last war, she returned to North America. She is said to have eventually divorced him because of his excessive drinking, but what is certain is that when he died, Marianne resigned herself to a remaining life without a partner. She remained in North America until her death, when in her nineties in 1992 but her true identity was unknown to most people around her, and apparently she was in terror of any fresh public interest in her links with Borley Rectory. It is obvious that she wished to be left in peace, and when one sees some of the results of publicity about her and her private life, one can perhaps hardly blame her.

Now, however, we must come to her time at Borley with Lionel Foyster. Much has been said about Marianne and her years at the Rectory, and it would be fair to say that she was a curious person, at least in the context of Borley. However, it would also be true to say that a lot of the criticism of her has arisen out of the attitudes of people who perhaps expected Marianne to be something she was not ... namely a very ordinary and conventional vicar's wife. That was something that really she would never be.

Numerous Borley folk, even today, refer to Marianne as 'that strange woman' and yet perhaps it is not entirely surprising that she might appear strange to a community made up of rather conservative and perhaps somewhat austere rural folk with old-fashioned ideas and morals. Marianne was of a rather different stamp, young and lively and fond of fun and bright lights and men. It is not at all unreasonable, in view of Marianne's origins, to suggest that maybe she found the Borley folk as odd as they thought her to be.

A number of points about Marianne seem quite plain. She had a rather inconsistent interest in children, having care of at least three whilst at Borley ... little Adelaide, young master Pearless who was Francois d'Arles' little son and brought to the Rectory as a playmate for Adelaide, and John Emery, a little baby who died only a short time after birth, and was buried in the churchyard at Borley. That death is known to have upset d'Arles and it is very likely upset Marianne as well. The book *The Ghosts of Borley,* tells us that Borley folk could still remember d'Arles weeping at the grave. But to return to Marianne . . .

She cared, as well as any reasonable wife would for her husband, Lionel, when he was ill, with either arthritis or heart trouble which was often. In general it seems that for the most part they co-existed peaceably enough as far as the disturbances at the Rectory allowed. In fact, it would not be at all unreasonable to take the view that there could be little amiss between a couple who could put up with that Rectory and its unwanted tricks for a goodly part of of five years, if not always willingly. There seems little doubt that Marianne found Borley Rectory depressing and isolated, but then so did Mabel Smith, and it seemed to be she who suffered the greatest inability to come to terms with the Rectory and its strangeness. Marianne, however, seems to have found ways of alleviating this lack of fizz in her life by occasionally taking herself off to something more lively. There has been much criticism of her for the various affairs in which she was involved whilst married to Lionel, and it is no secret that she enjoyed the company of various would-be suitors during those days. One correspondent described her to me as an 'adventuress of the first water', and others have referred to her as 'a little beast'. It is admittedly all too easy to condemn her as such on first impressions. Remember that even Harry Price viewed her as a fraud at the beginning of his sometimes stormy and foreshortened relationship with the Foysters. But as so often happens, there were two sides to the story, and it is claimed that Lionel Foyster not only knew all about Marianne's men friends, but is said to actually suggest that she should be looking to the future after his death. Foyster himself was well aware of his own failing health, and appeared to be liberal-minded enough to be concerned at the prospect of Marianne being left in lonely widowhood.

Against Foyster's apparent knowledge and acceptance of his wife's affairs, it should be mentioned that various people who knew the couple while they are at Borley, have suggested that Lionel Foyster was infatuated with his much younger wife and, in his eyes, she could do no wrong. If that is the case, then one could suggest that as the couple remained man and wife for twenty three years, the infatuation in this case was certainly positive. Were it merely a passing dalliance, it would not have lasted beyond a few brief weeks. Other dalliances were also in play. For a time she ran a flower shop with d'Arles, in a London suburb. This was a business entitled 'Jonquille et Cie' in Worple Road, Wimbledon, and she only returned to Borley at weekends.

It has been put that Marianne was responsible for phenomena that occurred during her's and Lionel's tenancy, fraudulently keeping things on the boil in order to give Lionel a reason to take her away from the place, which she supposedly hated. It would seem, however, that the more likely sequence of events was somewhat different. A number of points can be made about this.

1. Things happened at the Rectory during their tenancy which Lionel Foyster, the person most directly associated with Marianne, and Richard Edwin Whitehouse were certain of being genuine. Assertions made in *The Haunting of Borley Rectory* that Dom Richard's evidence was not valid because he had been suffering from a nervous breakdown were subsequently rejected by the monk, who described the allegations as nonsense.

2. It will be remembered that even Harry Price, when he and his party made known their feelings about Marianne and the phenomena, incurred the extreme anger of the Rector. He had been told on this occasion that, regrettably, it seemed some of the phenomena occurred only when his wife was not under controlled observation and that consequently, she could be responsible for these phenomena. Mr Foyster would have none of it, and I believe that the Rector was an intelligent man who would not have been seriously misled by fake phenomena.

3. It has been more reasonably sugges-

ted by Harry Price among others, that Marianne could have been an unwitting channel for the disturbances not by her own doing, but because she *may* have been a 'psychically tuned focus' through which disturbing energies already in being at the Rectory, were reactivated and to some extent enhanced. It has more than once been said that Marianne came from a family with a psychic background, so it might have been a good idea for Price to have tested her as a medium. If she was a channel for disturbances at the Rectory, and assuming that such phenomena surrounding Marianne were peculiar to Borley alone and did not occur anywhere else where she resided, then surely such happenings are or were valid as exclusive Borley Rectory pheonomena. The point about localisation of phenomena could be rather significant and will be gone into later.

4. The experience of previous and later occupants of the place would seem to indicate that Marianne was really rather irrelevant as far as the curious disturbances were concerned. Many of the Foyster phenomena had occurred before their tenancy, and continued after they had gone. The various assaults on inhabitants of the house give some examples of this point. The reader will recall the blow on the face received by Marianne, a similar attack on baby Adelaide and, reportedly, another on Francois d'Arles, who is said to have come down to breakfast one morning sporting a black eye. One should not forget also that during Henry Bull's time, one daughter in bed had her face slapped and that a much later visitor was bodily seized by unseen hands and thrown face down in a pool of dirty water at the back of the Rectory yard.

5. The one thing peculiar to the Foyster tenancy was the wall writing, not seen or at least not reported previously. Incidentally, there is nothing to prove that they had *not* already occurred before in earlier years, during the Bull tenancy for example? With so many people in the house in those days, a housemaid finding messages on any of the walls could well assume that one of the youngest Bull girls might have been responsible and thought

no more about it. But in respect of the Foysters, did the writing occur anywhere else that Marianne lived in? If not, then again they were valid Borley phenomena, Marianne being nothing more than an unconscious conductor for the energy that produced the scribblings. In other words, it seems feasible that Marianne *could* have been (and that remark is used with reservation) a channel through which the messages were created. However, one should at this point note that the wall writings also occurred in Marianne's *and* Harry Price's absence. In the *Ghosts of Borley,* the authors tell of how little Adelaide was a 'terror for scribbling', but it was also pointed out that the child was not only too young to be able to write any real words as such, also rather backward and, incidentally, not tall enough to reach the level at which some of the messages were found. It seems, therefore, that there is no clear proof at all that Marianne was responsible for the wall writings. Consequently, can anyone be at all sure that she was responsible, even unconsciously, for any of the phenomena? It seems not, unless one takes a more detailed look at the occasions on which Marianne herself was sometimes suddenly taken ill and even on occasions collapsed.

6. As others have thought, it seems to make little sense for Marianne to have persisted for five years in perpetrating fake pheonomena merely to get her husband to take her away from the place. When he did eventually quit the living, it was due to ill health. It would however be a fair comment that Marianne disliked the isolation of Borley Rectory, but then so did the Smiths, but when Marianne had a bout of being bored with the monotony of life at Borley, she dealt with it very simply by taking herself off to London.

It would seem that the only real pointer to any unconscious or latent involvement in the product of phenomena by Marianne, lies in those occasions when she collapsed in the Rectory and was seemingly rather unwell.

A rather interesting possiblity lies in the idea that Marianne collapsed, not through illness as such, but as a result of exhaustion arising from excessive output of psychic energy, when the phenomena were at their most violent phase. It is to be hoped that experts in psycho-medicine will be able to confirm this idea, or at least provide an answer to the problem in the near future.

A curious twist to Marianne's story, like that of Mabel Smith, was that many years later, when interviewed in America by Eileen Garrett, Marianne dismissed Borley Rectory's reputation as nonsense, but this completely contradicts the testimony of people like Dom Richard Whitehouse and Mr G. P. L'Estrange, two of the many people who were adamant that the phenomena was genuine. Marianne will probably remain something of a curiosity in relation to Borley, for whatever her true feelings were about her time at Borley Rectory, it seems that they will remain her secret.

Whatever one might think of Marianne Foyster's lifestyle, who could fail to be intrigued by this enigmatic lady? One of the co-authors of *The Haunting of Borley Rectory*, T. H. Hall, accumulated a large dossier on Marianne and offered it to the Harry Price Library but it was declined as being unsuitable for the collection, partly because it would not have been available for general inspection. I cannot help feeling that perhaps such details of a private nature that this dossier would be most likely to contain, would best be left unpublished and the remarkable Mrs Marianne Foyster, left in peace.

Nevertheless, in September 1979, the *Journal for the Society for Psychical Research* carried an article, in an abridged form, by Iris Owen and Pauline Mitchell, of the New Horizons Research Foundation, Toronto, Canada. It was based chiefly upon various statements given by Marianne over the years since the war. Not least among these was her claim that there never was anything to the Borley story and the place was not haunted when she lived there.

Interestingly, more details of her biography seemed to have come to light in the Owen & Mitchell report, though as Marianne showed herself to be totally contrary and unreliable upon the subject of her one-time home in Essex, one does

wonder how much even of her own stated biography is totally accurate.

Peter Underwood, in a reply he gave in June 1980, to the Owen & Mitchell report, considered that Iris Owen and Pauline Mitchell had dropped into the trap of taking Marianne Foyster at face value, which is risky to say the least, where the subject of Borley Rectory is concerned. The results of so doing are graphically illustrated by the difficulties one encounters when trying to square pre-war and post-war statements by Mabel Smith, until one realises and takes into account, how a combination of unpleasant experiences and the passage of time distorts the ability of a witness to recall the truth of what happened. That is something that many critics of the Borley Rectory episode, and of Harry Price, may need to learn and accept.

Another of Marianne's curiously contrary statements was that Lionel Foyster's diary of events at the Rectory was fictional, and that everyone in the family knew that to be so. This claim conflicts with everybody else's testimony to a point that, as evidence one way or the other, it is completely unreliable.

Marianne also stated in the Owen & Mitchell report that all the keys to the Rectory had been lost, and that consequently, anybody could get in or out of the Rectory at will. Her intended inference was that the phenomena were caused by local children getting into the Rectory and messing about.

This statement is as contrary as some of the others, because the next Rector after Foyster, the Rev. Alfred Clifford Henning, handed the keys to Price when the latter rented the Rectory in 1937. Furthermore, whereas Marianne claimed that local boys used the Rectory toilet after church, the general tendency of local people was to give the Rectory a wide berth.

Marianne also claimed that she was well liked by the Bull sisters, whereas they and their brother Walter made it plain more than once, in front of witnesses, as Peter Underwood tells us, that they could never take to Marianne at all. The reader will recall that many Borley folk used to refer to her as 'that strange woman', though as was pointed out previously, there was no doubt a good deal of judging Marianne by their own standards.

According to Owen and Mitchell, Marianne also suggested that both Lionel and the tenants of the Rectory cottage, Mr and Mrs Arbon, cashed in on the hauntings and strung Price along over the occurrences. It is quite clear however, from both Price's writings and files, and from both Hastings and Underwood's work on the subject, that Price did *not* consider the Foyster testimony essential to the story of Borley Rectory, whereas the happenings of the Smith period did, at least to Price, warrant more serious consideration. We do know that Price's view of the Foyster period did change in time and the intervening row with Foyster over Price's doubts about Marianne's veracity obstructed a clear assessment of the situation, until Sidney Glanville's work cleared the air.

The persistent suggestions that Harry Price was fooled by Marianne really can not be accepted, especially in the light of the row which resulted in Price being shown the door. In any case, this accusation suggests a level of gullibility on Price's part that seems out of character with the man. Marianne claimed that Price, after the row, turned up at the Rectory one night, uninvited, bringing with him a picnic hamper. Hastings tells us that he was in the area on one occasion after the split between himself and the Rector, so it is possible that he might have tried to revisit the Rectory, but is also recorded elsewhere that Price was not able to renew contact with the Rector until much later.

In the final analysis, having considered the Owen & Mitchell report together with that of the late Robert J. Hastings, and taken account of both Price's own views and those of Peter Underwood and the late Dr. Paul Tabori in their respective books, I conclude that Marianne cannot be relied upon for evidence and that consequently, the case of the haunting can neither stand nor fall on her testimony. Her husband's testimony, and that of people such as Dom Richard and very many others, is a different story altogether, and

one finds that it is their testimony that is the more honest in many areas of the story. Peter Underwood asked the question: 'What sort of priest was Foyster if he presented as fact an account of things that he knew to be bunkum?'. No, upon the Foyster period at Borley Rectory, Marianne's claims just will not do. On the other hand, to describe her as the villainess in the Borley story will not do either. Contrary she may have been, but she was very much a part of this extraordinary episode whether she herself believed the place to be haunted or not.

The other major published view of the Foyster phenomena, that of Messrs Dingwall, Goldney and Hall, *The Haunting of Borley Rectory,* can hardly be accepted as being completely accurate, having been shown by the report of Robert J. Hastings as being rather misleading in certain aspects.

The Owen & Mitchell report is more extensive and I can only present a small portion here of what it, and Peter Underwood's reply, contains.

How does one sum up Marianne Foyster? She was contrary, curiously wayward and, to a degree, a female Walter Mitty character. In spite of all the many versions she gave of her life at Borley Rectory since the thirties, she seems to be one of those extraordinary, sometimes infuriating but always fascinating characters for whom one can hardly avoid feeling some sense of affection. She must surely be regarded in very truth as one of the many enigmas of Borley Rectory.

A strange story about her after she left Borley Rectory reached the public through a short documentary programme on BBC Television in October 1994. It was a story that seems to be very much in keeping with her reputation for waywardness, and her penchant for changing the details of her life with each telling. As the story doesn't really have any bearing on the story of the Borley Rectory hauntings, it will suffice to say that through the persistence of a young man seeking his natural mother, Marianne's trail of assorted adoptive children finally led to a brother and sister long parted being reunited.

It will be remembered that Marianne

married a Mr Fisher, though at the time she was still legally married to Lionel Foyster. When she married Fisher, Marianne presented two adopted children as being her own, whereas in fact they were not hers, and were to end up, like Adelaide Tower, in care.

Readers will also recall that after Lionel and Marianne moved to Ipswich, Lionel was often mistaken for Marianne's father, chiefly due to his age. What came to light in the documentary was that Marianne encouraged this state of affairs by actually claiming that Lionel was her father. And yet, when one remembers how she had changed or denied so many aspects of her story throughout her life, this episode serves simply to reinforce her curious and wayward character.

This episode does, however, touch upon the hauntings at Borley Rectory in one way.

The writer has suggested that Marianne might have been acting as a psychic focus through which the disturbances at that time were being channelled. She has since apparently stated that she was not psychic though as with so much else that she has related about herself, one wonders whether even that denial can be taken at face value! But could it be that the entities active at Borley Rectory, instead of appealing to her for help, as has been thought, were in fact creating their havoc *in protest* at her presence there?

Whatever the truth of the matter, and however wayward and deceiving she seems to have been during those momentous years of her extraordinary life, Marianne was with all her apparent faults, deserving of a permanent place in the annals of Borley Rectory and its strange history!

There is one more character from this extraordinary period in the Rectory's history whom we must speak of, though what is known about him is little enough. A frequent occupant of the Rectory during the Foyster's time, was Francois d'Arles, a curious character by all accounts. His name was assumed, for he was in fact born Frank Charles Pearless on November 10th, 1894, in Bermondsey, South London and on Boxing Day, December 26th, 1918, he married Ada Ewens at West Hackney. For a time he lived in France, which is when he assumed the name Francois d'Arles, probably nothing more than a version of Francis of Arles, indicating perhaps that it was in that town that he lived. His marriage to Ada lasted until 1933, when in the November he was divorced. One cannot help but wonder whether this arose out of his association with Marianne, for between 1932 and 1934 he and Marianne ran the Wimbledon flower shop mentioned earlier, with Marianne only returning to Borley at weekends.

On August 8th, 1934, he remarried, to Jessie Irene Dorothy Mitchell, at Wandsworth Registry Office. That marriage lasted until October 11th, 1944, when he was again divorced. He later married for the third time, to one Jessi Steed and some time after the war, in 1955, he departed for Australia from whence he was to return in 1966, dying on October 10th of that year.

During the Foyster period, he lodged at the Rectory his small son, who acted as a playmate for little Adelaide Tower, and in addition, d'Arles stayed there frequently himself. It is even suggested that for a time, he dominated the Foyster household. Local people recall him weeping at the grave of the dead infant, John Emery, who died aged about five weeks, whilst in Marianne's care.

He also reported having been a victim of one of the periodic assaults upon residents of the Rectory, appearing for his breakfast one morning sporting a black eye and claiming that a ghost had struck him in the face in his room.

It is a pity that more is not known about this curious man, and indeed what is recorded about him here only came to light during the research for Peter Underwood and Paul Tabori's joint book, *The Ghosts of Borley*.

CHAPTER THIRTEEN

THE TENANCY OF HARRY PRICE

The author now turns to the man whose work at Borley forms one of the inseparable parts of the strange story of the Rectory, and about whom so much as been said since.

Ultimately, it matters little what one thinks of his work, or of the Borley story in general when one realises that Borley Rectory without the late Harry Price is almost as inconceivable now as would have been wartime Britain without Winston Churchill. That Harry Price and his Borley Rectory investigation has aroused controversy would be something of an understatement. On one side of the scales, there have been many attempts to prove that without Harry Price, the story of Borley Rectory would never have seen the light of day. In Sir William Crocker's *Far From Humdrum . . . A Lawyer's Life,* we are told that Price, disgusted and contemptuous of the unwillingness of many people to accept his debunking of some of the more dubious ghosts and various fake mediums, is alleged to have said "People don't want debunk – they prefer Bunk! Alright, I'll give them Bunk.' The inference is that he then proceeded to concoct 'Bunk' on a grand scale.

The other side presents a different story, of a man who totally believed in the work he was doing, who believed that without publicity, psychical research would not get the attention it should have. He could also be seen as a lone wolf, whose way of approaching the story of Borley Rectory was controversial, and in some ways inadequate and incomplete but *not* a deliberate or even unconscious fraud. After he was dead, and couldn't defend himself, the mudslinging started in earnest.

One of the main attempts to discredit Harry Price was contained in *The Haunt-ing of Borley Rectory*, by Dr E. J. Dingwall, Mrs K. M. Goldney and Trevor Hall, which also appeared as part of the *Proceedings of the Society for Psychical Research* in 1956.

In this work, the writers sought to prove, from Price's own records and from various witnesses, that Price had invented, misled, misquoted and exaggerated incidents in Borley Rectory, and more seriously that he was guilty of duplicity in his dealings with the Rev. Foyster and his wife Marianne. In relation to his attitude towards his chief colleague and assistant Sidney Glanville, he was also supposedly guilty of treachery regarding the excavations in the Rectory cellars in 1943. The allegations appeared to have succeeded until the appearance of the late Robert J. Hastings' report, on behalf of the S.P.R. in 1969. The relevant proceedings are contained in *Proceedings of The Society for Psychical Research* – Volume 55, March 1969, Part 201.

In this lengthy examination of the assertions made, R. J. Hastings demonstrated how the case fell down on so many counts because they had taken much of the documentary evidence out of context. In essence, by so often telling only half the story, the authors of the book had themselves presented an inaccurate and unconvincing assessment of the case. R. J. Hastings showed that, section by section, their allegations became at best weak and at worst unfounded.

The Hastings report was to become contemporary with another publication in which Harry Price, and more particularly the story of Borley in general, was viewed in a middle ground light, which left one with the feeling that Borley Rectory was indeed an enigma.

In their joint book, *The Ghosts of Borley,* published in 1973, Peter Underwood and the late Dr. Paul Tabori, looked at the story of Borley Rectory from a different standpoint, whilst making it clear that they considered the episode to be broadly acceptable as a genuine case of haunting. Peter Underwood, in common with others, has more than once expressed his doubts that Harry Price would seriously have risked his reputation by setting out to construct aspects of the Borley story for publicity or effect. Having noted both sides of the argument and examined Price's material in the University of London I am of the opinion that such a fraud would have been pointless and would have achieved only the briefest and most adverse publicity, no credibility and a total loss of public approval. Admittedly Price was not always an easy man for academics to understand, which is probably the root cause of much of the criticism against him, and he was often bad tempered, rather infuriating and inclined to be tactless, all of which is very far from evidence of duplicity, treachery or any other reprehensible activity. Psychical research was, and to some extent still is, the Cinderella of science and it is all too easy for the establishment to criticise lone specialists. There is another point that needs despatching and that is the idea that Price made large sums of money out of his presentation of the story of Borley Rectory. In common with most of the later inhabitants of the Rectory he spent quite a sum on the place and received, in return for some eighteen years work on the case, only a tiny return combined with ill health, which eventually killed him.

To clarify my views at this stage, I consider that on the basis of existing information, the way in which Price administered the investigation of Borley Rectory was in certain aspects, wanting of completeness. In my opinion, the scientific value of Price's work at Borley was limited, chiefly because it was not extended enough. In addition, he didn't keep enough personal control over the various stages of investigation, whilst in other ways he laid himself open to adverse criticism later, over the details of his methods by complicating much of the arrangements for those

enlisted to keep watch. The background to the little Blue Book produced by Harry Price as a sort of code of conduct for his investigators, has led to considerable criticism because of the view that its contents could lead to auto-suggested results. One could suggest that it might not be all that straightforward to decide how far an investigator should go in preparing or advising his assistants for their task.

Critics today of Price's work at Borley might ask: "Did he make errors of judgement in his management of the 1937/38 investigations team at Borley?", but one could suggest that, after so many years, we really cannot prove one way or the other. I do feel that the supposed case against Borley Rectory and Harry Price is not capable of being proved and that Borley Rectory's reputation as a haunted house is broadly plausible but that it warrants further investigation of the historical background, the ultimate purpose of this present work.

It is now time to turn to the man himself and his tenure at the Rectory. Before examining his investigations it would perhaps be of interest to newcomers of the story of this extraordinary man, to learn something of the sort of person he was and what made him tick, but such a study can only be but a thumbnail sketch. Harry Price, the son of Edward Ditcher Price from a family with a long association with Shropshire, was born in London on January 17th, 1881. For a time, during the early years of his childhood, the family resided in Crudgington, near Shrewsbury. They then settled in Brockley, in a house in St. Donyatt's Road, near the boundary with New Cross. In 1892, at the age of eleven, Price entered Haberdasher's Aske's Hatcham School, not very far from his Brockley home, and where he remained until he was sixteen. His great over-riding interest then, and for ever after, was two-fold, namely psychic phenomena and another more controversial subject, the tricks of magicians. The knowledge he gained certainly played a part in his later, and often controversial debunking of some of the many phoney Spiritualist mediums, to whom, as Sir William Crocker was later to relate, Price was a like 'a knife through the heart'. The episode of Helen Duncan will be remembered by older readers in this context. She was a medium of some long standing in the Spiritualist world, but was in the end, the subject of an exposure and finished up in court charged under the Witchcraft Act. Price was the author of a much argued about exposure of this notorious Scottish lady, whom he viewed as a monumental fraud. A few brief comments about this episode may be of general interest.

There are those who feel that Price's management of the Duncan story was invalidated by an over-riding desire for publicity in debunking Helen before the Spiritualist circles could get their teeth into the case. Whilst writers such as Dr. Paul Tabori and Robert J. Hastings have pointed out that what Price was trying to achieve was publicity for psychic research as a principle, it would be fair to say that the way in which he went about his work, did tend to leave him open to criticism. He was not an easy man to get on with, though this was not quite such a negative factor as some would have us believe, and his professional awkwardness was tempered by considerable generosity to others less fortunate than himself. One problem that reveals itself is that Price delved into so many different things that gaps and inadequacies were bound to occur. One could suggest that he should have employed more assistants or limited the scope of his work. He did at times exaggerate, a fact confirmed by Mr A. H. Wesencraft of the Harry Price Library, but the degree to which he might have done so over Borley Rectory is not so easily proved, in spite of Price's critics.

Throughout his life as a psychical researcher, Price was often, if not constantly at loggerheads both with the committed Spiritualists and the obstinate non-believers who seemed to be immune to any idea that paranormal phenomena had any serious scientific interest. Chief among the Spiritualists whom Price fell foul of, was the famous Sir Arthur Conan Doyle, creator of England's most revered fictional detective. Arguments between the two men are extensively described in Paul Tabori's biography of Price, but it is perhaps ironic that for many years, a Spiritualist circle were Price's London landlords.

Among other interests, Price was an avid collector of ancient coins. After he married and moved to 'Arun Bank', Pulborough, in Sussex, he began compiling a history of Sussex coins, on which he spent some twenty years, only to be forced to abandon the project when his collection of rare coins, stored at Pulborough Church, was stolen. As it was, Harry Price did write at some length about English coins in various published works.

It is sometimes suggested that it was because of his involvement in coins that Harry Price was able to plant the curious medallions that were found at Borley Rectory, but he had little or no interest in foreign coins or tokens. This point about the medals was also dealt with in the Hastings report, wherein the accusations concerning the medals were pretty soundly discarded.

Price was also greatly interested in mechanical equipment and engineering, having been in charge of an engineering workshop during the First World War, after being rejected for military service owing to a weak heart. He designed, made and used a goodly number of gadgets in his laboratory, a pioneer of its kind, which he founded, taking for himself the title of Hon. Director of the National Laboratory for Psychic Research.

The personality of Harry Price was an intriguing one. He was a stocky, rather oval faced man, best remembered in his later years with his bald head and rather dour expression. Early on in his life, he strained his heart and as a consequence, suffered from angina for most of his life. At various times, including the period when he was visiting Borley, he suffered from its symptoms and it is suggested that at the time of the Sutton incident at Borley Rectory, he was very probably in the grip of just such an attack. Had he not have been, then Charles Sutton might have found himself sporting a few broken front teeth, because another of Price's characteristics was his short temper. Those who knew the man have told how he could, and did, explode in response to any criticism that he considered to be unjustified.

One cannot help but wonder what exactly passed between Price and Lionel Foyster during the row about Marianne and the phenomena, more particularly because Price made no mention of the split in his books, and only wrote to Guy Smith that the Foysters would not permit him to visit again, without saying why. There does not seem to be any recorded evidence of what was said at the time, but there is a clue to the strain that was put upon relations between Price and Foyster in a letter that survives in the Harry Price Library. The background to this was that having previously undertaken not to publicise the case locally, Price proceeded to organise a lecture on the subject, which annoyed Foyster. But as we now know, this rift between the two men was eventually healed through the efforts of Sidney Glanville.

Among other features of his life, Harry Price was very fond of Germany, in particular the Rhineland and Bavaria, both of which he visited many times. It was in Germany that Price got involved in a performance that he might, on reflection, have done better to have left alone, namely the Brocken incident. This episode, which concerned the supposed transformation of a goat into a handsome prince, turned out, not surprisingly, to be a rather stupid hoax. Though Harry Price realised this, the popular press had seized upon it before he could debunk it and he was left looking rather silly over this incident.

Another episode which was never fully cleared up was that of the spirit child 'Rosalie'. Over this, Price was accused of fraud. His defence was that he had not concluded his work on this subject, and if such was the case, then accusations of fraud were somewhat premature to say the least.

At various times prior to the Second World War, Harry Price's files and his library, which he wanted to hand over to one of the big Universities, very nearly went to Germany; Breslau and Bonn among other places being considered as possible locations. Adolf Hitler was known to have a fascination for the occult and the paranormal, and there were various discussions between Price and those close to the Reich Chancellory, but thankfully all moves to transfer Price's collection and laboratory to Nazi Germany eventually fell through.Price was known to be upset by the approach of what he must have realised was the inevitable conflict between the two countries, and in a letter to a colleague just before the war, he expressed the hope that even at that late stage, the rift between Britain and Germany could be avoided.

The coming of the war did not stop Harry Price from carrying on his work though the library at the London University, which by now included his vast files and collection of books, was closed at the outbreak of hostilities. During the blitz, the Middlesex Library, to which the HPL is attached, received a direct hit but the contents of the Harry Price collection escaped with but a few torn pages. Price even managed to visit Borley during the conflict, which produced danger even in that remote spot, the Rev. Henning being nearly blown out of his car on one occasion when a retreating German bomber dumped a stick of bombs near Liston. Harry Price's health had deteriorated and as a consequence, any strenuous activity was quite beyond him. This is one reason why he was unlikely to have been able to perpetrate fraud regarding the bone remains found when the remnants of the Rectory cellars were dug out, under his supervision, in the presence of Captain Gregson and others, partly as a result of the suggestions of the Rev. Canon Pythian Adams.

Ultimately at the end of the war, Price attended the burial of the bones and the two corroded medals found at the same time, in the churchyard at Liston, by the Rev. Alfred Clifford Henning, in the presence of Mrs Henning, their son Stephen and himself. Later in 1946, Price set out his sequel to *The Most Haunted House in England*, but his heart trouble was become more of a strain and a danger. Though he had been advised more than once to take a complete rest, he was one

The courtyard passage and pump-wheel after the fire, *opposite above.*
The exposed cellar reveals the brick wine bins, *opposite below.*

of those who could not stop working, and regrettably in the spring of 1948, he suffered another heart attack and this time it killed him.

He was survived by his wife, formerly Miss Knight, whom he married in 1908, and who died in the 1970s. He was devoted to her throughout their married life, but she took no part in his work.

This is a much condensed account of the life of Harry Price, but those seriously interested should consult Dr Paul Tabori's biography, *Harry Price – The Biography of a Ghost Hunter,* for a fuller account.

Among reading matter which seeks to cast doubts about Harry Price's work are listed in the select bibliography, including Trevor Hall's *The Search for Harry Price.* The S.P.R. also possesses a good library, available to the serious but casual student.

We must now turn to Harry Price's tenure and work at Borley Rectory. Before turning to the period during which Harry Price held the tenancy of the Rectory, that is from 1937 to 1938, a look at his work on the case prior to this is needed.

Although there is some evidence to suggest that the Borley hauntings had already come to the notice of some London people, the S.P.R. included, it was as a result of appeals by the Rev. Guy Smith, culminating in an article in the *Daily Mirror* by a journalist, V. C. Wall, that Price was first introduced to Borley. Following this, the editor telephoned Price and suggested that he should investigate the occurrences at the Rectory, to which Price agreed. On June 12th, 1929, he packed some equipment, his secretary Miss Lucy Kaye, Mr Wall and himself into a car and headed for Borley, arriving in time to take lunch with the Smiths, over which the happenings were related by the Rector and his wife. The truth of what happened during that night became a blur in the mind of Mrs Smith many years later, when she became very reticent about it, even going so far as to state that she thought Price was to blame for all sorts of misdemeanors, in stark contrast to the esteem in which both she and her husband had held Price for very many years. During that first visit, Price took statements from the Bull sisters who had come

over from Cornard, and from Mary Pearson, Smith's maid, who in a magazine article was described as being a proven liar. Price's next visit was on June 27th, 1929, when various phenomena were reported.

On July 5th, 1929, Price returned to the Rectory with Miss Kaye and Lord Charles Hope, who later described Price as a rascal, but only after he was dead. During this visit, more phenomena was experienced.

It is now thought to have been on July 25th, 1929, that the reporter Charles Sutton, of the *Daily Mail,* went to Borley with Harry Price and Miss Kaye, and there is evidence to suggest that Sutton himself asked to be taken. Nobody at the time could have had any idea of the row that was to erupt over this visit in the years after Price's death.

At the root of the Sutton episode, was what was probably an incident that nobody except Charles Sutton thought much about at the time. Having arrived at the Rectory, which had been vacated by the Smiths about ten days before, the party proceeded round the darkened house with the aid of a hurricane lamp. During their perambulations, indistinct voices were heard, which Sutton described as sounding like an attempt at ventriloquism on Harry Price's part, a description based, it seems, upon a biased assumption. The one incident that later led to all the trouble, came when after the noise of various objects falling about in the darkness was heard, what was most probably a brick or a large stone went crashing down the stairs. With the benefit of hindsight, and with reference to the report by Robert J. Hastings, it now seems that what happened was that when the Smiths moved out, and furniture men moved some things into one of the rooms, they propped open a door with a brick or a stone. When all had departed, this door prop was forgotten and remained where it had been placed but then came the Sutton party with only one lamp between them in a very dark house and in the shadows, one of them, failing to notice the brick, very likely tripped over it or kicked it down the stairs.

But the light in which Charles Sutton

The main staircase, scene of various cases of poltergeist activity, *opposite above.*
The small summer house in the Rectory garden, *opposite below.*

viewed this, and the follow-up, was rather different. Some twenty years afterwards, writing an article in the *Inky Way Annual*, he said, (see page 79 of the Hastings report).

"Many things happened the night I spent in the famous Borley Rectory with Harry Price and one of his colleagues, including one uncomfortable moment when a large pebble hit me on the head.

"After much noisy phenomena I seized Harry and found his pockets full of bricks and pebbles. This was one 'phenomenon' he could not explain, so I rushed to the nearest village to phone the *Daily Mail* with my story, but after a conference with the lawyer my story was killed. The News Editor said:

'Bad luck old man, but there were two of them and only one of you'."

When preparing *The Haunting of Borley Rectory*, the authors asked Sutton for a statement about this incident, which he duly signed and sent to them, but it was omitted. Much of the Sutton material is set out in the detailed report in 1969 by Robert J. Hastings. The substance of the Sutton business is that after various stone throwing noises and the crashing brick incident, he grabbed hold of Price, finding, he claimed, pebbles and bricks in Price's pockets, but the most fallacious part of his remarks relate to the suggestion that when he was challenged, Harry Price stood there looking vacant and mumbled "What are you going to do?".

So what did really happen?

Once again we turn to Robert J. Hastings for a very likely course of events, related to the state of Price's health. The gist of Hastings' remarks is that Price could only have responded so feebly, if he was suffering from an attack such as angina, which of course we know Price suffered from. Further evidence reveals itself firstly in the point that Price continued to be on good terms with Sutton, which he surely would not have done had he realised that Sutton was accusing him of fraud, and secondly on returning to the

'Bull' at Long Melford, Price sat very silently in the lounge, as though trying to recover from an attack such as angina.

Whereas most people soon forgot about the stone and brick incident, Sutton emphasised it I feel, out of all proportion. As the matter is extensively covered in the Hastings report, I will leave it there, but it is worth mentioning that when Lord Charles Hope and colleagues visited the Rectory on July 28th, and again the following day, Price was ill and did not accompany them!

Price continued with his search for information and it was in June 1930 that he heard the story of the nun at the gate from the carpenter, Fred Cartwright. It has been suggested that this story only came out with the aid of a few timely pints of beer with which the carpenter was plied by Price, but what little evidence exists about Price's even meeting with Cartwright, seems to indicate that this is a groundless bit of inuendo.

Price's next visit came after he was visited by the Bull sisters in London, when they suggested that he should visit Borley again in view of fresh happenings surrounding their newly arrived cousin, Lionel Foyster.

But in the meantime, on October 9th, 1931, Foyster received a visit from a representative of the Society for Psychical Research, Mr W. H. Salter, who told Foyster that if Price's forthcoming visit could not be deferred, Price should be made to sign an undertaking against publicising the event. Mr Salter also offered the services of the S.P.R. if they were wanted.

It might seem to some readers that he was somewhat out of order and had in effect, gone behind the back of Price who was also a member of the S.P.R. In fact not until the appearance in the Proceedings of the S.P.R. of the material by Dingwall, Goldney and Hall in 1956, and the later counter examination by Robert J. Hastings in 1969, did the S.P.R. seem to express any interest. My comments on the Salter visit are a personal opinion upon the ethics of trying to persuade the Rev. Foyster to limit or halt another man's investigation and it should *not* be taken as an attack on Mr W. H. Salter himself.

The reservations about Salter's approach concern the principle, not the person.

It was the Foyster period that formed the background to Dingwall, Goldney and Hall's other main thrust in their attack on Price, inasmuch as they asserted that Price was guilty of duplicity in his dealings with Lionel and Marianne Foyster. Although this was comprehensively covered by Robert J. Hastings, some points concerning this period are worth looking at again.

On October 13th, 1931, came the visit to Borley by Harry Price and his party and as quickly as his visits to the Foysters had begun, they were just as quickly thwarted, because it was as a result of what he thought had occurred regarding Marianne and the phenomena, that Harry Price and Lionel Foyster parted on bad terms. Had he been so bamboozled, the Foyster row would never had arisen.

It is here, in the row with Foyster over the phenomena, that there lies the real answer to the gap in the visits by Price to Borley and his change of views concerning Marianne. As Hastings points out, Price was not able to visit the Rectory for some time, although he was in the district on one occasion in 1932, the reason for which is not recorded. However, it may have been on the occasion of the lecture by Price, to which Foyster took exception. Not until 1939, when Price had access to the findings of his chief assistant Sidney Glanville, was he able to resume contact with Lionel Foyster. As a result of those findings, Price altered his opinion of Mrs Foyster and the phenomena, viewing them both in a more favourable light.

In October 1935, Marianne and Lionel Foyster, he now badly crippled and in poor health, left Borley and for some eighteen months the Rectory was again empty, until the next period of Price's involvement, this time as a tenant.

By the time a new Rector had been found, the Church authorities had decided that the Rectory would never be used again by a parson, and the new incumbent, the Rev. Alfred Clifford Henning, was instructed to make arrangements for the place to be sold, though this was not the first time that the building had been put on the market. Accordingly, the parish of Borley, and that of nearby Liston, were merged, and Henning and his wife moved into Liston Rectory, which survives to this day as a private dwelling. The two parishes, together with that of Bulmer, have now been attached to and administered from, Foxearth Rectory for some years. Interestingly enough, at the time of the Rectory fire, according to his little booklet *Haunted Borley,* Henning and his wife were staying at Borley Place.

In the interim period, before the Rectory was finally sold to Captain Gregson, to Price's obvious delight, it became possible to rent the place and, by arrangement with the Rev. Henning, he proceeded to do just that.

There has been much criticism, over the years, of Price's tenancy of the Rectory, his motives and his direction of the investigating team during that time, but his stated purpose, as he himself saw it, was sensible enough. He told readers of *The Most Haunted House In England* that what he wished to do was to put in a team of fresh investigators, totally unconnected with all the previous aspects of the story, and people unknown to himself or any of the Rectory's previous occupants. Apart from setting up the project, Price decided to stay out of the investigation himself and leave it to the new team, with the chief intention of getting an independent assessment of the place and its odd features. He would maintain his interest from outside.

Accordingly, Price now set about finding a team of suitably academic, hardheaded, scientific and sceptical people and he therefore placed an advertisement in *The Times,* seeking volunteers for the task. The advertisement read as follows:

'Haunted House. Responsible persons of leisure and intelligence, intrepid, critical and unbiased, are invited to join a rota of observers in a year's night and day investigation of alleged haunted house in Home Counties. Printed instructions supplied. Scientific training or ability to operate simple instruments an advantage. House situated in lonely hamlet, so own car is essential. Write Box H989, The Times, EC4.'

As Price himself related, the response was extensive and very mixed. There were, inevitably, scores of bored Society types looking for action, cranks, and would-be inventors of all sorts of gadgets, out-of-work soldiers and folk expecting to be paid for their services. Inevitably, there were also the ignorant, abusive types ready to pour scorn on the work of someone whose field of knowledge was probably greater than theirs, but out of all these, Price found nearly fifty people who might be suitable, and these he proceeded to interview. Nobody was allowed on the team or near the Rectory unless Price had interviewed them first, and he made them sign a declaration form against revealing the results of their work, most particularly to the Press or lay members of the public. Price stated quite openly in his first book that as a legal document he doubted whether the form was worth the paper it was written on, but it was accepted by Price's team on the basis of a gentleman's agreement and Price related that none of his team ever abused his trust over the matter.

Among the team who over the next year carried out investigative duties at Borley, were the following:

Ellic Howe – Oxford undergraduate.

Sidney Glanville – Professional engineer and draughtsman.

Roger and Helen Glanville, Sidney's son and daughter.

Mark Kerr-Pearse, British pro-consul to Geneva.

Rupert Haigh . . . a cousin to Mark Kerr-Pearse.

Colonel and Mrs F. C. Westland.

Dr. H. F. Bellamy.

Mr de Lotbiniere – BBC Engineer.

Mr W. S. Hammond, accompanied by other BBC staff.

Mr and Mrs C. Gordon Glover (Gordon was later known for his *Countryside* programmes on BBC radio, which I can well remember).

Mr and Mrs Lloyd Williams, later to feature in a row about the nun.

Mr M. Savage, an early engineer for the fledgling BBC television.

Mr J. M. Bailey.

Mr C. V. Wintour.

Mr S. G. Welles – Oxford undergraduate.

Mr J. Burden – Oxford undergraduate.

Mr T. Stainton – Oxford undergraduate.

Dr. C. E. M. Joad, later of *Brains Trust* fame.

Mr E. Carter Jonas – RAF Flying Officer.

Mr Caunter – RAF Flying Officer.

Mrs F. A. Mansbridge.

Mr A. P. Drinkwater and three colleagues.

The final selection was of about forty-eight, of which it should be said that Mr Sidney H. Glanville was the most dedicated, and who was responsible for accumulating the details that went into the Locked Book of private information relating to the Borley Rectory story.

Prior to the appearance of the advertisement, Harry Price had visited the Rev. Henning at Liston Rectory on Wednesday, May 17th, 1937, to tie up financial details, such as the rent, and to arrange for the distribution of keys. One set of these was deposited with the tenant of the Rectory Cottage at Borley, Mr Arbon, a steamroller driver, with strict instructions that they were only to be given to visitors authorised by Harry Price.

An inspection of Borley Rectory was made during that afternoon, by Price and the Rev. Henning, but nothing unusual was seen or experienced.

The Times advertisement followed, and to effect some control over the conduct of his investigators, Price set out some specific instructions in the controversial Blue Book, a few samples of which still survive. This little work, irrespective of its merits or shortcomings, was indeed rather unique and some of its contents are related here.

There were twenty procedures to be followed. In the original copy, various place names were indicated by blanks, partly in line with Price's often argued over policy of keeping unauthorised persons out of the Rectory and the attendant investigations, but these can now be filled in.

In the context of the time, the case for keeping outsiders at bay could probably be argued either way with equal force, except that if one were conducting such an investigation now, it would probably be advisable to keep out the media, or at least attempt to be highly selective for some cannot unfortunately be trusted to report without sensationalising and invalidating serious investigations.

The general procedure instructions for Price's team ran as follows:

1. Attend carefully to all written and verbal instructions and carry out to the letter.

2. Each observer should provide himself with the following articles, in addition to night clothes, etc.: Note book, pencils, good watch with second hand, candle and matches, pocket electric torch, brandy flask, sandwiches, etc. If he possesses a camera, this can be used. Rubber- or felt-soled shoes should be worn.

3. When going on duty, search the house thoroughly, close and fasten all doors and windows. If thought necessary, these can be sealed.

4. Visit all rooms, etc., at intervals of about one hour, unless circumstances call for your presence in any particular part of the house or grounds. Before going on duty at each period, inspect grounds.

5. Occasionally extinguish all lights, and wait in complete darkness (varying your observation post), remaining perfectly quiet.

6. Make a point of taking meals at same times each day or night. Depart from this rule if circumstances warrant.

7. Make fullest notes of the slightest unusual sound or occurrence.

8. Take a note of exact times of all sounds or happenings; also make notes of your own movements, with exact times. Record weather conditions.

9. Frequently examine grounds, and, occasionally, watch windows of house from exterior of building.

10. If with a companion, both he and you should act in unison (in order to have a witness), unless circumstances determine otherwise. If several observers present, party can be divided between house and grounds.

11. For one half-hour before, and a half-hour after dusk, take up position in

Summer-house. Remain perfectly quiet, and watch the 'Nun's Walk' on far side of lawn. It is this path that a black, draped figure is said to frequent.

12. If phenomena appear strong, or if experiencing a succession of unusual events, immediately communicate with one of the persons whose telephone numbers have been handed to you. Detail exact happenings. Expert assistance, or further instructions, will be sent you.

13. Establish your base in one room, and keep all your equipment, etc., at this post. This will prevent you hunting for an article when wanted in an emergency.

14. Keep the electric torch IN YOUR POCKET ALWAYS, whether in or out of the house. Be careful with all lights, matches, cigarette ends, etc.

15. Should strangers call, be courteous to them. Do not permit them to enter the house; do not encourage them to remain; ON NO ACCOUNT GIVE THEM INFORMATION OR OPINIONS of any sort. This applies to villagers, hotel staff, etc., equally.

16. Re meals. You should come provided each day with sandwiches, etc., and hot drinks in a vacuum flask. Rest can be obtained on the camp bed provided, but excellent meals and beds can be procured at 'The Bull', Long Melford (2½ miles) or at Sudbury (2¼ miles). It should be possible to obtain sufficient rest during the 24 hours, but if two are on duty, take turns at resting, and wake your companion if anything unusual occurs. Leave your car in the appointed place, screened from the road.

17. When asked to take charge of instruments, examine them regularly with torch, and record readings and times in note book. Carefully note anything which may appear unusual. Change charts when necessary, marking on each the time it was changed and date.

18. Spend at least a portion of the day and night (in complete darkness) in the Blue Room.

19. No observer is permitted to take a friend to the house, unless permission has been given, and the necessary Declaration Form signed.

20. Your report and notes should be

posted to the Honorary Secretary, University of London Council for Psychical Investigation, 19 Berkeley Street, Mayfair, W1, as soon as possible after you have completed your 'watch'.

At this point, against the frequent criticism of the Blue Book for pre-suggesting phenomena to its readers, the reader's attention is drawn to an important instruction at the very end of the Blue Book, for it will be seen that Price warned his observers of the risk of apparent phenomena originating from natural causes. The instruction reads as follows:

IMPORTANT NOTE

'Although some- or all- of the above phenomena may be observed, it is very important that the greatest effort should be made to ascertain whether such manifestations are due to normal causes, such as rats, small boys, the villagers, the wind, wood shrinking, the Death Watch beetle, farm animals nosing the doors, etc., trees brushing against the windows, birds in the chimney stack or between double walls, etc.'

It makes no sense, in the light of this warning, for Price to have then presented a misleading account of his team's reports, especially when one remembers that he also told his readers where his files were deposited and could be seen! The details that follow, in which Price gave examples of what his team *might* experience, should be seen in the light of this warning.

Instructions were then included for recording bellringing, movement of objects, footsteps, forms or apparitions, raps or knocks, perfumes, lights, apports, disappearances and thermal variations. From this, it can be seen that the framework for extensive scientific quantification was there, but this part of the investigation was not, in my opinion, entered into in sufficient depth. Records of a number of happenings were indeed kept and the details were no less significant than the experiences of former occupants of the Rectory, but where Price can be reasonably criticised, is for not insisting upon much

greater detail of measuring and timing of phenomena, checking for electrical disturbances, or having some sort of visual graph or scale of the team's work prepared. With the benefit of hindsight, one can see now that the Rectory should have been filled with a wide variety of test equipment.

In order to set up a base room and collect the essential supplies for his team, Harry Price, accompanied by Mr Ellic Howe, motored down to Borley Rectory on June 2nd, 1937. Having obtained a carfull of supplies from Sudbury and deposited these in the library at the Rectory (chosen as the base room), and made all ship-shape, Price and Howe then inspected the Rectory throughout, and ringed every movable object in the place with chalk.

It was when they entered the Blue Room that they found their first curiosity. Hung up behind the door was a woman's tatty overcoat. In spite of several enquiries in various quarters, nobody seemed to know anything about it. Price left the scruffy souvenir where they had found it and at one stage it was reported to have disappeared entirely and then turned up in another room. Later in the day, they two men made another inspection of the house and as evening wore on, they decided to make a night of it. After some time resting in the library, Price and Howe were disturbed by tapping noises coming from the passageway outside the room, but an inspection revealed no obvious cause. They were later further disturbed by two loud thumps, followed by the sound of a slamming door. Another search, this time of the upstairs quarters, again revealed no obvious cause. The grounds were then inspected and the house watched from the outside for some time without any result. The night had now turned chilly, even though it was June, and abandoning the idea of staying the night, the two men packed and returned to London, leaving the Rectory set up for the forthcoming investigation tem, with crockery, books, a lamp and fuel, etc.

On June 16th, 1937, Price and Howe again visited the Rectory and during an evening inspection, discovered that two of their control objects which had been placed inside chalked circles had moved out of them, in one case to a point several feet away. Price later commented that as the movement of these objects appeared to have occurred while he and Howe were absent from the building, no valid comment could be made.

One of the complaints made by Messrs Dingwall, Goldney and Hall, in *The Haunting of Borley Rectory,* was that Price's editing had resulted in the reports being presented inaccurately. They were attempting to show that this was, in their view, yet another pointer to the dubious nature of the story of Borley Rectory and of the integrity of Harry Price. Against these allegations, Hastings made the following valid observations.

Firstly, he stated that Price reserved the right to edit his observers' reports where he felt considerations of space justified this action.

Hastings also pointed out that Price's intention in writing *The Most Haunted House in England,* was to present the case to ordinary members of the public rather than to those of a purely academic turn of mind. Basically, what Harry Price wanted to produce was something that was easy to read without descending to a level of undue simplicity, or as he put it, neither too scientific, nor too 'popular'. Price's editing of the reports was hardly a deliberate aim to mislead, and he did tell his readers where his files, the sources and basis of his book, had been placed.

In connection with aspects of the life of the Bull family at Borley Rectory, Mr T. H. Hall in particular, made much of Price's editing of the seance results, documented by Sidney Glanville and placed in the Locked Book, which after the war was handed over to Hall having persuaded the then head of the Harry Price Library, Doctor Pafford, that Glanville had given the book to him.

The full text of the seance results in the Locked Book included the names of people who had come to light during the seances themselves. Only two of the names were repeated by Harry Price when he included the seance results in his books, and they were, respectively, Katie Boreham and Marie Lairre. Other names were replaced in the books by blanks, excepting the Waldegraves, who had long since ceased to have any living connection with Borley. Trevor Hall's main criticism of these results related to suggestions that somebody died there as a result of poisoning. The inference usually put upon this was that the victim was either Katie or Harry Bull, but Price *did not* name Harry Bull as such in his books. Why should he have given the names of Katie Boreham and Marie Lairre? There is one very simple answer, I believe, and it is this. Firstly, there *was* a Katie Boreham of Sudbury who died in the same year as that given by the Katie that Price told us had *allegedly* come to light during the seance sessions. The relevant point here also is that the real Kate Boreham was many years dead, as the Parish Records seemed to show, and it is doubtful whether Price even thought about any living Borehams. Therefore, there would be little objection to naming her. Incidentally, no complaints seem to have been made at the time by any member of the Boreham family.

Secondly, Marie Lairre was an unproven personality, and if she was real and further *if* she had died sometime during the 17th Century, then there was surely no worthwhile objection to the name being given in Price's books. But when it came to those parts of the results that seem to relate to members of the Bull family, then Price really did have no choice but to withold names because various relatives of those concerned were still alive and others not long departed. It should not be forgotten that at the time the Glanvilles carried out the seances, Harry Bull in particular, had only been dead ten years and his brother Walter, some of his sisters and relatives from Pentlow were still going strong. In the final analysis, the accusations against Harry Price over his editing of the reports, both of the seances and the observers' logs, really amount to little better than inuendo and irrelevance.

Price's tenancy of Borley Rectory lasted until 1938, and a precis of occurrences during the period covered by his team of investigators is included in the chapter that deals with the hauntings. In the end, two main points motivated Price's decision to view his team's work as being finished. The Church was anxious to finally dispose of the place and at the same time, Price himself felt unable to provide further money to continue his tenancy.

The next important period of involvement for Harry Price, came in 1943, when, after a period of trying to overcome the practical problems, he was at last able to get the excavations started on the site of the ruined rectory. Price was accused of 'calculated treachery' over this period, by not inviting his associate Sidney Glanville to the dig, but quite apart from any other considerations, there would have been nowhere for him to stay. All local hotel rooms were full and Mrs Henning at Liston Rectory had only limited room, in the end, only enough space to accommodate Price and his secretary. Furthermore, relations between Price and Glanville at that time, were on a business rather than an acquaintanceship level, as is obvious from the tone of their correspondence. Another serious allegation made against Price in connection with the excavations was that he had planted the bones found beneath the cellar passageway in 1943. First of all, he was physically unable to indulge in any such activity, for by that time, he was even having difficulty in walking. The digging at Borley was done by Mr Jackson, a local labourer, assisted by the Rector, Mr Henning, under Price's authority, which in turn was the result of permission from Captain W. H. Gregson who was planning to sell the ruin for demolition.

One of the claims made by Messrs Dingwall, Goldney and Hall also was that there was supposedly proof of Price's dishonesty regarding the bones, in that later examination of the cellars revealed the remains of a battery lighting set, the inference of this find being only too obvious. However, like so many of the accusations against Price, this amounts to precious little when one learns that Captain Gregson often showed visitors round the ruined Rectory, and it was made clear

by Robert Hastings that it was very likely Gregson who installed the battery lighting to aid such tours.

The medals found with the bones were another source of complaint by Price's critics for again he was accused of having planted them. This point has already been dealt with earlier, in referring to the fact that in spite of an avid interest in English coins and tokens, Price was not interested in foreign articles of this sort. This, coupled with the knowledge that he had lost his collection of coins some years before, makes nonsense of that accusation. It should be remembered that medals were found at the Rectory twice during the years of Price's investigation, once in 1929 and again in 1943. One medal in each case was foreign, French in fact, and here again, the critics accused Price of using these to build up the French Nun legend, which becomes ridiculous in the light of the fact that Price told the readers in his first book, that he *did not* believe in such tales.

Price began his investigations in June 1929, and was still answering correspondence on Borley a few days before his death in 1948, a total of nearly twenty years involvement in the case.

During the Foyster tenancy at the Rectory, he had become suspicious of Marianne's part in the saga, said so to Foyster, and got shown the door for his pains. That row was the main real reason for the gaps in his involvement with Borley. Later, in the light of Glanville's findings, Price's views changed, thus making nonsense of the duplicity accusations.

Two fair criticisms can, however, be made against Harry Price's work at Borley. In my opinion, Price did not carry out enough scientific work at Borley Rectory. There were some minor experiments with various bits of equipment such as Bellamy's electrical contact breaker, which was triggered off by falling books, but the place really ought to have been covered with every reliable piece of scientific equipment that could be obtained, and monitored continuously.

It is also clear that Price did not devote anything like enough effort to the historical possibilities beyond Georgina Dawson's theories and the intriguing scenario of Canon Pythian Adams, something that I will attempt to deal with later.

However, I do feel that Price's involvement in Borley Rectory and his lengthy investigation, so far as it went, was *not* dishonest and that, furthermore, Price presented the case in good faith. No doubt the arguments will rumble on for many years, but the foregoing comments, apart from relating his work to the newcomer, also presents the considered opinions of the author, based on the available evidence.

However, before we move on, there is one matter to which some attention should be given. At the beginning of this chapter, details have been provided that include the place of Price's birth as London. Many people for long believed that Harry Price was born in Shrewsbury, and indeed until very recently, the writer himself was basing his own text upon that apparent fact. Those familiar with the work of Price will probably be aware of the claim by Trevor Hall that Price invented a Shrewsbury background and birthplace knowing this to be demonstrably false. I have carried out an extensive investigation and research into this matter and find that the assumption that Price was born in Shrewsbury arose, not from a deliberate invention by him, there would be no reason for this anyway, but from an apparent error on the part of his biographer, the late Dr. Paul Tabori. The chain of evidence has revealed itself to be as follows:

1. In *Search for Harry Price*, Hall asserts that Price was born at 37 Red Lion Square, Holborn, and that his mother, at the time she became pregnant, was under-age. He also states that the Central Registry of Births, Marriages and Deaths supplied him with Price's birth certificate as proof of Price's lies.

2. Unable to locate proof of Price having been born in Shrewsbury, I referred back to the Registrar General and applied for a search, detailing in the application both the London birth claim, for 37 Red Lion Square, and the popular belief that Price came from Shrewsbury. The Registrar General's Office searched both 1881

and two years either side of that year before informing the writer that they were unable to trace a certificate for a Harry Price *or even a Henry Price* anywhere in that five year span. So perhaps his certificate has been lost in the archives, perhaps during the transfer of the department from its former home in Somerset House.

3. Hall castigates Price for stating that his father was a Shrewsbury paper manufacturer, when supposedly he was an unemployed London shopkeeper. Hall goes on to claim that there was no paper mill in Shrewsbury, or any trace of a Price in any Shropshire papermaking establishment. However, he omits to relate the existence of paper merchants Cox & Wright at Shoplatch, near Shrewsbury, and also fails to mention the existence of a paper mill at Tibberton, which lies very close to Crudgington.

4. In a collection of newspaper cuttings in the Harry Price Library, I found one concerning an interview with Harry, between the wars, in which he states quite plainly that he was born in London, though his family had a long association with Shropshire.

5. Because in his *Confessions of a Ghost Hunter*, Price recalled watching 'Sequah', an Indian medicine man, performing in Shrewsbury market, I contacted the Wellcome Foundation, that has in its possession an archive on Sequah, which is in itself a fascinating story.

6. Sequah, as he first existed, was William Henry Harvey, and in spite of often claiming to be American, he is believed to have come originally from Yorkshire. The Sequah medicine man routine, performed round the country from a gaudily gilded and decorated horse-drawn wagon was not one man but several. To capitalise on his initial success, Harvey founded a company of these travelling medicine men, all of whom were entitled 'Sequah', and who had to face a steadily increasing battle with copiers of the quack-medicine routine, until the company, Sequah Limited, finally ceased operations. Ultimately of course, medicine selling of this kind, and the often dangerous dentistry also carried out at these shows, was made illegal.

All this took place during a period when Price was a small boy and from William Shupbach, of the Wellcome Foundation the writer learned that a 'Sequah' did visit Shrewsbury, so young Price was quoting a childhood memory of seeing a spectacle that obviously made a great impression.

7. One other cutting in particular is of interest. It consists of a handbill for an open day to be held at Tibberton School, about 1908, and to which Harry Price was invited to give a phonograph demonstration. Tibberton Paper Mill, and Cox & Wright, the paper merchants were both functioning during the late 1880s.

8. It is obvious that Price as a small boy, spent a considerable amount of time in Shropshire. His grandfather had at one time owned a large house at Rowton, which is in High Ercall parish, as also then was Crudgington, and the possibility is, that unless these stays in Crudgington were only for holidays, young Price may have attended Tibberton School, which would be one reason for his being invited back later to one of the school's open days. It is also quite within the realms of probability that Edward Ditcher Price, Harry's father, held some connection with Tibberton Mill.

9. Price relates how he was virtually apprenticed to his father in the paper trade. Long years afterwards, Price's closest associate in the Borley story, and his near neighbour for many years, Sidney Glanville, told Paul Tabori that Price had an extensive knowledge of the paper making business. It must be pretty obvious that this knowledge came from his father, thus vindicating another part of Price's own statements about his background. Further proof of Harry Price's knowledge in the paper business exists in the drawings of a paper corrugating machine that he designed.

As far as the writer is able to discover, the one place where Harry Price is stated to have been born in Shrewsbury is in Paul Tabori's biography of him. A probable reason for this is that Tabori misunderstood the Shropshire links with Price's family, misinterpreted also Price's description of the Sequah spectacle, thinking this referred to the day Price was born, and thus wrongly created the error that has persisted ever since.

To assist my search for reliable information, I enlisted the help of a local researcher in Shrewsbury, Mrs Desarka Davies, who duly searched the Tibberton School Records, and also made local enquiries with regard to the registers of Crudgington School. In the Tibberton records, she could not locate Harry Price. In the case of Crudgington, an initial quick search was made by the headmistress, Mrs Corbett-Jones, again without finding a Harry Price, but in this case, Mrs Davies was of the opinion that something could have been missed, and a closer check might be advisable. Mrs Davies also failed to locate references to Edward Ditcher Price in what little local information is available about Tibberton Paper Mill. As this mill was subsequently in the hands of a firm in Birmingham, as was another paper mill at Great Bolas, it seemed that here again, this aspect should be further investigated.

However, on one important point, Mrs Davies did indeed score a hit! In an old copy of the *Shrewsbury Chronicle* for Friday, November 1st, 1889, there was a poster advertising the arrival of 'Sequah' in Shrewsbury. The only point on which this differed from Price's stated memory of 'Sequah' was, that whereas Price recalled having watched him in Market Square, the bill poster gave the location as a plot adjacent to the Abbey Foregate. It should be realised that Price's memory of this event, as he told it in *Search For Truth,* was related in 1940, some fifty or more years later! Furthermore, it is quite probable that the medicine man would have paraded his gilded wagon through the streets of Shrewsbury on arrival, and very likely passed by the Market Square, where a considerable crowd of people would have collected.

This find by Mrs Davies provided an essential piece of evidence that turns Price's memory of a possibility into a certainty that he did indeed witness Sequah in Shrewsbury.

To conclude this investigation into a period of Harry Price's life, it remains to link in with his father's paper trade background, but before giving these details, there remains the matter of Crudgington School. The writer himself contacted the headmistress, Mrs Corbett-Jones, and asked her to make a thorough check of the registers for the 1880s. She could not find any mention of Harry or a Henry Price.

And so to the paper trade links. The paper mill at Tibberton, started by a local owner, was later sold to a firm from Birmingham, Martin Billings & Co., of Livery Street, who also owned the paper mill at nearby Great Bolas. The writer was provided with evidence of the existence of Tibberton Mill by the Guildhall Library in London, and they suggested contact with Birmingham City Library in any attempt to trace surviving records of Martin Billings & Co. This the writer did, but only to discover that no records of the company have survived. We are therefore left with only one possible chain of evidence that could tie up with the few documented facts. Hall claims that Edward Price was a commercial traveller. The writer suggests that Edward Ditcher Price may have been an agent for the paper making industry, and in that capacity, may very well have been in close association with companies such as Billings. In any event, to have functioned as a sales agent of some kind in connection with this trade, Edward Ditcher Price would certainly have needed a sound working knowledge of the industry.

The other possibility is that Edward Ditcher Price owned or managed a paper trade company in London, rather than in Shropshire, which would explain why evidence of him cannot be found in business archives relating to Shropshire. It does seem that the links with Shropshire were more to do with family rather than business. There is also, of course, the possibility that Edward Ditcher Price was involved in specialist hand-made paper production, as until relatively recently, there were various tiny enterprises of this kind throughout the country, often unknown to the public at large.

One final observation concerns young Harry Price's attendance at Haberdashers Askes School. If, as Hall alleges, Edward Ditcher Price was an out of work London shopkeeper, where did he find the money for young Harry's school fees? True, he might have won a scholarship to go there, but then he did remain there for five years or so, and the writer cannot help but observe that Trevor Hall's attempted demolition of Price's reputation is itself a doubtful exercise, and does little to reveal the truth of the matter. In the final analysis, only one person knew the truth of the entire sequence of events, and that man took his life's mysteries with him to the grave in March 1948!

CHAPTER FOURTEEN

GREGSON AND THE FIRE – THE RECTORY'S LAST TENANT

If the strange events reported to have occurred at Borley Rectory during its existence have resulted in countless theories and much speculation, not to mention open refutation and counter accusations, then this can certainly be said of the varied versions of how this rather unprepossessing and isolated house came to its untimely end in February, 1939.

Following the conclusion of Harry Price's tenancy of the Rectory in 1938, the church authorities were finally able to dispose of their dubious liability, for one could hardly consider the rambling great barn as an asset, once and for all. On his arrival in 1936, the Rev. Alfred Clifford Henning had made it quite plain that the did not want to reside in the place, and even if *he* had been prepared to accept the bleakness and lack of comfort in the old Rectory, one could well imagine that Mrs Henning would have had something to say upon the subject. In fact, according to Henning's little paperback book *Haunted Borley*, his wife was none too keen on the Borley living from the word go. Although the Smiths and the Foysters had spent some money on tidying up the old Rectory, by the time the Hennings came, it was already reverting to a state of progressive dilapidation.

Harry Price could not satisfactorily maintain it, as quite apart from living in Sussex, he was also in poor health and quite unfit for any strenuous activity. After he ended his tenancy, the place remained empty until December 1938. On the 16th of that month, Borley Rectory was purchased by Captain William Hart Gregson, retired and late of the Royal Engineers. With it, Gregson purchased about 3¾ acres of grounds, the cottage at the rear of the building and the farm buildings. For

this, we are told, he paid the princely sum of £500, a figure previously quoted to Price. Having thus acquired the Rectory, it is told that Gregson proceeded to insure it for £10,000, which it might have been worth properly modernised, wired for electricity, etc. In the state in which it was in 1939, however, one doubts whether the church would have got more than a thousand for it from anyone.

Gregson moved in initially to the stable cottage, with his two young sons Allan and Anthony, and apparently renamed the place 'The Priory', which certainly, if inaccurately, reflected the associated history of the place. It is thought that something in the contract of sale prevented it from being referred to as 'Borley Rectory' once its use as such had finally ceased.

About ten weeks later, on the night and early morning of February 27th and 28th, 1939, the Rectory caught fire and was so badly damaged that without immediate and extensive repairs, it became a complete wreck. It was left roofless and largely unattended except for some makeshift temporary repairs to the upper flooring carried out by some Polish officers who visited the site. After the worst that an East Anglian winter can produce in such an exposed position, followed by further seasons exposed to the elements, the ruined Rectory began to collapse, becoming dangerous to anyone who ventured inside its remains, and in 1943, Gregson sold it for demolition and shortly after, workmen began to pull it down. When Harry Price and an American photographer, Mr David Sherman, visited it for the last time in 1944, an occasion that later led to another attack on Price's integrity by one of that day's party, Price was shocked to find that all but the rear wing and the cellars had gone, and with it the last reminder of the wealth and grandeur of the family of Henry Dawson Bull.

What concerns us now, however, is exactly how the Rectory came to burn down in the first place. Captain Gregson gave varying accounts of the fire, starting with that given to Harry Price not long after the fire. In this, our illustrious Captain told how, on the night of the fire, he had gone into the Rectory to sort out some of his books. A number of books that he had already stacked, securely as he thought, toppled over on to an oil lamp which landed on the floor, smashed, and sent burning oil all over the place. Another version of events was that he stacked his books on a drawing board laid across a couple of cabinets to dry them out by the warmth of an oil lamp, the books having become affected by damp. Gregson, in this report, stated that in the course of sorting out his books, he noticed a copy of *Chambers Encyclopaedia* which had escaped his previous attention. He made to pull it out from the pile and in so doing, caused the stack to topple, knocking the oil lamp flying. Later in 1947, when Gregson broadcast on the *'In Town Tonight'* programme, he said nothing about books, but felt that an oil lamp which should not normally have fallen over did just that, and scattered burning oil with unfortunate results. Both the earlier versions of the course of events have been fairly commonly accepted as valid by some enthusiasts of Borley Rectory in general. Less convincing, perhaps, have been the often propounded ideas that the fire was a belated manifestation of the 1938 'Amures threat' to destroy the Rectory, a threat that came about during experiments with a planchette at a sitting with the Glanvilles eleven months to the day prior to the fire.

In the local press at the time, mention was made of the 'Ghost Room' over the library, going up in flames. This would have been the Blue Room, but in fact one slightly curious aspect of the progress of the fire was the apparent speed with which it took hold, bringing down the roof and completely wrecking the upper front part of the house before the fire brigade could get to grips with it. Gregson could not, in truth, tackle the fire himself because he could obtain no water without resorting to the pump. In any event, his only means of getting his pumped water to the flames would have been by bucket and that, against a fire of burning oil, would have been of very limited effect if not completely useless. If one takes the time occupied in trying to dowse the fire himself, and adds to that, the time taken to run to the nearest telephone and get through to Sudbury Fire Brigade, it is not hard to see how the place was potentially lost before the fire brigade could reach it. Sudbury Fire Brigade were called at approximately 12.15 a.m. and arrived in about fifteen minutes. The blaze was brought under control in about an hour and a half, after which the tender remained to damp down the remains and ensure that the fire did not restart. All their efforts were, in the end, to little avail. The fire had done its worst and Borley Rectory, save for the rear part of the house, was for all practical purposes a write-off. It could subsequently have been salvaged or rebuilt, at considerable cost, indeed many a Borley fan including the present author, bemoans the fact that it wasn't salvaged, but as we know, no attempt was made to clear the mess or replace the ruined floor and gutted roof and the Rectory became a pathetic and unsafe ruin.

Now, however, we come to an aspect of the fire at Borley Rectory that has, in more recent times, thrown a cloudy shadow over the whole incident and Captain Gregson's tenure at the Rectory. In due course, Gregson filed an insurance claim for accidental loss by fire to the tune of £7,356. The claim was taken up by William Crocker, a solicitor concerned with insurance matters and Colonel Cuthbert Buckle, a loss adjuster. It is out of this that there has since arisen probably the most discrediting assessment of Captain Gregson and Borley Rectory in terms of the supposed purpose of Gregson having perpetrated an insurance claim of a fraudulent nature. As told by Crocker, the story of Gregson and the fire shows the Captain in a very poor light.

Writing in his memoirs in 1967, Crocker (now Sir William Crocker) told his side of the Borley Rectory episode in Chapter 23 of his book, *'Far From Humdrum . . . A Lawyer's Life'.* It makes interesting reading.

The basic line of Sir William's account goes as follows. Having distrusted Gregson's versions of how the fire occurred, and having taken rather a dim view of his having insured a house and possessions worth at the most £500 for £10,000, and of his having paid for it by a mortgage of £600 raised for the purpose, Crocker and Buckle began to have their doubts about the claim. Ultimately, their rejection of the claim as it stood was based, among other things, upon the results of a careful examination of the wreckage from the fire, some of which was put through sieves for close scrutiny.

Among other things, Gregson had bemoaned the loss of a collection of coins valued at £50. According to Sir William Crocker, a search of the gutted Rectory produced precisely one Victorian farthing. Secondly, Crocker concentrated upon, of all things, Gregson's underclothes, which he described as being highly priced, initialled, and existing in large quantity. A chest of drawers containing these garments was found to have charred outwardly in the fire but the clothes in it were so tightly packed together that there had been insufficient air inside to cause the contents to be more than vaguely scorched. These garments were, it is said, thin and darned, worn out and fit only for the rag basket. The inference here is, of course, that in insurance terms, the value of Gregson's property within the house was virtually nil. The upshot of the whole episode, was that the insurers bluntly refuted what they considered to be an impudent claim, stating that, as far as they were concerned, Gregson had set fire to the place himself. It was then made known that for the sum of £750, the matter could be settled on a nuisance basis, out of court. Sir William, in his memoirs, commented upon the fact that this would have been much less than their costs in debunking Gregson in court and achieving, as Crocker put it, 'an empty judgement against this man of straw'. Accordingly, disgust and chagrin

being duly swallowed, like some nasty medicine, they paid out on that basis, and there was an end to it as far as Sir William Crocker and Colonel Cuthbert Buckle were concerned.

To the author, however, there are aspects of Sir William Crocker's assessment of Gregson and his intentions which strike an incomplete note, at least in respect of the relatively little detail related about the Captain in print.

Whilst it should be clearly understood at this point that there is no intention on the author's part to question the integrity of either Sir William Crocker or Colonel Buckle over their handling of Gregson's claim for the loss of Borley Rectory, both men doubtless dealing with the case as it appeared to them at the time, one is given to wonder whether or not, upon looking again at the case, the view of Gregson and his role in the story of Borley Rectory is totally valid and correct? So far as the existing chronicles of Borley Rectory are concerned, there are various aspects of this episode that would seem to have been given less than close attention. There are a number of potential questions that occur to the present writer for a start.

What was the view of the officers of Sudbury Fire Brigade concerning the Borley Rectory fire? This I have so far been unable to ascertain.

What was Gregson like as a person, particularly in the context of his ownership of the Rectory?

Would he have been likely to set fire to his own home, especially to a building with the post war potential of Borley Rectory, which once the war and resulting shortages were over, could soon have been turned into a desirable residence, worth a substantial sum?

Was the Captain then in such financial dire straits that he took such an appalling course of action in order to obtain funds?

Finally, considering the reputation of the Rectory, does it not seem certain that it would have been of greater financial benefit to Gregson intact, rather than as a blackened ruin?

It seemed to the present writer that an attempt ought to be made to answer some at least of these questions, and also to provide something about the life and character of this, the last owner and resident of 'the most haunted house in England'.

When we come to delve into the story of Captain Gregson and the fire at Borley Rectory, it becomes obvious that the late Captain William Hart Gregson was not all that he seemed. When Harry Price was compiling *The Most Haunted House in England* in 1939–40, not having known Gregson until he had bought the Rectory, he obviously took the Captain at face value and indeed, at the time he would have had little reason to view Gregson in any other light. Had Price known then what can now be related about Captain Gregson, then the story of the Rectory's destruction would very likely have read very differently in Price's books. The passage in Sir William Crocker's memoirs has been known about for some time, but beyond that, very little has been written about the Gregsons.

After having faded from the scene for some years, one of the Captain's two sons, Anthony Hart Gregson, was recently rediscovered living at Cultus Lake, B.C., and this through the efforts of Richard Lee Van Den Daele, of Shipley in West Yorkshire. Anthony Gregson, in a letter to him stated quite bluntly that his father had set fire to the Rectory for the insurance money.

Furthermore, according to this same letter, Captain Gregson is portrayed as very much the 'man of straw'.

Gregson came, it appears, from Rusland Valley in the north of England, where his father was a local preacher, but at the time he purchased the Rectory in December 1938, he was living at Maldon in Essex. During the thirties, Gregson became involved with Sir Oswald Mosley's British Union of Fascists and became a sort of area organiser for them in the Maldon district. On one occasion, however, his activities brought him into conflict with what Anthony Gregson describes in his letter as 'a mob', who were incensed at the appalling treatment meted out to hapless tribes-people in Ethiopia by Mussolini's air force. The late Captain, 'man of

straw' indeed, thought that discretion was the better part of valour and changed sides. In due course, he became a garrison engineer with the Royal Engineers at Southend-on-Sea.

Of his handling of Borley Rectory, Anthony Hart Gregson says this of his father:

"my father Capt. (Retd.) W. H. Gregson bought Borley Rectory as a real estate venture around 1937 at which time it was classified by a prominent spiritualist, Harry Price, as the most haunted house in England. When this didn't pan out, he torched it for the insurance."

According to the same letter, Gregson became involved with the Mosley bunch after the Borley episode, but this conflicts with, among other things, evidence in the form of letters to and from Price and the Rev. Henning, revealing that Gregson was living at Maldon, where he had been a B.U.F. area organiser, *before* and not after the Borley period. When, in 1943, Gregson finally sold the shell of the burned out Rectory to a Mr Woods for demolition, he and his sons departed, not back to Maldon in Essex, but to the similar-sounding WALDEN in Yorkshire, not far from Rusland Valley from whence the Captain had originally come. His two sons went into the forces, Anthony serving in Europe whilst the other, Allan, was posted to East Africa where, his brother complains, he had an easy billet.

In his letter to Richard Lee van den Daele, A. H. Gregson describes his father as 'an upright citizen', in connection with his joining the British Union of Fascists, but his actions in 1947 could hardly be classed as such, it was in that year that despising the Socialist point of view and partly it seems because he was a landlord owning about 25 slum dwellings, he and Allan Gregson departed for Tasmania.

According to his own story, Anthony Gregson decided to get to Canada by stowing away aboard ship and finally came to Discovery Mine, a gold camp in the North West Territories, from where he later claims to have stolen part of a gold shipment by substituting lead for the gold bars. He was not apprehended until 1957

105

in Tasmania, the year of his father's death, whereupon he was sent back to Yellowknife in Canada to face a two year prison sentence.

That at least is the picture of the Gregsons and the fire, given by Anthony Hart Gregson. However, without supporting evidence from the other son, Allan, this discrediting assessment of the case is not necessarily the end of the story. Richard Lee van den Daele managed to trace Alan Gregson, now living in Tasmania, and the latter's response and version of events directly contradictts the insurance fraud suspicions! Allan Gregson's memories of the night of the fire turn the whole episode on its head again, because in his letter he says:

"Although we'd bought the property and taken possession in late 1938, we lived initially in the flat above the coach-house, pending redecoration and furnishing of the Rectory (not all 20 rooms of it though). A great deal of our furniture, etc. was stacked in the entrance hall and stairwell temporarily. There being no electricity or gas, our lighting was by oil lamps which were not pressure lamps. One of these was an argand type brass table-lamp which was carried into the rectory any evening when we required to fetch one or our books or other articles. On one such evening my brother and I were in the flat, it was about bedtime, and my father wanted a book or document from the Rectory; apparently he stood the lamp on a table or box while he rummaged about, and then a stack of books suddenly keeled over onto the lamp, overturning it, breaking the glass and spilling kerosene which then caught alight and speedily ignited surrounding articles. Like most households, this one didn't have ready-use firefighting equipment and so my father immediately sent us boys to the nearest telephone (Borley Green) to call the fire brigade from Sudbury."

This contradicts Anthony Hart Gregson's version of events, of which Allan says that his brother tended to suffer from 'over-exposure to James Cagney', but there are aspects of Allan's account of the night of the fire which raise questions. The first concerns the storing of their belongings in the Rectory prior to having it redecorated. In a house with wooden floors and stairs, what on earth was all that gear doing stored in the hall near the main stairs, the worst place of all to store books and paper in the event of a fire, unless it was never the intention that the Rectory should survive to be redecorated? The second point that arouses suspicion to the outside observer is the despatching of both boys to the nearest phone. If *one* of the two boys had stayed with the Captain, they just might have stood some chance of containing the fire until the brigade arrived. Nobody could really be blamed for thinking, as I am inclined to suspect, that with both boys out of the way, Gregson could have made *sure* that the place was well alight! It should not be forgotten that in the space of about fifteen minutes, the time taken for the Sudbury Fire Brigade to get to the Rectory, the place was far enough gone that they were unable to save it. The evidence against Gregson may well be considered circumstantial, but when we stop to take stock of the evidence, the conclusion that the fire was deliberately started for financial gain is hard to avoid:

1. Gregson bought the Rectory for some £500, and then insured it for £10,000 ... twenty times the purchase price.

2. During his short ownership of the place as an intact house, books and other belongings were stacked in the hall, near to the main staircase. If a fire started in the hall, as it did, the danger that it would roar straight up the stairwell and set the upper landing alight very quickly was so obvious that the stacking of their belongings there was monumentally risky.

3. One of the two sons states quite bluntly that Gregson bought the Rectory as a real estate venture, and when it didn't pay off out of its reputation, he set fire to it for the insurance.

4. When the fire broke out, the Captain sent both boys to phone for the fire brigade, whereas if one of them had

stayed, the fire might have been contained.

5. Gregson gave different versions of how the fire had started to the insurance assessors, and on the basis of an examination of the remains of the Rectory, the insurers refuted the claim, in the end settling with Gregson out of court for £750 because it was probably economically more expedient than the costs of trying to fight the claim in court.

6. This view of the insurance claim side of the episode was confirmed by Sir William Crocker, who was directly concerned with the claim, although it should be added that Crocker had a jaundiced view of Borley Rectory's reputation as a haunted house.

Against this evidence for the acceptable cause of the Borley Rectory fire, there is also *some* evidence for the *possibility* of a paranormal cause for the fire:

1. During the tenancy of Lionel and Marianne Foyster, a skirting board in an upstairs room caught alight and had it not been for the fact that people in the Rectory smelled burning and went to investigate, that fire might well have got a hold. It has been alleged more than once that this was not the first time that a minor fire had started in the Rectory without obvious cause.

2. At a planchette session operated by Helen Glanville at her home in Streatham, a threat was made by a 'communicator' whose identity has never been established, that the Rectory would be burned down, thus revealing the cause of its infamous reputation, supposedly surrounding an act of murder.

3. Eleven months to the day after the planchette prophesy, the Rectory caught fire and was gutted beyond repair.

4. During the fire, at least one witness insisted that two figures could be seen watching the Rectory burn, whilst Gregson was equally insistent that only he and the firemen were there. Two figures were reported to have been seen actually standing in one of the windows of the burning building, of which one appeared to be a man in a cloak, whilst the other was just a blurred form.

A psychic colleague to whom the writer recently mentioned the possibility that

Captain Gregson had set fire to the Rectory for reasons of insurance fraud, responded by saying:

"No, I don't think he actually started the fire, but it happened as a punishment for his having bought the Rectory for an insincere purpose, i.e. to try and make money out of its reputation."

The lady had not been reading about or studying the story of Borley Rectory, and had never heard of Gregson until the writer mentioned his interest in the case. How much, if any, value the lady's thoughts have in deciding the case of the Rectory fire is hard to say, but when viewed in the context of the Rectory's rather unfortunate history, the fire could *perhaps* be viewed in the following light:

Borley Rectory and/or the site upon which it stood was at some time the scene of a human tragedy. Those spirits who had been involved in that tragedy tried many times through physical disturbance and seance contact to persuade those who came afterwards, to excavate and reveal the truth of what had happened. When this was not done, the final resort of causing the place to be burnt down so that someone could then unearth evidence of a tragedy was finalised. In the arrival of Captain Gregson, and his dubious reasons for buying the property, the entities saw their means of revealing the truth by fire, and Gregson became the instrument of their intention. Once the deed was done, Gregson's part was finished, as far as the entities were concerned, leaving him to face the disapproving opinion of a doubting insurance assessor.

In the light of what has been revealed about Captain Gregson and the Rectory fire, it seems that we may never know whether the fire was a fraudulent act or whether it was another of the Rectory's long saga of weird happenings, or whether it was an extraordinary coming together of destiny and human motivation. The writer will leave his readers with the thought that a seemingly normal event was the trigger that achieved a paranormal purpose!

CHAPTER FIFTEEN

JAMES TURNER AND THE RECTORY COTTAGE

It is with a picture of the life at the Rectory Cottage of James Turner, the writer and poet, that the author will conclude his look at the inhabitants of Borley Rectory and its attendant stable cottage. There is little doubt that many strange things have happened there since the fire, including oddities experienced by the Bacon family who lived in the cottage for a time, but these we will have to leave for another time.

James Turner purchased the Cottage, the ruins of the old Rectory cellars and much of the large garden early in 1947. He lived there for three years, market-gardening for a living until 1950, when he and his wife moved to an even more remote hamlet, Belchamp Walter. The couple eventually moved out of the area to Bodmin in Cornwall. James was an interesting man, a lover of poetry for which he is best remembered, a writer and sometimes a painter.

James Ernest Turner was born in Foots Cray, Kent, on January 6th, 1909, and was educated at Queen's College, Oxford. Regrettably, he passed on in 1976. By his own admission, he was never a rich man, and seems in recent years to have been out of the limelight. According to Mr A. H. Wesencraft, who met James, he had some personal interest in the occult and wrote, among other things, *Ghosts in the South West*, as well as articles in *The Listener*, *Punch* and the *Sunday Telegraph*, and had at one time, been a schoolmaster in the north of England.

In 1950, he published an extraordinary and quite delightful book entitled *My Life With Borley Rectory*, which claimed to detail some months of hair-raising experiences in the Rectory Cottage. It has to be said that the book is a very readable and delightfully hilarious tall story.

The central characters were an extraordinary old housekeeper called 'Prescott', and an even stranger wild Irish pianist called 'Ryan'. The would-be villain of the piece was a girl whom, in the story, Turner supposedly married, though in real life he married his wife Lucy in 1936, after which they lived for a time at Staplehurst in Kent. The plot in this charming book revolved around attempts to steal Borley's lost church plate which had supposedly been thrown down the well in the remains of the courtyard. What a wonderful tale it was! Tales of old chests crashing down the stairs in the middle of the night, bottles flying in all directions and ghostly figures vanishing behind the church were the backbone of this work, well worth a read if one can still find a copy. In the published works about Borley, James Turner had plenty of genuine material for his excursion into novels, but his tenure at Borley was, in truth, not without curious interest in itself. An interesting result of his time at Borley was the low wall he built, conforming to the outline of the old Rectory itself, and within which Turner laid out a sunken garden. Sadly, all that has now been destroyed, and like the great Rectory itself, become a memory of the past.

The Rectory cottage still showed signs of its former use as a coach-house in the wheel ruts in the brick floor of both kitchen and dining room. It had been the resting place of the Bull family's own carriage, itself referred to in that household as the 'phantom carriage', according to a more recent but confusing testimony by Marianne Foyster. It was an amusing send up, if true, by the Bull sisters, of the weird coach and bay horses so often reported as careering noiselessly across the Rectory lawn or clattering unseen up the lane outside. James Turner himself was apparently not much impressed by the stories about the coach, and by all accounts didn't really believe them. He did, however, feel that there was indeed something odd about the place, which is hardly to be wondered at, considering its past history, and even allowing for prior knowledge of the Borley Rectory story.

While his book, *My Life With Borley Rectory,* was a satirical exercise, James Turner's autobiography, *Sometimes Into England,* is a different kettle of fish. Some interesting details were provided by Mrs Lucy Alice Turner, James's wife, in reply to my enquiries. The salient passages from her letter to me read as follows:

"Dear Mr Banks,

Thank you for your letter. I was interested to hear about your proposed book on Borley but I am afraid I can't be of very much help in giving you any fresh information. It is a fascinating place and the interest in it never seems to die down.

I can't say we ever saw anything in the way of nuns, phantom coaches, etc., though we used sometimes (on hot summer days) to hear the sound of children's voices and laughter in the old orchard – rather charming really – were they the Bull 'children'? Who knows? – and one hot afternoon I was sitting in the old driveway with the Rectory remains on my left – all very peaceful and quiet when I was rather startled to hear heavy footsteps, but a few feet away, as though someone was walking on bare boards! And one evening – or rather late at night – we came home and in the headlights of the car we saw a lean grey cat dash under the car – we got out thinking we had run it over but nothing there! And of course there were the usual sounds of smashing crockery in the kitchen and once when I was washing up, the sharp crack of a pistol, just above my head."

Regarding the odd business of the grey cat, there is, of course, the possibility that a real cat on being struck by a car, could have been thrown into a hedge or to the side of the road, but against this, having got out of their car to look under it for the injured animal, it seems quite reasonable to suggest that James and his wife would also have looked around for signs of the animal.

Whilst one might feel that prior knowledge of Borley could lead to the experiencing of phenomena, the writer feels that James and Lucy Turner's experiences as related, only serve to confirm occurrences already recorded long before. In addition, the experiences of Edward Cooper and his wife during the First World War, show us that the stable-cottage as well as the Rectory had its fair share of strange happenings.

The phenomena, if phenomena it was of the laughing children, is rather intriguing and in spiritual terms it does rather suggest a period in the old Rectory's history when the Bull children were young. This also prompts me to take a look at the character of the Rectory itself in respect of the disturbances. Harry Price was among those who have commented upon the apparent change from the atmosphere of the Rectory during the heyday of the Bull family as compared to the less than pleasant atmosphere in the place during its declining years. One could find some sympathy with the idea that when the Bull children were young, Borley Rectory was a happier place, the ghosts and phenomena being accepted as part of life in the house, whereas later inhabitants found such happenings someting of an intrusion into their lives to say the least, and the Rectory itself a cold, run down and rather depressing place, much in want of domestic servants to assist in creating a more friendly and lively environment.

There are many ways of looking at the apparent change in the atmosphere at Borley Rectory over the years. Those who are interested in the spiritual side of hauntings might, for example, find some common ground with the idea that the large and, generally happy Bull household soaked the building with an atmosphere that percolated through another dimension to the spirits of those departed characters from the history of the site, thus perhaps providing an open channel of contact coupled with some degree of stability. The Bull family, though surprised sometimes by the phenomena, accepted them and maybe even vaguely understood them, possibly without realising it. When the Bulls were gone however, those who came after were to all intents and purposes strangers, who could not come to terms with the phantoms and strange happenings, and because of that, they caused the whole aura of the place to change, and become a scene of rejection and defensiveness, resulting in the increase in disturbances. One wonders whether in fact, some sort of break in family unity resulting from the departure of the sisters from the Rectory in 1920, was the catalyst that caused a change in the atmosphere, because it was after this that the whole picture had taken on a different look.

James's own attitude to the reputation of his home was a trifle contradictory, because in *Sometimes Into England*, he expressed the feeling that most of the stories attached to the place were little more than local tell-tales that often surround old and rambling houses. But he told A. H. Wesencraft that he did consider there to be something most odd about the place.

On one occasion Turner himself invited a visit from a theatrical group who staged a play in the old Rectory grounds, based upon the role of the Waldegraves in the Borley saga, including parts about the elusive nun. There was something of a hope among those present that the ghost nun herself might be induced to appear but on this occasion the sad faced little phantom failed to respond, though her reported appearances had not ceased for she was sighted some time after Turner and his wife had left the place in 1950.

Turner does mention in his autobiography, minor incidents such as pressure indentations in chairs in the mornings, such as would be left by a cat sleeping in them, though this sometimes happened when Turner's cats had not been in at night. He also tells of the noise of smashing crockery, but dismisses it as nothing out of the ordinary. We know of course that this phenomenon was of old lineage at Borley Rectory, and that consequently,

James's poor opinion of its significance does not really carry any weight one way or the other.

One incident did occur while he was at Borley, however, which even he had no answer for. About a month after a terrific storm which did much damage in the area, including ripping the steeple off Foxearth Church, James was sitting by the priest's door of Borley church, whilst outside on the road by the gate, a young couple were standing talking. Then there came the sound of someone walking up the path to the church, with one step sounding slightly heavier than the other. This was also accompanied by the sound of a swishing garment but there was nobody to be seen, except for the young couple by the gate. Not long after this incident, a lady visitor to the church heard the same footsteps following her up the aisle. She had come to look at the recently refurbished altar, but she got no further than the Waldegrave tomb before hearing the footsteps. She took fright and walked out of the church.

In more recent years, it has been the church that has more often than not, seen any reported unusual incidents, but mostly auditory.

One of the reasons for James Turner having come to Borley in the first place was his intention to grow mushrooms in the dilapidated sheds at the back of the property. Although he made a good start, things generally did not work out and two successive failures of crops left him short of money, and an attempt to grow flax also failed. When a buying agent inspected what looked at what was thought to be a good crop, the buyer refused to accept it, because it had become infiltrated with weeds. To make matters worse, vibration from low flying jet aircraft wrecked the mushroom racks, for which the Ministry of Defence refused to pay compensation.

In 1950, James and his wife decided that Borley was just not an economic proposition, so they put it up for sale, and rented a cottage in the 'outback' at Belchamp Walter. For a long time, there were no takers for the empty Borley Rectory cottage, until it was purchased, mortgage and all, by the Bacon family, whose experiences there appear in *The Ghosts of Borley*.

CHAPTER SIXTEEN

BONES AND A TUNNEL:
AN ARCHAEOLOGICAL ASPECT

The present writer feels that here is a good opportunity to bring together the details of the two major excavations carred out at Borley Rectory following its destruction by fire in 1939.

Harry Price described the digging in his second book, *The End of Borley Rectory,* with notes covering the excavations he supervised during the middle of the war, when bone fragments were found under the remains of the Rectory cellars. The most important find, the jawbone fragments which have since become known by popular belief as the remains of the nun Marie Lairre, were analysed, photographed and later, in 1945, officially buried by the Rev. A. C. Henning at Liston. It was over the period of the excavations that Harry Price was heavily criticised by Messrs Dingwall, Goldney and Hall.

But the second major archaeological discovery at Borley was when workmen busy in the lane outside the Rectory grounds, broke through into a tunnel beneath the road, the existence of which had been part of local folklore for many years. These finds in their turn were later described by Peter Underwood and Paul Tabori in their book, *The Ghosts of Borley.*

The digging in 1943 was carried out under Harry Price's auspices, partly as a result of the fascinating scenario set out by Canon Pythian Adams, and in the presence of Captain Gregson and the Rev. A. C. Henning, who assisted with the work, helped by Mr Jackson, a local labourer. Price himself was limited to overseeing because he was physically unable to indulge in any strenuous activity.

For some time, the non-availability of accommodation locally and the fact that the Rector was unable to find anyone to help with the excavation, led to a con-siderable delay in starting the excavations. It was Canon Pythian Adams who later attached considerable importance to digging up the Rectory cellars in line with the results of *his* theories, and this in later years, was twisted by Price's critics, who suggested that it was only when Adams urged the necessity of carrying out the digging that Price got on with the job. In fact, these comments by the Canon were made *after* Price had carried out the excavations. Furthermore, the later comment about Price's attitude towards his associate Sidney Glanville in not inviting him to the dig, fails to be of value when one learns that the Rector's wife confirmed some while later that there was virtually no accommodation available in the area and she had only enough room at Liston to put up Price himself. Their helper at the dig, Jackson, had his own home locally.

Eventually Price got over the problem of accommodation when the Rev. and Mrs Henning offered to accommodate him at Liston Rectory, and things were at last able to get under way, Henning obtaining the loan of a bricklayer's sieve from Sudbury to help sift through all the rubbish that they would doubtless find.

Because of the war, The Bull at Long Melford and virtually all accommodation in Sudbury was taken up by service personnel, and there were restrictions on the letting of rooms and the provision of meals. Petrol rationing was in full cry, making any travel for non-essential purposes difficult and travelling by train was far from comfortable. Price, it should be recalled, lived in Sussex, so any visit to Borley involved several hours of crammed trains, air-raid alerts, queueing and slow progress, not to be taken lightly by a man whose health was less than perfect.

However, things eventually began to move and the dig was begun. Price had received Captain Gregson's permission to undertake the excavations, which became a matter of some urgency by early 1943, for Gregson was offered a post abroad and was anxious to dispose of the remains of the Rectory. Price realised that whoever purchased the ruins would most likely pull them down to salvage the bricks, mostly still in good condition and of a quality in short supply during war-time. In addition, of course, Price might have found a new owner uncooperative regarding allowing part of his property to be dug up.

Work on the excavations began on August 17th, 1943, but by that time, other people had turned up either to help, or to analyse what might be found. Among these were:

The Rev. A. C. Henning and his wife.

Mrs A. English, formerly Miss Beenham and Price's secretary.

Captain W. H. Gregson and two nieces.

Dr. E. H. Bailey, MRCS, LRCP, a pathologist.

Mr R. F. Bailey, a barrister.

Flying Officer A. A. Creamer, DFC, LLB.

Jackson, a local labourer from Borley.

Mrs Georgina Dawson, originator of the theory about Arabella Waldegrave.

Having arrived together with some stonemasons hired by the Rector, the party first tried to find the entrance to the sealed up crypt of Borley Church. Price himself hoping that some clues as to the fate of Arabella Waldegrave might lie therein. A huge slab, thought to cover the entrance to the crypt, was heaved out with a block and tackle, but beneath it they found only sand embedment and no trace of any crypt. What they did discover, however, was that the stone was the base of a pre-Reformation altar and at some time in the past, it had been repositioned upside down. Further inspection of likely places for an entrance to the crypt was made, but for Price, this was rather a secondary point to the Rectory itself and the search for the lost crypt was, for the time being, abandoned. Neither the crypt nor the lost Borley Church plate have so far been located. One cannot help but wonder whether, if the crypt could be discovered, so also might the lost plate. At a time when there might be a threat of the plate being stolen, by Cromwell's men for example, what better solution than to place the plate in the crypt and then seal it, hoping to retrieve it during better times.

To return to the story. Price was anxious to tackle the remains of the Rectory and so proceeding to enter the cellars, began by clearing the area where they expected to find the shallow well tank, into which one of Price's colleagues had nearly fallen in 1929. To Price's undoubted mystification, the whole tank had vanished! In spite of clearing large amounts of debris and probing the ground, no trace could be found of it. So the search for it was left and Price turned his attention to one of the wells, which Jackson proceeded to empty. Up came a strange assortment of bits and pieces, including all the usual rubbish: ash, potsherds, old bricks and in this case several old wine bottles, with which the old Rectory seemed to have been more than amply provided, followed by empty tins, broken glass, broken cutlery and a big brass preserving pan. It should be remembered that Herringham owned a Rectory on this site, though he used Borley Place, and later excavation revealed that traces of an even older building were extant on the same site. One can but wonder what interesting articles might have been discarded from the old Waldegrave Rectory, the existence of which seems to be almost certain in the light of documentary evidence and later site investigations.

However the party's next major find proved to be more recent and all were surprised when Jackson handed up a splendid cream jug, made of silver, absolutely black but otherwise quite undamaged. Later, back at Liston Rectory and with the aid of some cleaning materials, Price cleaned it and later had it valued by a London silversmith, who dated it about eighty years old. How did such an article come to be buried in such fashion? Broken or worn out household junk one would expect to find, but a silver jug?

At a depth of about six feet, Jackson hit what seemed to be well-bottom, because he had reached old bricks of the same type as those used at the side or body of the well shaft. These they could not break through and yet this well bottom raised something of a puzzle. Why so shallow a well? It set Price to thinking that they might have come upon merely a false bottom, but concealing what? This mystery was never answered and neither was that of the well tank. So far as the tank was concerned, Price could only surmise that at some time during the previous few years, somebody had removed the tank, or filled it in, and bricked in the space where it had been, except that nowhere could they actually find where any replacement floor bricks had been inserted. Some people since have suggested that Price was mistaken as to the exact position of the well tank, but it does seem a bit odd that he should fail to remember the position of something that related so strongly to some of the theories about the ghostly nun, surely the most important of all the various mysteries about the place.

Although he never mentioned having done so, it is not beyond the bounds of possibility that Gregson could have filled in the tank, though why he should wish to obliterate all trace of its former existence is a mystery. He did report having covered over the well in the cellar, because in spite of the fact that he had locked the cellar behind him, the wooden lid that he had placed over the well, was found thrown off and lying some distance away. Did Gregson then fill in the well tank? If he did, we will never know.

During 1937, Sidney Glanville and Mark Kerr-Pearse, both taking duty turns as members of Price's team of watchers, did some exploratory digging in the cellar, at a point roughly beneath that of the cold spot on the first floor landing, but without finding anything of interest. Did they fill in the tank at that time? There seems to be no valid reason why they should. One is left with only one answer that makes any sense: that either Foyster, Henning or Gregson, or perhaps somebody from the Church authorities, had the tank filled in and didn't bother to record the fact. The

mystery of the well tank is one of the enigmas of Borley Rectory that seems destined to remain thus. Now, however, we return to the excavations.

Having come to a halt in the small well, the group now turned its attention to the cellar passageway and it was here, at a depth of about three feet, that they found the remains that were later to lead to much argument, after Price's death in 1948. First, from out of the blue clay, came part of a jawbone. Price, at that point, didn't really know from what creature it came, but Dr. E. H. Bailey, who was assisting, identified it on sight as human. Almost immediately, Jackson unearthed part of a skull, and that was clearly human. Price tells us what Dr. Bailey had to say:

'The jaw bone is the left mandible, with five teeth in good condition, and probably belonged to a woman. The other bone is from the left side of a human skull and is the parietal and temporal bone.'

Upon his return to London, Price submitted both these fragments to a well-qualified dental surgeon, Dr. Leslie J. Godden for further professional appraisal on the 19th August 1943. The skull was in a very decayed state, due to the type of subsoil at Borley and the same was also true of the jawbone.

Initial examination of the jawbone by Dr. Godden indicated that it had probably belonged to a young woman of about thirty, which makes one wonder about the validity of suggestions that it belonged to the nun 'Marie Lairre' who, according to the planchette experiments, was nineteen at the time of her supposed death. Without being dismissive of Harry Price's abilities and knowledge, it does seem to me that there are aspects of the fragments the significance of which he may well have missed. For instance, a rather disturbing thought is that according to the death certificate, Kate Boreham of Sudbury, who died at Easter of the year named by the planchette communicator 'Katie', was thirty one years of age. After all the theories about Katie, and the allegations by T. H. Hall that the whole business about Katie was nonsense, was it her skull that Price had unearthed at Borley? Was there after all some accident or misfortune concerning one of Borley Rectory's servants, and if so, if it *was* Kate Boreham, why was the body buried in the foundations of the Rectory? If such was the case, then something else becomes possible, namely that the details upon that death certificate now in St. Catherine House, Kingsway, are false! The very idea seems terrible, and yet if one looks into the social background of many wealthy families in Victorian times, then one sees why and how such a thing *could* conceivably happen.

Price made the point that lime-clay subsoil, like that at Borley, would tend to cause a more rapid decaying of bone than some other soils. Taking that into account, is it not possible that the bones could be less than a hundred years old? One must remember that the carbon dating technique was not then available, and to the chagrin of many interested persons today, it is a fact that requests to the Parish to have the bones exhumed from Liston churchyard, would almost certainly result in a refusal. The writer himself, early on his researches, learned from a local resident that various folk had asked if they could dig up the bones for fresh examination, only to be told no! Not that one should blame the church authorities for refusing requests for exhumation because it would not be fair to expect them to put up with people digging up the churchyard, only to find that nothing could be proved from the bones anyway.

But what about their true age? Once again, one thinks of 'Katie'. She supposedly died in 1888. Kate Boreham of Sudbury most certainly died in that year. Could the lime-clay of Borley have caused decay at a rate which gave the appearance of an age, when found, of a hundred years or more to bone fragments that were then only fifty seven years old?

The writer approached the Home Office Forensic Science Service for some guidance, and they suggested approaching Professor Bernard Knight, an expert in pathology of the University of Wales, attached to Cardiff Royal Infirmary. Advised

of the circumstances surrounding the discovery of the skull fragments, Professor Knight gave some valuable insight into the difficulties attached to trying to date bones. His remarks show, above all, that Harry Price was working blind in his opinions about the bones and the ageing thereof. Professor Knight expressed the view that Harry Price was too optimistic in terms of his accuracy in dating the bone fragments, and commented that the longer he had worked on this subject, the more he had come to realise that it is, in fact, next to impossible to get an accurate estimate of the time of death.

Another point made was that though much has been made of the effect of various kinds of soil on the decaying of bones, in practice this is an insignificant factor when it comes to trying to date bone fragments, and cannot be relied upon at all. Only very acidic peaty soil has an effect more pronounced than other kinds of soil, and as the Professor demonstrated by example in his letter, even a single bone can show great variation, depending on just how it has lain in the ground. Even radio-carbon dating is fallible, and under certain chemical conditions can give a bogus result.

Taking the Professor's views into account, it does not seem possible to prove with any certainty, that the Borley skull fragments could be older than they appeared. Therefore, although readers will realise from the 1943 dental surgeon's report, that there are some aspects of the bone fragments which suggest some basis for the nun stories, Price's interpretations were much too optimistic in scientific terms. The most likely reason for this, would not be that Price was inventing evidence, but more likely he was presenting his ideas on the strength of knowledge of the subject based on what amounted to some widely accepted but technically misleading scientific information.

Further to the bone fragment queries I submitted to Professor Knight, a photocopy of the dental report, with photostats of the illustrations from *The End of Borley Rectory* were also sent to him, and he in turn passed them to Dr. David Whittaker, of Cardiff University, a dental expert. The relatively poor reproduction of the photocopy limited his field of opinion about the jawbone and Doctor Godden's views on it, but he made the following points.

He was not prepared to guess the sex of the person to whom the jaw had belonged.

The root ends or pieces of the lower wisdom tooth, No. 8 in the 1943 report, looked to have completed their growth and Dr. Whittaker was of the view that this suggested an age of at least 24 years and that an age of 19, the would-be age of the murdered nun, was most unlikely. He further thought that the wear on the 1st and 2nd molar teeth indicated an age nearer thirty rather than about twenty. He also asked whether there was any information as to how the bone had come to be cut or broken through the canine area, which seemingly had not been noticed by Price and rather surprised me.

For the benefit of readers, the complete report is reproduced here. It makes rather interesting reading, not least in respect of the allegedly miserable expression upon the face of the nun when seen by witnesses.

'REPORT ON EXTERNAL APPEARANCE OF JAW

General. The fragment consists of all the left side of the lower jaw from and including the distal wall of the left canine socket. All the appropriate teeth are present, viz., first and second premolars, first, second and third molars. The professional method of writing these is 4̄5̄6̄7̄8̄. As a specimen, the condition is good, but the outer plate of the first premolar has been lost POST MORTEM.

Dental. The teeth are well formed and free from decay. A fair amount of tartar is present. 7̄8̄ are slightly out of alignment owing to lack of room for 8̄. There is a well marked attrition which increases from 4̄ to 6̄, where it has destroyed the biting surface of the enamel cap, and then decreases in 7̄ and still more in 8̄. It should be remembered that 6̄ is the oldest tooth of the five and erupted at six years or earlier. There is some absorption of bone, particularly around 6̄, but not enough to indi-

cate gross paradental disease.

Deductions. From the slenderness of the ascending ramus, and the moderate degree of development of the muscle attachments, I believe the jaw to be that of a woman. From the condition of the teeth and bone, I put the age at death at round about thirty years, with more probability of its being under than over. The diet contained a good amount of roughage and probably some finely divided grit. I cannot assess with any accuracy the age of the specimen.

REPORT ON X-RAY APPEARANCE OF JAW

Teeth. The large pulp chambers suggest the lower end of the probable range of age mentioned in the previous report. Notice the loss of the biting surface of the enamel cap in 6̄, and the calcific deposits in the pulp chamber. (The presence of these pulp stones, so well defined in a patient so relatively young is a point to be noted. Their presence is consistent with the chronic inflammatory condition to which the tooth was exposed – see X-ray photo). The anterior root of 6̄ shows evidence of infection, very likely arising from the fact that the anterior horn of the pulp approaches very closely to the denuded biting surface of the tooth.

Bone. There is a large area below 6̄, and extending deep into the jaw, of infected bone. It doubtless arises by spread of infection of 6̄. It is extensive and indicates an infection of some severity. It is in close association with the canal which carries the main nerve of the area.'

Dr. Godden forwarded two of the X-ray films to Price and the accompanying note reads:

'The condition indicated on both the films I have sent you, and on those I still have, could be responsible for anything from a persistent mild ache to any one or any combination of the following: a raging toothache; a persistent severe neuralgia; pain in and anterior to the ear; pain above the eye or down the side of the nose. Which of these really occurred I can-

115

not say; but the fact that the disease is so deep-seated and is in such close association with the mandibular nerve, does suggest that the owner of the bone had a good deal of pain from it.'

Interestingly enough, as Harry Price intimated in *The End of Borley Rectory,* the details given by Dr. Godden have a good degree of consistency with the nun theory in that nuns in the days of Marie Lairre, e.g. 1667, would have lived on a diet of very rough food containing quantities of stone-ground flour. At the same time, Godden's remarks about the probable age of the person at the time of death, throw the whole matter of whose bones they are, right back in the ball-park. We began by wondering whether, if the bones belonged to someone of about thirty years of age, they were possibly those of the elusive 'Katie', but in the light of the dentist's remarks that the person could have been considerably younger, we are brought back to that most puzzling character, the 'Borley nun'. There remains, of course, the possibility that during the days that we associate with the story of Marie Lairre, the late 17th century, people might have aged more quickly than they do these days, owing to poor diet, lack of cures for common illnesses and bad hygiene conditions. One could therefore suggest that a nun of about twenty years of age or so, especially if exposed to hard living conditions, could look much older. This would surely be all the more likely if the young woman was suffering some illness, and of course any prolonged pain, especially in the mouth or any part of the face, would result in a very careworn look.

Digging recommenced on August 18th, and during the course of that day, two more unusual objects were dug up, leading in later years to more criticism of Harry Price. The artefacts were a pair of medallions, one of poor quality gold and one of copper. Upon the latter was, on one side, the words 'O Mary Conceived Without Sin, Pray For Us Who Have Recourse To Thee', and on the other side was an 'M' in monogram form with a pair of hearts surrounded by stars.

The little gold medallion, very badly damaged by time and corrosion, was intact enough to display very faintly, the figure of the Virgin and beneath it, the word 'Pax'. On the other side were more religious symbols, which included stars as on the copper medallion. Price showed both of these medallions to the Rev. Father M. J. Moriarty, of Westminster Cathedral. The copper medallion proved to be an example of the Miraculous Medal of Catherine Laboure, and briefly, the story of Catherine Laboure is:

She was born 'Zoe Laboure' in 1806, in Fain les Moutiers, France, and after a lengthy sequence of events she became a nun with the Sisters of Charity at Châtillon in April, 1830. During her life as a nun, she saw three visions of the Virgin Mary. Sister Catherine, as she then became, died in December 1876 and in May of 1933, under the auspices of Pope Pius XI, she was beatified. As part of this ceremony, her body was exhumed and showed no sign of decomposition. Two elderly women who had, as little children, been under her care, recognised the body immediately as that of Sister Catherine Laboure.

We should also consider another medallion which came to light in the Rectory during the first year of Price's investigation, 1929. Price reported finding two medals at the Rectory, but that illustrated in *The Haunting of Borley Rectory* was a St. Ignatius Medal, given to children on their confirmation. It appears to have originated in Paris in 1799, five years after the French Revolution finally caught up with all the English convents in France, resulting in their being sacked or expelled. Curious that this medallion should have been struck at such an unfortunate period for the Catholic church in France. Was the mystery of the nun something to do with the French Revolution, and not with 1667?

In his second book on Borley, Harry Price suggested that both the medallions found in the ruins in 1943 could well have been the property of an immigrant Italian workman possibly employed by the company that built the Rectory in 1862-3 and he lost them whilst digging the foundations. Italian workmen were quite commonplace in England during the mid to late 19th century, and of course, one at least if not both of the curious marble fireplaces in the Rectory is thought to have come from Italy, via the Great Exhibition of 1851. One cannot help but wonder whether an Italian worker at the Rectory site was involved in some unfortunate emotional incident or an accident, which left a disturbed atmosphere about the place, thus contributing to the psychic disturbances.

Certainly to a devout Catholic, the loss of either or both religious symbols could have proved to be a shock and greatly upsetting, they were, after all, physical signs of his committed acceptance in the spiritual faith. Similar losses have been accepted as traumatic for some, and as such, form the basis for poltergeist phenomena and events closely aligned to those experienced in the Rectory.

We now turn to the post-war digging on the Rectory site, which revealed another curiosity, the tunnel under the road, popular in local folklore for years. In fact, part of a tunnel had been found during Harry Bull's time by a local man, Mr Farrance, when he broke through brickwork in the grounds of Borley Place, but his impromptu exploration of the tunnel was terminated when his candle guttered in the stale air. Looking back it is lucky that Farrance didn't set off a pocket of methane gas with his candle. One popular tale was that a tunnel once stretched from Borley to Bures, indeed Price tells us that traces of a tunnel or tunnels had been found along a line between the two places, though in civil engineering terms such a long tunnel does seem something of a tall order.

Before giving a summary of the post-war excavations, I would remind readers that some details can be found in *The Ghosts of Borley*.

Selective digging was carried out in the grounds of the Rectory during 1946-7 on behalf of the Rev. Henning, who had hopes of finding lost church plate, but he was not successful. It was James Turner who was one of the first to re-excavate the old well, previously examined in 1943 by Harry Price. With the help of some friends, he cleared out a mountain of junk from the remains of the cellars and opened up both the main wells but failed to find any tunnel or drain leading off therefrom. The deep well was in a dangerous state, but Turner got down inside and confirmed that there was no opening leading from it.

The next Borley investigator was Philip Paul who dug extensively during 1954, '55 and '56. At one stage, he even unleashed a mechanical excavator on the site and during this period, an interesting find was a number of pre-18th century bricks. It was during these excavations that more was found of much older foundations, which lends more weight to the suspected existence of a much older building on the site, older than the Herringham rectory that stood there before the Bull pile was built, and possibly even older than Borley Place. The existence of the Herringham rectory is now well established by the Chelmsford tithe map of 1841, which was unearthed by Mr L. Sewell of Long Melford, who also carried out some excavations at Borley at this time. A story arose about a pair of iron gates alleged to have been discovered in the cellar, and which were said to have opened out onto a blank area, but nothing has ever come to light to confirm or refute this tale.

However, it was in September 1957 that the legendary tunnel was found by accident, providing an answer as to why the lane between the two Rectory gates sounded hollow when heavy vehicles passed over it. It was discovered that the roof of the tunnel was only twelve inches below the road surface at one point. One wonders what might have happened if, during the war, the Army had routed heavy tanks through Borley. Examination showed the tunnel, of very small dimensions internally, to be lined with old fashioned Tudor style bricks of the ancient two inch pattern. At one point the tunnel dipped in a very curious fashon and in all, it stretched from inside the grounds of Borley Place to the area of the old Rectory farm. To this day, the full extent of the tunnel has yet to be discovered for the excavators of 1957 could get only just so far, due to sections of the tunnel having collapsed.

Readers might wonder about any possible connection between the elusive crypt of the church and the tunnel, more particularly in connection with the various stories about the past history of the site. For example: We know now that in the time of Henry VIII, the Waldegraves were responsible for the maintenance of a Rectory at Borley and also that old bricks, possibly Tudor, were found in the cellar remains, in the fabric of the remnants of a building older than Borley Rectory and possibly older than the Herringham rectory (not Borley Place which Herringham also used).

The Waldegraves, and most particularly Sir Edward Waldegrave, were Catholics, and of some influence. King Henry VIII especially, and later Edward VI, and of course, Queen Elizabeth I, all rounded upon the Catholics with a vengeance and it is something of a miracle that Sir Edward lived to be released from his first sojourn in the Tower instead of having his head lopped off, though his second term of imprisonment there at the pleasure, or more correctly the displeasure, of Queen Elizabeth proved to be terminal!

In the various documents from the *Calendars of State Papers Domestic*, relating to Waldegrave's arrest and imprisonment after being betrayed by John Cox, there are dark suggestions of various plots against the Queen. Did the Waldegraves construct the tunnel as a means of escape or concealment perhaps?

It is a curious coincidence that they would have been about the only people in Borley in those days with the resources to construct such a passage. It was in such dangerous times that priestholes and escape routes were common in many a wealthy man's home.

But to conclude this section, there are some other more minor excavations that ought to be mentioned. During 1937, Sidney Glanville and Mark Kerr-Pearse made a small exploratory dig in the cellar of the Rectory, which of course at that date was still intact if rather dilapidated. They dug out a spot beneath the area of the 'cold spot' that was found on the first floor landing, but nothing of any value was found. More curious, however, was the discovery by Glanville that the cats cemetery had been disturbed. It was found that an area of about five feet across had been turned over, and some of the little head boards flung into the undergrowth. Glanville redug the spot and fond bones that were neither of man nor cat, but looked as though they might belong to farm animals. Somebody or something had seen fit to disturb and rake over a private pets cemetery. Who and why has never been satisfactorily explained.

Further digging could have provided a definite answer as to whether there *was* a plague pit on the site, as was believed, and as seems at least possible in connection with the monastery story. Is it, however, too much to hope that one day, some enterprising individual might seek to discover the full extent of the tunnel under the road?

What does survive from the great Rectory? Not very much sad to say. The big Rectory bell was presented to Harry Price by Captain Gregson during the excavations of 1943, and it is now in the care of Peter Underwood, who also has an inkstand made by the late Harry Bull. The huge oak gateposts from the lower drive gate also survive, now 120 years old, cracked and bleached but otherwise more or less intact.

As far as I can ascertain the last substantial item from the Rectory, the huge pump, disappeared for scrap. The medallions found under the cellar passageway in 1943 were buried with the bone remains at Liston in 1945, whilst of the silver cream jug which Harry Price painstakingly cleaned, the writer can find no trace.

At the time of demolition, particular care was taken to rescue the big dining room fireplace with its monks heads, and it was duly laid aside – only to be smashed to pieces, by whom it has never been discovered. It was indeed a sad end to the 'Most Haunted House in England'. Even the writer cannot help but feel a sense of regret that of Henry Bull's massive Victorian rabbit warren, not one brick survives, though, I understand, a roof tile is used by an adult tutor for psychometric tests.

CHAPTER SEVENTEEN

THE MONASTERY CONTROVERSY

At the root of many of the stories and legends about the origins of the ghosts at Borley Rectory, was a popular local belief that the site on which it was constructed, had once been the location of a Benedictine monastery. Since the death of Harry Price, no evidence has been presented to prove, or disprove the existence of a monastic establishment at Borley, or of a nunnery or convent at Bures, both of which form the background to the exciting but rather fallacious story of the 'Novice of Bures'. The general opinion these days is that there was no monastery as such at Borley.

A fairly popular view locally is that the idea of a monastery at Borley, was most likely developed from local gossip to explain the presence of the spectral nun in the Rectory grounds. As the monastery idea was popularly believed in the district for so long, the fiction-from-gossip idea does seem, at least to the writer, somewhat weak and lacking as a final and conclusive explanation of the truth about a monastic background to the story of Borley Rectory.

In my opinion, the one common answer in both cases, is that in order to really convince, any such story or legend has to originate from, or be based upon, at least some grain of truth. In the case of Harry Price, despite frequent attempts to discredit his work, his presentation of the Borley Rectory episode to the public at large was, on the balance of evidence, founded solidly on a goodly quantity of truth, originating from the experiences of many people, at least in my belief.

When one comes to examine more closely the available facts about Borley's monastic associations, one finds that whilst the idea of a 'Borley Monastery' is erroneous, so also is the idea that its existence is, or was, an entirely fictional concoction. The truth of the matter is that beneath a layer of folklore and legend, there lies a less spectacular but no less interesting basis of reality. The end result of what is now known about Borley's past associations with the monasteries, is that historically, the dismissal of 'Borley Monastery' requires some qualification.

Several accounts of the Borley Rectory episode indicate that sometime between 1362 and 1364, King Edward III granted the Manor of Borley to an order of Benedictine monks who held it until the Dissolution, after which it was in the hands of the Waldegrave family for some three hundred years. What those past chroniclers of Borley discovered now appears to have been a classic misinterpretation of one part of a very interesting chain of events concerning Borley's links with the monastic world. Before examining these, we do need to go back in time to discover what seems to have been the first documented involvement of monks in Borley's affairs, in fact back to the year 1248 AD.

At that time, it would appear that part of the district of Borley was under the wing of the order of Benedictine nuns of the monastery at Barking, or to give it its old rendition 'Berkynge' and of which all trace has long since vanished. In 1248, the Abbess of Barking was Maud, a daughter of King John, and who held the post until 1252, when she was succeeded by the Lady Christina de Boseham. During the period in question, a legal dispute arose between the then Rector of Foxearth, and the Barking establishment, concerning tithes due for the estate of Little Borley from one Humphrey, son of Walter.

In the British Museum's Department of Manuscripts, wherein several items that relate to Borley, Bures and the Walde-graves can be found, there has survived a document concerning this episode. In it, judgement was given in the dispute by the masters Gilbertus Perdris and Fulco of Dovoria, acting on behalf of Father Fulconis Bassett, Lord Bishop of London.

As far as the writer has been able to ascertain, Little Borley is believed to have occupied the area now known as Brook Hall, so of course there is not necessarily any involvement in the history of the site of Borley Rectory, though if Barking Mon-astery held title to land at Little Borley, it may well have held land elsewhere in the parish.

The major monastic involvment in the affairs of Borley came in 1301, and has caused much misinterpretation since.

In that year, King Edward I granted to the Prior and Convent of Christ Church, Canterbury, title to the Manor of Borley, in exchange for lands that they had pre-viously held at Westcliffe in Kent. The Prior and Convent were then required to render to the Exchequer the sum of £10 per annum, being the stated difference in value between Westcliffe and Borley. Westcliffe was valued at £30 per annum, Borley at £40, hence the difference to the Exchequer.

As recorded in the Canterbury charter, the payments feel into arrears and as a consequence, in the year 1364, the Prior and Convent made over to King Edward III lands held in the Isle of Sheppey in Kent and thereafter, the Manor of Borley was charged with an annual pension to the Exchequer of £4.5s, and that state of affairs continued until the Dissolution. Ownership of Borley Manor by the Priory is also evident from returns of 1303 and 1346. The Prior at Canterbury in 1303 was Henry of Eastry.

The patronage of the church at Borley as given in the Canterbury charter is in some doubt, stating the Lord of the Manor to be the patron of the Church, while according to *Repertorium* Vol 2, p75, the patronage remained with the King.

However, the Canterbury document tallies with the British Museum copy in this respect. Morants *History of Essex*, Vol II (London 1768) p317, states that the advowson of the church was vested in the Crown until 1364, when King Edward III gave it to the Prior and Convent of Christ Church, at Canterbury. It is from here, it seems, that the inaccurate recording of the alleged monastery of 1362 could very well have arisen, or at least partly.

On March 20th, 1539, the Prior and Convents holding seems to have lapsed, and on 21st May 1541, King Henry VIII granted the estate of Borley to the Dean and Chapter, who being unable to finance its upkeep, reassigned it to the King on 23rd Nov, 1545. Not long afterwards, it was apparently given to Sir Edward Waldegrave of Bures, the ill-fated Sir Edward who was later to perish in the Tower of London.

It would now appear from a general concensus of opinion, that in the general administration of the Borley estate during Canterbury's ownership, the only time monks would have been involved directly with the place would have been during the initial period of ownership, when a report on the state of the place would have been needed by the Priory at Canter-bury. For all main practical purposes, day to day running of the manor would have been in the hands of a land steward or tenant manager.

Now, however, we come to something more interesting than even the time of the Canterbury Priory ownership of Borley. It has been fairly well established that there was not a monastery as such on or close to the site later occupied by Borley Rectory. Why, then, did this *supposed* community persist for so long in local folk-lore and folk history?

One possibility lies in the fact that whilst there was no monastery in Borley itself, there was supposedly a Priory on the opposite side of the River Stour, on land that geographically butted onto Borley's parish boundaries. What is more, acording to a local historian Georgina Dawson this Priory was of a Benedictine order. It was suggested that this Priory had access to land, or 'free warren' in Borley. If this was indeed the case, then one very obvious source of the stories about an old monastery in Borley reveals itself. Further to this, one should add that if this monastery did in fact exist, there arises a number of questions that require answers.

1. Is there any documentary evidence of such an establishment?

2. If it did exist, to exactly which order did it belong?

It would for example, be rather interesting to discover whether the place was of an English or an Alien order. If this last point about an Alien priory establishment was found to be admissible, this would be of obvious interest in connection with the story of Borley Rectory, for Alien orders that once existed here were, almost always, French. An example would be Boxley Abbey in Kent, which was run originally by monks from Clairvaux in France.

It is worth remembering that Harry Price was convinced at the time of writing his second book on Borley, that the nun which so bemused those interested in the story was, if she lived at all, a French girl.

The reader will discover later that there have been many candidates for the identity of the elusive Catholic sister, but for the present, it is the supposed Stour Valley priory that must occupy our attention.

Historical archives do indeed suggest that Georgina Dawson's findings were sound because there were not one but *two* monastic orders no great distance from Borley. On the basis of available evidence, however, neither of them appears to have housed any nuns, though one of these two orders is of considerable interest.

One of these monastic communities was in Sudbury, by the Stour, close to the present day Sudbury Cricket Ground. Part of the remains are built into premises now occupied by a Masonic lodge. It was dedicated to St. Saviour and was founded in about 1248, it is believed by Baldwin of Shipling, and was of the Dominican order. Sudbury Friary, which was its official title, lasted until 1538 and was chiefly known for its theological studies.

More interesting in relation to the Borley story, however, is the now well-proven existence, until 1538, of another rather more obscure order, in fact a very small Priory cell, which had its premises close by the present day main road between Sudbury and Long Melford, near to what is now St. Bartholomew's Lane, so named after the order.

It was, as Mrs Dawson had stated, of the Benedictine order, and was founded by Wulfric, Master of the Mint to King Henry I. The existence of this is apparent from an entry in Dugdale and it also appears in a gazette entitled *English Mediaeval Monasteries – 1066 to 1540*, published in 1979.

St. Bartholomew's Priory was older than that in Sudbury itself, having been founded in 1115. Of this Priory, only the ruins of the church now survive, the Prior's lodging having been destroyed in 1779.

It becomes apparent that here indeed, at last, lies the most probable answer to the persistent stories about a Borley Monastery.

Two main points now need to be examined concerning St. Bartholomew's Priory. Georgina Dawson stated that the priory had 'Free Warren' or access to woodland within Borley's boundaries, and therefore, it would be interesting to learn just what the priory possessed in terms of local land or land rights.

Also, one would naturally be curious to know whether anything in the Priory's history involved Borley, and the site of Borley Rectory in particular.

Readers will recall that mention has already been made of a long standing belief that part of the grounds had once been a plague-pit, wherein had been buried victims of that scourge of the Middle Ages.

The period during which the Priory was in existence did indeed ocver those years in which this country, and especially South East and Eastern England, was ravaged by appalling epidemics of bubonic plague.

By far the worst of these was that of the autumn and winter of 1348-9.

It is thought to have begun in China, or Cathay as it was then known, in 1346, as a result of the failure to bury the victims of a famine. The disease then spread through the caravans of merchants returning overland from the Far East, and eventually, crews of ships returning to England from the Continent, brought the plague to England.

When it struck the results were nothing less than disastrous and it hit monasteries and nunneries just as badly as it hit the towns and villages. None but a few totally enclosed orders were safe from the consequences.

Very wet weather during the late autumn of 1348 helped the disease to spread out of control and in a contemporary account, Cardinal Gasquet tells of the disease 'killin by midday many who had been fit and well in the morning'.

In East Anglia alone, the plague is alleged to have wiped out some 60,000 people in the Norwich area alone. The inference here for the fate of the monks of Sudbury Priory is very obvious and it is virtually inconceivable that either Sudbury itself or Sudbury Priory could have escaped the plague unscathed.

So, how does this relate to Borley and its supposed plague pit?

We will assume that during this epidemic some monks of Sudbury Priory contracted the disease. When one realises that some monasteries used to shelter the poor and the wayfarer in times of bad weather, or at night when it might well be unsafe to travel the open road, it becomes obvious that it would need only one traveller who carried the plague, to set the black death loose among the hapless monks.

Faced with this, and the resultant deaths among them, what might the brothers do? They might simply consign the bodies to their own graveyard, or perhaps even burn them, but even at that early date, they might have been aware enough of the idea of isolation to protect those not affected to have their dead taken out to a more remote spot to be buried.

What better place than upon an isolated and at that time possbily unoccupied spot on a knoll a good mile from the Priory itself across the river.

Although it may not be possible to prove this, the theory does not to the writer, seem at all impossible. In this case the legend may very well fit the history without any journalistic assistance.

There is more concerning the fate of the monks of Sudbury Priory that lends weight to a connection between the Priory, the plague and the plague pit on the site of the Rectory. Georgina Dawson began by stating the existence of a Priory on the opposite side of the River Stour to Borley, no great distance away.

We know now, both from Dugdale and from Roy Midmer's gazetter that in this statement she was indeed correct. She also stated that the Priory had access to land in Borley.

The main difficulty in this lies in our not being able to know just where the boundary lay between the land held by the Prior and Convent of Christchurch, Canterbury, who held title to the manor of Borley at that time, and any possible land owned, held or tenanted by or on behalf of Sudbury Priory.

Therefore, it is of course possible that the site of the Rectory could have belonged to either party, or of course, to neither. Alternatively, as both the Canterbury order and Sudbury Priory were Benedictine, it is just possible that they might have shared some land.

In any case, insofar as the site's use as a plague pit is concerned, the tiny community of Borley itself could well have buried victims of the plague on that site, away from the cottages, some of which almost certainly date back to the 15th and 16th centuries and probably replaced even older structures.

When the epidemic of 1348–49 eventually burned itself out at the end of the latter year, as far as the monasteries were concerned, the deaths of so many monks and nuns, whole communities in some cases, so damaged these communities that, in the opinion of many historians,

The controversial 'flying brick' illustration of April 1944. Note the position of the workman on far left, and levitated brick right of centre. (For detail, see close-up between p114–5), *opposite above.*
The landing outside the Blue Room, *opposite below.*
The coach house as it is today, *page 124, above.*
Edward Bull's Rectory at Pentlow, birthplace of Henry D. E. Bull in 1833, *page 124, below.*

they never really recovered.

In many ways, it is a miracle that a small priory such as that which now concerns us, survived those dreadful days at all, more especially when one learns that there were further outbreaks of plague in 1361 and 1368.

By 1665, and the Great Plague, Sudbury Priory had of course, been suppressed, but one cannot help wonder just how many victims of the Black Death might have been consigned to that knoll above the Stour Valley, and to the graveyard of Borley church?

How short a time it was between the Great Fire of London in 1666 and the alleged death at Borley of Marie Lairre the nun, in 1667, a story that will occupy a later chapter.

What do the available records have to say about this little Priory whose history, to date, seems to have been so scantily told?

In fact, details as to what land holdings this tiny Priory possessed are scant indeed. The Ecclesiastical Taxation of Pope Nicholas IV, AD 1291, states that Sudbury Priory had property in the Deanery of Sudbury. It also held some other possessions, among which were properties in Acton (Suffolk), Chelveton, Clare, Kedington, Melford, Thorpe and Wratting. The holding of Clare is of some interest in the overall story, because Clare lay out in the countryside beyond Borley, and itself in later years had an order of monks since re-established in recent times and functioning today. No mention is made of Borley in this list.

The reader might well, at this point, feel that this lack of mention of Borley in the list of Sudbury Priory's holdings proves that it held no land there. Historically, this may be true, but lack of a listing for Borley among Sudbury's books is not proof one way or the other of course. But the writer asks his readers to remember the statement by Georgina Dawson that the Priory existed and *had free warren in woodland in Borley.* We have seen how the existence of the Priory is proved from known recorded history, and as I intimated earlier, I see no real reason to doubt the comment about the woodland rights either, though it would, of course, be of interest to know the source of Mrs Dawson's evidence. It is a somewhat peculiar coincidence that it should have been Clare to which Fred Cartwright was going to work, when he came upon the ghostly nun outside the Rectory in 1927.

To conclude, therefore, the writer suggests that Sudbury Priory held either title or right of access to some small portion of land in Borley, the suggestion of which may have attracted Mrs Dawson's attention through knowledge of the Clare holding. It remains to be seen as to whether or not the writer's submission results in the coming to light of any fresh information concerning this matter.

Marianne Foyster at Worple Road, Wimbledon, in the thirties. Note the bottle – some things change little, *page 125, above.*

Two of Price's best-known co-investigators, Roger Glanville and Mark Kerr-Pearse. Roger's father was Sidney Glanville, Price's chief associate, *page 125, below.*

Harry Price, Borley Rectory's famous and controversial pioneer investigator, *opposite, above.*

The Rev. Alfred Clifford Henning and his wife stand on the site of the courtyard passage. An early post-war photograph. Note remains of the pump and the stable cottage behind the couple, *opposite, below.*

CHAPTER EIGHTEEN

A LOST GHOST AND SIR EDWARD WALDEGRAVE

It seems perhaps rather strange that the one person so well known to the history of Borley should have been all but passed by in the search for the identities of the ghosts of the Rectory, and yet this individual cries out to be set in his due place as an almost certain character in the Borley Rectory saga.

The reader would need to search hard for any hint that Edward Waldegrave from Bures, one of the earliest Waldegrave Lords of the Manor at Borley, could conceivably be one of Borley Rectory's ghosts. Only in *The End of Borley Rectory* is there a brief mention of the fate of Sir Edward, and a suggestion that the psychometrist Fred Marion was referring to Sir Edward when, from a piece of touchwood found in the Rectory, he drew the sensation of a tall disillusioned man who became an enemy of people in the church. I cannot help but wonder whether the personality that Marion thought he had detected was that of Harry Bull rather than Sir Edward Waldegrave, but for the present it is Sir Edward that must concern us. By all normal and traditional standards, when one examines what history has to say about this devout and powerful Catholic baronet, one is hard put to avoid the idea that he of all people must rate a placing as one of the strange spectral inhabitants of the now vanished Rectory.

There will be those who may be inclined to dismiss such an idea as fanciful nonsense, an understandable attitude in many ways, and yet if no one takes as a basis for argument's sake a belief that ghosts seem to be a visual end product of a sense of injustice or persecution by someone long since dead, then Sir Edward's known history presents the researcher with some very strong ammunition on the side of Edward being the ghost.

Although his exact date of birth does not appear to have been recorded, his age at the time of his death, 44 years, gives at least the year of Edward's arrival upon the scene, and that is 1517. In *The Ghosts of Borley*, he is recorded as having inherited Borley from his father but elsewhere, including the local historical guide to Borley Church, the documentation tells us that he came originally from Bures, where the Waldegrave family seat, Smallbridge Hall still stands.

However, acording to the *Dictionary of National Biography*, (O.U.P.) Edward did in fact inherit lands from his father at Borley. His father was John Waldegrave. What very probably happened was that young Waldegrave inherited land other than Borley manor from John Waldegrave and only later, at the time of the Dissolution did he come to Borley Hall.

Edward Waldegrave was born the second son of John Waldegrave and Lora Rochester and he was also a descendant of Sir Richard Waldegrave of Bures, at one time Speaker of the House of Commons. As one of this line, young Edward would ultimately have inherited Smallbridge rather than the Manor of Borley, and it would seem to be as a result of the Dissolution that Edward Waldegrave came in the end to little remote Borley. In 1546, King Henry VIII enacted the final repossession of the Manor of Borley from the Dean and Chapter of Christchurch, Canterbury, not apparently by force but by consent, since the Dean and Chapter could no longer afford the estate's upkeep. Shortly after that, the Manor of Borley was given to Edward Waldegrave.

Sir Edward, as he later became, was Master of the Great Wardrobe to King Philip and Queen Mary and was also at one time Chancellor of the Duchy of Lancaster. He was also one of the represen tatives for the county of Essex who gathered at the meeting of Parliament on January 20th, 1557. Waldegrave also held the position of a senior member of the household of Princess Mary Tudor, herself a Catholic and who spent some time imprisoned because of her faith, an unwanted experience that ultimately led her to round upon the Protestants and earned her the unenviable title of 'Bloody Mary'.

In 1551, Waldegrave was ordered to enforce the prohibition on the celebra- tion of Catholic Mass in Mary's household, and perhaps not surprisingly even in those dangerous times, Edward Walde- grave refused.

He was promptly sent to the Tower of London a close prisoner under the authority of Henry's successor, Edward VI, but the sickly boy King Edward did not long survive his coronation and for- tunately, for Waldegrave at any rate, Queen Mary succeeded to the throne. After he had become ill whilst still a prisoner, Waldegrave was granted partial release to what amounted to house-arrest at his home at Borley Hall before finally being set at liberty by the new Catholic sovereign. Not only was Waldegrave now free, but he was by the grace of Queen Mary, soon to be a very wealthy man as well. Among properties given to him was what was to become the main base of the Waldegrave family, at Chewton Mendip in Somerset.

When Waldegrave objected to Mary's marriage to Philip of Spain, he was repor- tedly bought off with a pension of 500 Crowns. All this however, was to prove to be something of a lull before the storm. Queen Mary died suddenly on November 17th, 1558, and though the persecution of the Protestants was to end as a result, the subsequent arrival upon the scene of Elizabeth was to signal a time of equal terror for those of the Catholic faith, to which the Waldegraves solidly remained loyal.

With the rise to the throne of Queen Elizabeth I, the enigmatic daughter of Henry VIII and Anne Boleyn, Catholic hopes in the person of her half-sister Mary

Queen of Scots, received a serious blow with the Scottish monarch's confinement in Fotheringay Castle, where she was eventually to end up on the block in 1587.

More trouble now lay in store for Edward Waldegrave. Staunch Catholic as he was, he refused to accept the Oath of Supremacy, making Elizabeth sole head of the English Church, and also rejected the Act of Uniformity. As Sir Thomas More had already found to his cost during Hen- ry's reign, this was to be a fatal mistake.

Whether Elizabeth had decided as a result of his rejection of the Oath to have Waldegrave's head for treason, or whether she was more concerned to have him convicted of the 'crime' of Popery in carry- ing on the forbidden Catholic practices, is not clear, but on or about April 20th, 1561, having held Mass with his wife, his physi- cian Dr. Fryer and others of his household at Borley Hall, he was arrested and again consigned to the Tower of London. This time however, he was not to emerge alive. A letter preserved in the British Museum Department of Manuscripts tells of Walde- grave's arrest and imprisonment, the writer of the letter was Sir William Seyntlow and the recipient Sir Nicholas Throckmorton.

According to most recorded versions of events, Edward Waldegrave died in the Tower on September 1st, 1561. It is as this stage that the possibility of 'Waldegrave the Ghost' comes into play, not so much because of his imprisonment and death, but because of the way in which his downfall came about, and the persecu- tion that lay behind it. When one learns of his ultimate fate after his death, then it becomes clear as to a cause for his ghost to appear near the site later occupied by Borley Rectory, if not actually in the Rec- tory itself.

According to the authors of *Ghosts of Borley*, Waldegrave was buried beneath the Tower Chapel but other accounts tell us that though this is what happened to begin with, he was subsequently exhu- med and brought back to Borley, where his family tomb survives in the Church.

Ironic, is it not, that a devout Catholic should end up buried in a Protestant church at a service where the Book of

Common Prayer was used. That alone would be anathema to the Waldegraves, the last straw, a persecution and an insult upon a grand scale.

Among many other aspects of the story of Sir Edward, we need to find out exactly how he died, because this bears considerably on the possible answer as to which of the strange spectral figures seen near the Rectory could reasonably be identified as his ghost. A learned local resident of Borley who helped with a number of historical details, intimated in a letter to the writer that Sir Edward Waldegrave was eventually executed for heresy.

Is there evidence to prove or disprove this suggestion? Some are of the opinion that he had fallen ill, and indeed this was the view of the archivist of the Public Records Office, based upon the fact that during August, 1561, William Paulet, Marquis of Winchester, requested the wardship of Sir Edward's son, if Waldegrave himself died. The opinion of the PRO was that this indicated the natural death of Sir Edward, rather than his execution. The Marquis of Winchester's letter was dated August 8th, 1561, which is just about four and a half months after Waldegrave's arrest, thus supporting the natural death theory. But it is worth while pondering for a moment upon some other aspects of the case that could suggest otherwise.

In those days prison conditions could be very harsh, though it is a fact that several of the more illustrious of the Tower's unwilling occupants were allowed some personal comforts, books, servants, reasonable food and so on. It is also true that the majority of inmates found themselves incarcerated under exactly the opposite conditions, and many died from illness and gross maltreatment. Santitation in those days was appalling and such medical knowledge as existed was often crude and sometimes based on horribly erroneous fallacies. One wonders whether Edward Waldegrave died as a result of illness after a period of just over five months? One might well consider that he might have been ill at the time of his arrest to have perished during his confinement. His medical adviser, Dr. Fryer, was present at Borley Hall when Waldegrave was taken, but there is no direct evidence to date to tell us whether Fryer was there in his capacity as a physician, or whether he was there to take part in the banned liturgy as one of this staunch Catholic family.

There are other questions which arise. In requesting the wardship of Sir Edward's son, did William Paulet perhaps know the likely consequences for his friend if the baronet was found guilty of Papist activities, or did he suspect that an informer had been planted in Waldegrave's household? If he did suspect the latter, he was not far wrong. It would not be unreasonable to suggest that the Queen had made up her mind to get rid of a rich and powerful potential enemy anyway by having him despatched to the next world, a man whom she must have considered to be guilty of treason in refusing to accept the Oath of Supremacy, and guilty of heresy under Protestant law.

If Waldegrave was to be executed, he may have known what was coming and made haste, as far as he was permitted, to settle his affairs for he certainly made a will, recorded in the Public Records Office.

Also we should not ignore the possibility that Sir Edward may have been consigned to the less than tender mercies of the Tower's rackmaster to extract a confession of either treason or heresy or both. One of the greatest difficulties in examining the fate of Sir Edward Waldegrave, is the apparent paucity of day-to-day accounts of what happened to many of the Tower's prisoners. The PRO, for example, informed me that they had no records from the Office of the Lieutenant of the Tower before the beginning of the 1600s.

If Waldegrave was either racked or executed or both, then this, coupled with his eventual burial under Protestant rites could be viewed as having compounded an injustice that could never be atoned for 'spiritually', until and unless his persecutors were themselves brought to book.

Like hundreds of others Sir Edward Waldegrave could be considered a victim of gross religious persecution and injustice, and his premature demise was never avenged. When looked at from a psychic viewpoint by those who retain an open mind about the theory of a conscience or consciousness that survives physical death, there could be said to be a good reason for the ghost of Sir Edward Waldegrave to be seen at Borley. There still remains the problem of discovering the exact cause of his death.

One of many people contacted in trying to get at the answers, was the well known historian, A. L. Rowse, author of many works upon Mediaeval England. He told me that Waldegrave died naturally but did not feel disposed to elaborate upon the subject.

We turn once again to the Rectory and the site upon which it stood. We need at this point to refer to the excavations on the site at the time the tunnel was found. If one looks at the layout of the old foundations found at Borley, and recalls that the Waldegraves were responsible for the upkeep of a Rectory at Borley from the time of Henry VIII onwards, it becomes almost certain that there was a Rectory or chaplain's house there which existed before Borley Place was built, a house which now seems almost certain to have been pulled down to make way for Herringham's Rectory. Oddly enough on the 1841 tithe map, Borley Place is also shown as being a Rectory and it is usually stated locally that at the time Henry Bull arrived, Borley Place was the official Rectory. He certainly used it as such until the new Borley building was completed in 1863.

Like a number of people, I strongly suspect that the tunnel found under the lane outside, connected the old Rectory with the church. Parts of this tunnel were found some years before the main part, by a local man named Farrance, working in the grounds of Borley Place and tunnels such as these were not uncommon in Tudor times, and used as a means of escape and concealment.

Just suppose that Waldegrave himself became suspicious of the planting of a Queen's agent in his household at Borley Hall. As a committed Papist himself, and having been in trouble earlier for his beliefs during King Henry's time, he must have known full well that he ran the risk of being spied upon. *The Calendars of State Papers Domestic,* in those entries that refer to the arrest and arraignment of Waldegrave and Sir Thomas Wharton, hint darkly at various plots against the Queen. It is known that although not really a cruel person by nature, she was prepared to deal harshly with anyone whom she may have believed was trying to aid any moves to remove her from the throne in favour of her Catholic cousin Mary. There can be little doubt that had they been approached for support in such a plot, the Waldegraves would not have been unsympathetic, indeed they would have stood to gain considerably from any new Catholic monarchy as Sir Edward had already benefited by the grace of Queen Mary. Against this background, how tempting it would have been to Elizabeth, or more probably to some of her more unscrupulous ministers, to have Waldegrave watched. As patron of Borley Church, it is not inconceivable that Waldegrave had the discreet connivance of the Rector, who he paid, thus being able to use the Rectory for business of a dangerous nature, where any dubious servant in his own household could be kept away. In spite of such precautions, it is possible that someone could have discovered the tunnel and used it to listen in on Waldegrave.

The problem with this is that if the Rector at that time, the Rev. William Cooper, did conceal the perilous activities of the man who was his paymaster, then he himself ran the risk of being found out. But he continued as Rector until four years after Waldegrave's death, being succeeded in 1565 by the Rev. Stephen Luskyn. There was always the possibility that he himself could have betrayed Waldegrave to protect his own safety in a rather dangerous situation, which would at least have saved him from being denounced as a heretic and for having collaborated with a Papist. In fact, when the betrayal did come, it was from a different quarter entirely.

Ther was, and still is, a persistent popular idea that the Bull family were descended from Anne Boleyn. Tradition has it that in the aftermath of the execution of

Henry's wayward queen and some of her rakish associates, the surviving members of her family changed their name to Bullen to avoid further persecution at the hands of Henry and that in time, the name was further shortened to Bull.

It does not seem impossible that members of the Bullen or Bull family might have tried to regain some of their lost glory by betraying Waldegrave to the Protestant establishment. Anne Boleyn is said to have kept a house at Bulmer, which is no more than two or three miles from Borley and it is known for certain that the Bull family proper held a lot of property in the district for a very long time, Henry Bull's father Edward owning the massive and outlandish Rectory at Pentlow, four miles from Borley.

It would be ironic indeed, assuming that the Boleyn-Bullen-Bull chain was valid, that another descendant, Henry Dawson Bull, should build a new Rectory on the Borley site some three centuries later.

There was always in the writer's mind the possibility that Waldegrave was betrayed and the reader will shortly discover that that is exactly what did happen. It is certainly not unreasonable to take the view that the old Rectory at Borley was the scene of the start of Waldegrave's undoing; events that left an entrenched atmosphere upon the site. If his betrayal had been assisted by members of the Bull family it would, in Spiritualist eyes, have meant that the building of another Bull house on that very site three centuries later, very likely set in motion the disturbances for which the Victorian Borley Rectory was to become famous.

We have to look back now to the time of Edward Waldegrave's arrest. It is here that we find the proof that he was betrayed and from historical records, we now learn who it was who did so.

According to the *Calendars of State Papers Domestic,* Waldegrave's own downfall came in the Spring of 1561. On or about the 17th April of that year, Edmond Grindall, the Bishop of London, informed Sir William Cecil of the Privy Council that the arrest had occurred of a Papist priest, John Cox, alias John Devon and also expressed the view that 'the Privy Council

would surely punish him for his magic and conjuration'.

Under interrogation by Hugh Darrell, who was a Justice of the Peace for the county of Kent, Cox/Devon admitted to the celebration of the forbidden Mass, firstly at the home of Sir Thomas Wharton of Newhall, Essex, and to being received in the house of Sir Edward Waldegrave at Borley, as well as other places, where he saw various 'papish books and superstitious ornaments', this having seemingly taken place about four days previously. One can but wonder who had betrayed John Cox in the first place.

Evidence quite plainly shows that by April 19th or 20th, Waldegrave's freedom was at an end. Certainly by that date, Sir Edward's home at Borley Hall had been searched and the Earl of Oxford had sent letters found there to the Privy Council.

The interrogation of Edward Waldegrave and his wife Frances went on throughout June and July of 1561, details appearing in the *Calendars of State Papers* of the indictment and conviction of Waldegrave at the Commission of Oyer, held at Brentwood, Essex, before the Earl of Oxford on June 3rd, 1561. During July, Waldegrave was answering the various charges brought against him.

A study of Thomas Parker's letter to Sir Edward, in which Forster the fishmonger and the price of Rhenish wine were among the topics, reveals a very likely candidate for Cox/Devon's betrayer, the manservant Goldney, whom Sir Edward was considering taking into his household service.

According to Thomas Parker, who knew much of this man's character, Goldney was a lying, deceitful and cunning individual, and something of a past-master at securing a situation for his own advantage at the expense of others. It is possible that upon the basis of this unsatisfactory estimation of Goldney's character, Sir Edward would have had no more to do with the man and sent him packing, but if Waldegrave *did* in fact employ Goldney, it seems plausible for such a cunning rogue to easily play turncoat upon payment of a few fortuitous crowns by interested parties, and reveal all to some agent of the Queen.

Thomas Parker's letter to Sir Edward was written in November 1560, and in April of the following year, Waldegrave was arrested. If he was, as is at least possible intent upon backing a Catholic reformation against Queen Elizabeth, and he would certainly have benefitted personally from the rise of a new Catholic monarch, then he was never to see a fulfilment of that quest.

As the writer suspects, Goldney seems artful and conniving enough to persuade Sir Edward Waldegrave into giving him a chance in his employ, but this was soon to cost the Baronet his liberty, and eventually if indirectly, his life.

Turning now to the search of the houses of Sir Thomas Wharton and Sir Edward Waldegrave, we find a suggestion that Waldegrave may very well have been involved in a movement against the Protestant establishment, though as to whether this proves that he was directly involved with active treason is open to question.

In his letter to Sir William Cecil of the Privy Council, the Earl of Oxford states:

"Upon search of Sir Edward Waldegrave's house, I found among other things, certain letters whereof I have sent your Lordships one already, and the rest by these bringers, by which letters diverse presumptions of scheming minds and doings towards the state and government are imparted. I have called him before me twice to understand what he would voluntarily confess of his disorders, which in no ways he would until last, and then as little as might be, which I have certified amongst the confessions."

The last portion of the letter leads me to wonder whether, as Sir Edward would not answer as to his actions 'until last', he ended up being physically 'persuaded' to make a confession, bringing to the surface once again the question as to whether he died as a result of his interrogation, or whether it was just due to terminal illness.

Another curious link in this whole affair is revealed in the letter, inso far as it stated that the priest, John Devon, was the parish priest of Pentlow and to have been in possession of items of holy service that belonged to Pentlow church. How ironic, it is that some three hundred years later there should come another Rector of Pentlow, Edward Bull, whose son Henry was to build and occupy a Victorian Borley Rectory upon the site that was perhaps occupied by the Rectory for which Sir Edward Waldegrave had been responsible.

An interesting point about the Earl of Oxford's letter is, that it seems to indicate that whereas Sir Thomas Wharton was guilty of religious offences, such as having taken part in Mass and being in possession of implements of heresy (crucifixes, images of Mary and other such articles) and therefore illegal under Protestant law, Sir Edward Waldegrave was in much more serious trouble, being in possession of apparently treasonable papers.

The matter of heresy, the conduct of forbidden liturgy, with which Sir Edward was charged, is well illustrated in the confession of John Cox/Devon the priest, given before the Justice of the Peace, Hugh Darrell:

"The said within John Devon Clarke (sic) sayeth that on Tuesday next following the Friday within written, he came to Sir Edward Waldegrave, Knight, to his house at Borley in Essex and there made his abode one month in the company of Doctor Rambrege, late Dean of Lichfield, and daily did eat and drink at the only table of the said Sir Edward Waldegrave."

The author has modernised the Elizabethan spelling and some of the archaic grammar of these documents for the benefit of readers, but they are otherwise exactly as originally written. I am indebted to Mrs P. M. Winzar, of Charing in Kent, who translated the appalling handwriting of the original documents into readable English, whilst retaining the old spelling and punctuation.

During Devon's sojourn at Borley he

was also given money by Sir Edward and received from Lady Frances Waldegrave a book of the Sarum liturgy, which was the form formerly used at Salisbury.

An interrogation of another man concerned with this period of anti-Papist persecution, one Thomas Wood, reveals the conviction held by the authorities that there was a Catholic reformation plot brewing against the reign of Elizabeth I, also a fear that the French, in collusion with Scotland, were supporting the Catholic side in plans against the Protestant State.

There is a curiously familiar ring in terms of the Borley story, in that this link between Borley and France, popularly believed in connection with the story of the ghost nun of Borley Rectory, should have surfaced in connection with the time and circumstances of Sir Edward's downfall!

Having had some insight into the course of events that brought about the undoing of Borley's Lord of the Manor, we are still left with the unanswered question as to whether he met his death through illness or whether he was in fact executed?

Sir Edward Waldegrave made his last Will and Testament during August 1561 and this gives the only definite pointer to just how he died. There is little doubt that the five months or so of his captivity in the Tower could have been sufficient for him to become ill enough to have died as a result, though it seems just as likely that he could have been already in poor health to have perished in that time.

To date, I have been unable to find any records of the Tower of London that might state exactly how Sir Edward died. We cannot prove that he was executed, but it is known that during his first imprisonment he became ill and was eventually freed to house arrest before final pardon, so that he could well have become ill again.

As to possible torture, again there is no written evidence as such, but there is just that one line in the Earl of Oxford's letter which gives a faint hint that Waldegrave might have had a confession extracted from him.

It is not possible, in terms of history, to prove that one of the ghost figures seen at Borley Rectory was that of Sir Edward Waldegrave. What the writer does believe though is that there is sufficient historical evidence about the life of this enigmatic baronet and his eventual downfall, to suggest that he represents a very strong candidate for the identity of one of the strange figures seen during the long history of the Rectory disturbances. The case can be summed up as follows:

1. Sir Edward Waldegrave was a committed Catholic, and was in serious trouble with King Henry VIII for refusing to carry out duties that would amount to an acceptance of anti-Catholic persecution.

2. Having once been imprisoned for his beliefs, it is not unreasonable to suggest that when another Protestant monarch came to the throne, the authorities decided that this powerful and influential Catholic should be watched as a potential enemy of the Church and the State.

3. It is now certain, from written records, that Waldegrave continued to follow Catholic rites and that during the spring of 1561, a fellow Papist and, what is worse a priest, betrayed Waldegrave to the authorities. As a result he and Sir Thomas Wharton were arrested and brought before the Earl of Oxford at Brentwood, charged with heresy and, very possibly, with treason.

4. Following his indictment, and almost certainly because of his refusal to accept the Protestant Oath as well as other offences, Waldegrave was sent to the Tower, for the second time in his life. Whilst a prisoner there, he died, aged 44 years.

5. Following his death, he was in effect the victim of a posthumous gross insult in being buried by a Protestant Rector, whose living had been in his gift as Lord of the Manor, in a Protestant grave.

6. There is clear evidence, both from the *Calendars of State Papers Domestic* and from the Calendars of Patent Rolls, that Waldegrave was responsible for the upkeep of a Rectory at Borley, which archaeological evidence tells us very likely stood on the same site as the Bull rectory. It is also not beyond the bounds of possibility that Waldegrave himself made use of the Rectory, possibly because of the existence of someone among the staff of

Borley Hall whom he may have suspected of being a spy.

7. Waldegrave was betrayed, died and was buried in an alien church by a man who himself used the rectory for which Waldegrave was responsible, and thus this site, upon which another rectory was to be built some 300 years after, was to become part of the scene of his downfall, hence the apperance of his ghost in the grounds or the house itself.

8. Ethel Bull was disturbed by a man sitting upon her bed, dressed in very old fashioned costume and wearing a tall hat. Such clothing was very much in vogue during the reign of Queen Elizabeth I, during whose time Waldegrave died. Ethel Bull was also taken by surprise by a tall figure of aman seen in one of the upstairs corridors of Borley Rectory.

Finally, Marion the psychic received from a piece of touchwood, the impression of a tall man who became disillusioned with his life and who was troubled by people in the Church who became enemies to him. Though the impression could perhaps have been connected with Harry Bull, the writer thinks, as did Harry Price, that the contact was that of Sir Edward Waldegrave.

Upon the basis of those details, and the evidence quoted, there seems to be a fair basis for stating that Sir Edward Waldegrave is very likely to have been one of the ghost figures of Borley Rectory, and was possibly seen at least twice by one of the Rev. Bull's daughters. I do feel that we may now have found a lost ghost of Borley Rectory, but for the present, we must leave the story of Sir Edward Waldegrave.

Facsimile of planchette script. Received 14 December 1937. From *The End of Borley Rectory*.

CHAPTER NINETEEN

THE ENIGMAS OF MARIE LAIRRE: A SEARCH FOR THE BORLEY NUN

Of all the spectral figures reported as having been seen at Borley Rectory over the years, the one that has resulted in more theories and puzzles than any of the phantoms, must surely be the nun. The writer has related how the dining room side window was allegedly bricked up because the nun stared full-face at the family at meal-times or, as suggested by Price, she was looking at the curious fireplace with its carvings of monks' heads.

Readers will recall the extraordinary incident in 1900 when some of the Bull sisters came face to face with the nun in their garden. Then there was Fred Cartwright the carpenter, who insisted that he had walked right past her as she stood by one of the Rectory gateways in 1927. She was seen on a number of occasions after that and there are those even who claim to have seen her face clearly enough to venture the opinion she was, or had been, crying.

However one takes the reports about the nun, all seriously interested parties in the historical side of the Borley story, from Harry Price onwards, have voiced the obvious questions; Who was she? Why did she appear at Borley? What became of her, when and how?

It is hardly surprising that the Borley Nun should be the focus of more than one spectacular story and a number of very plausible theories. Although some of these stories and legends are illogical in terms of any historical accuracy, they form a fascinating part of the Borley story and for the interest of the newcomer to the episode, they bear retelling.

The most spectacular and seemingly the most fallacious of all these stories is that which relates to the Novice of Bures, a story that varies in its content from one account to the next, and which was shown to be very doubtful to say the least. Basically, the background to the tale was that during the 13th Century, there was a monastery at Borley and a nunnery at Bures, which lies some six or seven miles from Borley. Both statements as such, are from evidence available, erroneous. However, supposedly a beautiful young novice from Bures became acquainted in intimate fashion, with a lay brother at Borley, which would in reality have incurred the most severe censure on the part of the monastic authorities, and the two eventually took it into their heads to elope. The lay brother supposedly enlisted the assistance of a fellow monk to have a carriage waiting in the woodland at Borley, in which the couple proceeded to effect their escape. They were pursued at once, upon their escape being discovered, and caught. The party were taken back to Borley, where the lay brother and maybe the coachman were beheaded and the hapless novice condemned to be walled up alive somewhere in the monastery grounds. A thrilling tale indeed, and one which has shown itself since to be a yarn in the best tradition of English folklore and as told, it is just that!

To begin with, the doubts about the Bures and Borley monastic establishments have already been stated, although as explained also in the chapter on the monastery controversy, not without some qualification.

Secondly, the carriage of the story is completely out of historical period. Carriages as such did not appear until the 15th Century and at that very early date, they were of the crudest kind and totally useless for the sort of escape or rapid travel of the kind envisaged in the story of the novice of Bures.

Finally, it has long been the common opinion that English nuns at any rate were *not* punished for sins against their vows by being walled up alive, though there is some evidence to suggest that this act of cruelty was inflicted upon nuns in some foreign countries.

A much more plausible line of thought concerns the story of the Catholic sister of Le Havre, variations of which form probably the best known of all the more sensible theories about the Borley nun. Basically, this theory was arrived at as a result of several factors, among which were the efforts of Canon Pythian Adams of Carlisle. He took as a starting point the wall writings at the Rectory, examples of the planchette results obtained by the Glanvilles, and some of his own general knowledge of the various religious houses, and produced a theoretical and fascinating sequence of events that ran as follows.

He considered that the story centred upon a scandal in one of the religious houses of former times, possibly one associated with the Orders of Cambrai. His suggestion was that at a time when members of the Waldegrave family might be in France with members of their Catholic cousins, one of the men came into contact with a young woman in a convent in Le Havre, surreptitiously no doubt, as any open approach would surely have been rebuked by authority. By some means, the girl was induced to leave the convent in the belief that she was soon to become young Waldegrave's wife. She was then supposedly brought to Borley, in secret, and there placed in the care of family servants at the old Borley Manor house that, according to tradition, stood upon what later became the Rectory site, and which now seems fairly well established as having actually existed as a Rectory or chaplain's house.

Supposedly, young Waldegrave then went away on other business, leaving his potential bride alone among strangers in what was to her a foreign land. She waited for his return, standing by the Rectory gate each day watching for his carriage, and growing increasingly sad and distraught. When eventually he did return it was only for the young girl to discover that he had found a more profitable match, and that not only was this unfortunate French girl no longer wanted, but was indeed an obstruction to Waldegrave's plans. As such, Waldegrave then decided that as she might well protest at her betrayal, she must be done away with, whereupon he had her strangled and her corpse thrown down a well in the grounds.

Among many things which led Canon Adams to this extraordinary view of what might have happened, were the results of several sessions by Helen Glanville, her brother Roger and Sidney Glanville with a planchette and table tipping experiments both at Borley Rectory and, on one occasion, at Helen's home in south London. During the course of these sessions, it is reported that contact had been made with the spirit of a young French novice, Marie Lairre. Her story was a very confused one. She claimed to have come from Le Havre, to have been a nun at Bures and to have been killed by 'Waldegrave', and/or by someone called Henry at Borley on May 17th, 1667, when she was 19 years of age. She said she had been buried in the grounds.

Both the above theories, that of Canon Pythian Adams and the planchette revelations of Marie Lairre, seem now to be historically more plausible, especially in respect of the coach and horses, which make no sense at all of the 13th Century tale of the novice of Bures, but does make some sense of Marie Lairre of Le Havre, assuming of course that the carriage and its reputedly headless driver relates to the nun at all. At this stage, I wonder whether the coach and horses is a pointer to something that happened much later. That we have still to try and discover.

The name that emerged during those sessions in 1937 has remained ever since and the Borley nun is always known as Marie Lairre. The name has even been applied, by some sections of the popular press, to the seemingly impossible 13th Century novice of Bures.

In 1947, in a letter of February 17th, a Mr G. S. Taylor told Harry Price that he had received a message from 'beyond' that

Marie Lairre was born on September 27th, 1647 in either Caudibec or Caldibec and that she had entered a nunnery of St Francois de Sales in Le Havre. Unfortunately, the name 'Caldibec' had appeared in the planchette messages, extracts of which appeared both in *The Most Haunted House in England* and in *The End of Borley Rectory*, written by Harry Price. MHH was published in 1940, EBR in 1946, so Mr Taylor would have had ample opportunity to see both books.

If the nun had in fact been received into a convent in Le Havre, then the proper name of the town from which she supposedly came would have been Caudebec, or to give it its full title, Caudebec en Caux, on the Seine between Havre and Rouen in Normandy. Personal enquiries made in Caudebec en Caux revealed the biggest barrier to unearthing any evidence about the case of the Borley nun in France. This obstacle was the result of the Nazi occupation, for like so many other Normandy towns including Le Havre and Caen, Caudebec en Caux was all but flattened during the fighting, with the result that the town's archives, housed in the Town Hall, were virtually a total loss. All that survives about the details of Caudebec's past is now in the care of the regional archives of Seine Maritime, at Cours Clemenceau in Rouen. The results of subsequent investigation there, were that there was nothing to substantiate Taylor's theory about the nun Marie Lairre having originated from Caudebec in 1647 or at any other time. It also revealed that there was no proof of the existence of a convent of St. Francois de Sales in Le Havre.

I then consulted the municipal archives of Le Havre itself, which showed that St. Francois was a small parish church, and that the name 'Lairre' was common place in Normandy in the 17th Century. Le Havre did have one order of nuns at that time, namely the Sisters of St. Thomas de Villeneuve. As I discovered later, no foreign order had any connection with the houses that we refer to as the Sisters of Mercy in Britain, and as far as can be discovered, the nuns of Le Havre were not of this order either.

A local historian, Mrs Georgina Dawson, claimed sometime before the war, to have found evidence that the Borley nun was from neither Bures nor Le Havre, but was in fact an obscure member of the Waldegrave family, whose life was something of a puzzle because whilst most of the Waldegrave daughters can be accounted for, seemingly one of them vanished without trace. According to Mrs Dawson, Arabella Waldegrave, as a baby was taken to France with her family when they followed the deposed King James II to the continent as loyal Catholics. In due time she was placed in a convent at Pontoise, and allegedly, several years later, she was expelled for some misdemeanour. After that all trace of her was lost, but one suggestion was that she had been enlisted as a spying agent for the Stuarts and by some course of events came to Borley and was killed there. Ther are allegations to suggest that her mother, Henrietta, was also thrown out of the French court supposedly for spying.

Arabella Waldegrave and Marie Lairre were brought together in a rather fascinating theory put forward by Mary Lycett of Surbiton, Surrey, who wrote of her ideas on August 17th, 1952. So, to quote from her letter:

'The Borley Nun

Arabella Waldegrave, the grand-daughter of James II by his natural daughter Henrietta Waldegrave, married to Baron Waldegrave of Chewton, Devon (Here, Mary has made an error, the Waldegrave seat of Chewton Mendip being in Somerset. IB.) In 1668 she is taken by her parents to France, where as loyal subjects, they follow James II. She is placed by her impecunious parents in the convent of Pontoise, to be educated.

Although an English order, French is the main language spoken by the pupils, consequently Arabella is more French than English, which language she speaks and writes as a foreigner.

Against her inclination she is destined by her family to become a nun. Her novitiate commences in a Parisian convent and she takes the name of 'Soeur Marie Lairre' (could it be Lazarre? ML) and ceases to be Arabella Waldegrave.

Somewhere, she has met her handsome cousin Henry Waldegrave, son of Philip, Lord Waldegrave of Borley. They are in love. Marie Lairre is removed to a convent near Le Havre but before her vows are taken, Henry Waldegrave effects her escape and they make for the port to board a ship for England.

By mere chance they meet Marie's mother, Henrietta Waldegrave, now an active spy for the Hanoverian party. She has become embittered by poverty and the fact of James II's neglect to recognise her claim to relationship. Marie implores her mother's help, but this is given only on condition that she will assist her mother's plans. Marie promises, without fully realising what these are, and Henrietta entrusts valuable documents to her to take to London. Marie is sworn to secrecy. The lovers are married and sail for England, arriving at the little port of Langenhoe in Essex.

Henry places Marie in the care of old Amos, his wife and a young servant maid, Janen, at the old disused Rectory of Borley. Eventually, he tells his father of his marriage and a terrible scene follows and Henry is sent away. Marie is kept in strict seclusion, nobody is aware of her existence and Lord Waldegrave prepares to send her back to France.

The poor girl pines in solitude. Grief and remorse torment her. She goes to the gate each evening, longing for the coach to bring Henry and effect her release. She has the documents to deliver and this she must do without Henry's knowledge, for he must know nothing of Henrietta Waldegrave's plans.

The faithful Janen helps her, and persuades her sweetheart Enoch, to obtain a coach to take Marie to London. One dark night Enoch drives the coach to the old Rectory and awaits Marie and Janen, but just as they are getting in, Lord Waldegrave, Henry and Amos spring out of the bushes and surround them. Enoch is stabbed to death by Henry in jealous fury, and Marie is imprisoned in a small priest's cell in the old crypt, approached only by a secret passage.

The horrified Waldegraves find the documents and discover the act of treachery by one of their family. Poor Janen is murdered to silence her, and buried hurriedly in the old plague pit. Marie is harshly treated, starved and taunted. Finally even water is denied to her to induce her to confess. Henry, infuriated by her obstinacy, strangles her and her body is carried at the dead of night and thrown into the deepest part of the stream. Later, fearing discovery, the Waldegraves dredge the stream and scatter Marie's bones under the floor of the now completely deserted Rectory, which is closed for over a hundred years.

The Waldegraves have performed, in their eyes, an act of justice on their fair but frail relation, Marie Arabella Lairre or Waldegrave, whom they imagine to have tarnished the family honour and to have betrayed both her religion and her king.'

* * *

I must offer a note of caution. If one studies the Pythian Adams scenario and then Georgina Dawson's apparent revelations concerning Arabella Waldegrave, and takes into account some of the ideas resulting from the planchette experiments, it becomes apparent that Mary Lycett's theory is something of a mix of the two. Canon Pythian Adams' suggested chain of events and the apparent course of the life of Arabella Waldegrave were both detailed in *The End of Borley Rectory,* by Harry Price, published in 1946. It is rather a pity that Mary Lycett's theory came to light after and not before Price's publication, for had the latter been the case, it might have carried more clout as a possible train of events.

A number of questions arise from her ideas though.

Firstly, assuming that any of the theories about the mystery of the nun have basis in reality, was she a novice or a professed nun?

If she was a nun, was a request to be released from her vows submitted to the Cardinals in Rome for their consideration?

If that was not done, did she of her own volition leave the convent willingly, or was she abducted?

There seems to be one possible answer, however. Towards the end of the 17th century, there arose among religious orders on the continent, a dispute over the matter of confessors. According to the archives of Darlington Carmel, this resulted in a great upheaval among the exiled English nuns in France and the Low Countries. The opinion expressed to me was that some associated incident *could* be connected with the Borley nun. The upshot of this dispute was that Rome imposed secular clergy, which was not without its darker moments.

Herein lies the possibility that the character of the Borley nun is a ghost of conscience, due to some possible involvement in this upheaval in her lifetime, and not the ghost of a victim of murder or some other unfortunate event. In this connection, one's attention is turned perhaps to the two daughters of Sir Nicholas Waldegrave of Borley, and of them there will be more to tell.

During a search through Sir William Dugdale's *Monasticon Anglicinum* (London 1817), a check was made of the few foreign houses listed, including French establishments. Included among these was a short entry concerning a small monastery at Lyre in Normandy. The writer was struck with the similarity of the name Lyre, as compared with Lairre, the name of the supposed Borley nun. It seemed doubtful that such an error could occur in the interpretation of the French language in France itself, but in England, where so many words once of Norman French origin have been corrupted, it seemed at least possible that the name Lairre had arisen out of a misinterpretation, either by the planchette users at Borley or even earlier.

Was it possible that the name Lairre, so long accepted as being the name of a person, was in fact a corruption of the name of a place? For example, had the name progressed: Lyre-Lire-Lirre-Lairre? If so, then what of the other names from the planchette? Fadenoch or Father Enoch for example. Should it have been read as Fadeneau or Fadeneux? – a French monk or cardinal perhaps?

Lyre, or to give it its full name, La Nouveau Lyre (the New Lyre) is a tiny, almost unknown town on the River Risle,

lying roughly in an area bounded by the cities and towns of Evreux, Conche and L'Aigle. In fact the small community consists of two scattered parts; the New Lyre and La Viexille Lyre, the latter place being about a mile from Lyre proper and being a scattered village, not unlike Borley. As recorded in Dugdale, Lyre lay within the diocese of Evreux and in 1046, William Fitzosbern, Senechal of Normandy, founded the monastery at Lyre. Its foundation was recorded by the French historian, William of Jumieges and in the *Nuestra Pia* list, 37 Abbots of Lyre are named.

Lyre monastery was still in existence in 1650 and the supposed date of the murder of Marie Lairre at Borley was 1667, seventeen years later. More questions now reared their heads.

Firstly, was it possible that there might be a link between the names of Lyre and Lairre and secondly, did Lyre monastery have any connection with East Anglia, particularly in relation to either Borley or Bures?

Also, did Lyre monastery have an attachment of nuns particularly in the mid to late 1600s?

I made numerous enquiries and found nothing to connect Lyre with Marie Lairre and Lyre monastery was host to no nuns. So the involvement of Lyre, as a possible source of this elusive young nun who seemed to be so often pleading for help from the occupants of Borley Rectory, faded away.

However, the disposal of Lyre did not necessarily mean an end to the possibilities of an interconnected place mix up. In Belgium, there is another town with the same name, though in this case it is spelt Lier. The case for Lier near Brussels seems to be somewhat more interesting. The salient point here is that daughters from among the Waldegrave family became nuns with the Brussels Benedictines. Arabella Fitzjames, said to be the youngest child of King James II by Arabella Churchill, whose family had links with the Waldegraves, started as a novice on April 16th, 1689 and was professed a nun on April 30th, 1690, at the age of sixteen.

Apollonia Waldegrave entered the Brussels order in 1623 at the age of 15, and was professed a nun the following year, but before going any further, let us just take a closer look at Arabella Fitzjames. Mary Lycett's theory talks of Arabella, daughter of Henrietta Waldegrave, being taken to France by her parents with the unseated James II, and placed there in a convent to be educated. She would have been just a child then. If Arabella Fitzjames was sixteen in 1690, born in 1674, and she is the Arabella described by Georgina Dawson and Mary Lycett, then at the time of the Waldegraves' supposed flight to France with the King, she would have been fourteen years of age. That would have been in 1688. One wonders whether Arabella of Pontoise, instead of being thrown out of that convent for some misdemeanour, was sent on to Brussels to continue her vocation. If so, and assuming that someone had an eye on her as a prospective wife, is it not likely that her parents might well send her elsewhere to try to forestall her suitor's plans? It would not have been beyond the resources of so powerful a family to make certain that if her lover attempted to follow, he might be detained en-route on some pretext. For the moment, however, we move on to another Waldegrave nun.

Joanna Waldegrave entered the Brussels Benedictines in 1663, at the age of fifteen and was professed a nun in 1666. It is here that Joanna Waldegrave was set to become of special interest in connection with Borley Rectory. That date of 1666 is of remarkable interest. The planchette contacts of Borley allege that Marie Lairre was murdered there on May 16th or 17th, 1667. Was Joanna our ghost nun? If so, how came she from Belgium, or more correctly the Spanish Netherlands, to Le Havre – if she did?

Another curious thing revealed itself here. The planchette and the table tipping experiments produced, among other things, the names of Janen, and Jeane Waldegrave. However, was it perhaps the name Joanna that was meant to be conveyed to the sitters at those sessions? On top of all this, the Borley nun, or Marie Lairre as the case may be, is supposed to have been 19 years old at the time of her murder, if murder it was. In 1667, Joanna

Waldegrave would have been 19 years of age!

There was something else about the Glanville seances that lead the writer to wonder about Joanna Waldegrave, and would refer to one of the planchette messages reproduced from *The End of Borley Rectory*. On page 226 of that book, Price illustrated one of the planchette answers from a session, the details of which he received on December 14th, 1937. The scrawled writing has been accepted as the word or name 'Lairre', but is it? Is the 'L' in fact a badly interpreted 'J'? If one takes 'J' as being the letter, then the rest of the word cannot be Lairre, and what has been taken to be part of the letter 'L' immediately adjoining the first letter, in fact looks more like an 'O' and the rest can most certainly be transcribed as :'ANNE'.

If the entity was trying to write 'Joanna', then the result could well end up as Joanne, Jeanne or Janen, but against this suggestion, we have to put a very pertinent question. If the nun could be Joanna Waldegrave, what has Marie to do with it? Could this in fact be a mixing of communication from the 'entity' in which variously her baptismal name was being interconnected with her religious name, e.g. Joanne Waldegrave/Sister Marie, and therefore Joanna Waldegrave cum Sister Marie du Lier, rather than Marie Lairre. However, where was the mother house of the Brussels Benedictines? What was Joanna Waldegrave's newly acquired religious name, presumably bestowed upon her according to monastic tradition upon her elevation to the status of a professed nun?

Further possible clues to a link between Marie Lairre and Lier in Belgium lay in entries in the French monastic directory of Dom L. H. Cottineau.

Lier, in what in 1667 would have been the Spanish Netherlands, now known to the modern world as Belgium, was possessed of three religious houses as is detailed by Dom Cottineau. In his scenario, Canon Pythian Adams was of the opnion that whatever monastery or convent the Borley nun came from, it was very possibly tied up with the mother house of one of the orders of Cambrai. Whatever one thinks of the Canon's theory as it stands, his observations about the orders of Cambrai become more attractive than might previously have been thought. One of the religious communities of Lier was under the authority of Cambrai and thus is presents some more interesting possibilities.

At this stage there have accumulated some important milestones on the trail to the identity of the Borley nun.

If the planchette details were a pointer to the truth, the Borley nun was supposedly named Marie Lairre.

Traditionally, there has been reason to suspect that she might either be a member of the Waldegrave family or be connected with it in some way. There were and had long been, various suggestions that this girl was brought to Borley from the continent, possibly from France.

Upon examining one particular planchette message originally taken to read 'Lairre', it now seems possible that the word was meant to be 'Joanne' or 'Joanna'.

Other planchette replies produced 'Janen' and 'Jeanne', also at one stage 'Jeanette'. There now arises the possibility that instead of 'Lairre', the word could be 'Lier', a place, not a person. Lier not far from Brussels, possessed a monastic order related to Cambrai, which attracted the attention of Canon Pythian Adams.

A Waldegrave daughter, Joanna, became a nun with the Brussels Benedictines. The supposed date of the death of the Borley nun was May 17th, 1667, at the age of nineteen, and in 1667, Joanna Waldegrave would have been nineteen years of age. This offers the possibility that for the identity of the Borley nun, we have Joanna Waldegrave, latterly Sister Marie of Lier, altered possibly as a result of the difficulties of planchette communication, to Marie Lairre, by which name the ghost has been known ever since.

However, was it to Lier that Joanna came as a novice? If so did she ever leave? If so, why? What could have happened to her after Lier and was she brought first to France and then to England?

Contact with the Rijksarchief d'Etat of Brussels revealed further clues. To begin with, there was indeed a family link between the Brussels Benedictines and the Waldegraves who were closely involved with a number of religious houses on the Continent. In a standard Belgian volume of reference, *Monasticon Belge* (Liege, 1890), there is a section by L. Van Meerbeeck concerning the English nuns of Brussels, in which one finds that Theodosia Waldegrave, who died in 1719, was at one time Abbess of Brussels. Curiously enough, she became a nun with the Brussels Order in 1663, the same year in which Joanna Waldegrave is supposed to have joined the house. The date of her death is of course later than the supposed time of Joanna Waldegrave, who would have been nineteen years old in 1667, the date the Borley nun is said to have met her death. However, if one Waldegrave was involved with Brussels, there is no reason to suppose that the other girls from the family did not follow the same path. Even if the suggestion about Arabella Fitzjames, Apollonia Waldegrave and Joanna Waldegrave proved to be incorrect, we still have evidence that other Waldegrave girls were involved with the Brussels house. According to a volume in the archives of the Carmelite Nuns of Darlington, whose sisters during the period in question maintained a house in Lier, Theodosia introduced one other girl from the family into the Brussels Order, her niece Elizabeth, the daughter of another Edward Waldegrave, this time from Staningill in Norfolk.

The reference to Elizabeth is to be found in *Soeurs d'Irlande et de Grande Bretagne* by Louis Fournier. Let us look for a moment at the Brussels Benedictines themselves:

Their foundation could be said to be a result of the suppression of all such orders in England, first under King Henry VIII, and then during the reign of Elizabeth I. In 1597–8, the Brussels Benedictine order of English nuns was set up by Lady Percy, daughter of Thomas, Earl of Northumberland. It was given the approval of Archduke Albert in 1597, and the blessing of Pope Clement XIII two years later. Lady

Captain Gregson at Borley, standing in front of the bricked-up dining-room window, *opposite above.* A close-up of the 'flying brick' incident, April 1944, *opposite below.*

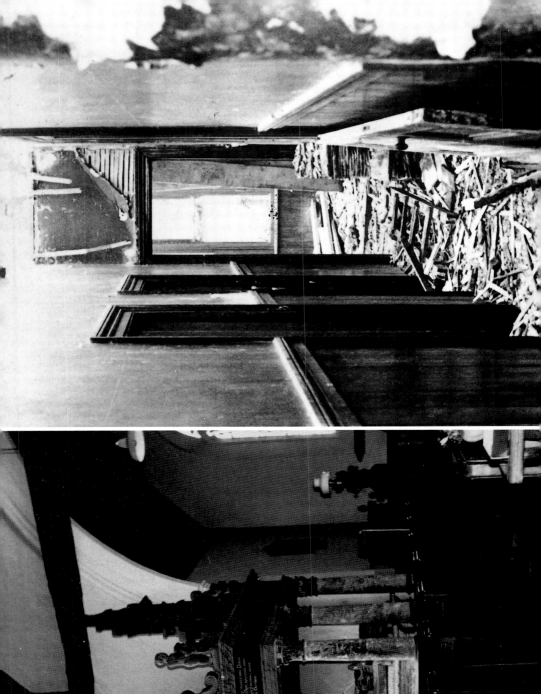

Joanna Mary Berkeley assisted Lady Percy in establishing the order. It is interesting to note that Sister Berkeley bore the two names 'Joanna' and 'Mary', both of which suggest clues to the Borley nun.

In *Archaeologia*, Vol 13, page 261, f9, published in 1815, by the Society of Antiquarians, Abbe Mann tells us that:

'This was the first new convent erected on the continent by religious persons of the English nation. It took place in the year 1598, by the zeal and industry of Lady Mary Berkeley, who was the first Abbess of it, and of Lady Mary Percy, Benedictine nun.

Besides their regular duties as religieus, they were occupied in the education of young ladies. On the approach of the French to Brussels, in June 1794, these religious ladies fled out of the Low Countries.'

In fact, the Brussels sisters reached England via Rotterdam, but the rather interesting point here, is that on escaping the French, these nuns eventually re-established themselves at East Bergholt in Suffolk, a mere 18 miles from Sudbury and, right on Sudbury's doorstep, lay lonely little Borley with the Waldegrave seat and an old Rectory.

When one learns of the nuns' flight, then the French Revolution medallion found at Borley Rectory in 1929 comes into the limelight and suggests that the whole episode of the Borley nun may date from much later than the planchette messages indicate, and once again that like the name Marie Lairre, the date of 1667 is a misinterpretation. If indeed the Borley nun is connected with the French Revolution, then two things become apparent. Harry Price's thoughts and the reporting of the medal would be vindicated, and also some sense could be made of the theories about the black coach and bay horses associated with Borley, because at least by the time of the departure of the nuns from Brussels, carriages more like that reported at Borley would have become more commonplace.

Let us now turn to another interesting point.

In 1623, forty years prior to the date of the supposed entry into the Brussels order of Joanna Waldegrave, the lady Frances Gavin and two other nuns, *all from the Brussels order,* set out to found a new cell in Cambrai, France. This house survived until abolished by the French in 1793. It was for all of its existence allied to the English Congregation of St. Benedict, under Father Rudifind Barlow, president of the congregation. Frances Gavin or Gawen's mother was a Waldegrave, Catherine Waldegrave to be exact, but there does not appear to be anything in the archives to suggest that Catherine Waldegrave was ever a nun.

For the moment, however, let us return to Joanna Waldegrave. In seeking clues to any connection with Lier and the Brussels Benedictines I wrote both to the Belgian national archives in Brussels and to the Flanders archives in Antwerp. From Brother Boniface Hill and from Dame Veronica Buss, of Stratton-on-the-Fosse and Oulton abbeys respectively, I was able to discover that Joanna Waldegrave did indeed exist, but here, the theory of Joanna Waldegrave-cum-Marie of Lier comes unstuck because Joanna Waldegrave was none other than Sister Theodosia, already mentioned, and who died, not in 1667, but in 1719. However, it still seems odd tha the planchette writing should look so much like the name 'Joanna' or 'Joanne', and so set the thought about Lier *before* I learned of the existence of Theodosia and that she was Joanna Waldegrave.

Research into the archives of the English nuns of Brussels, has revealed that a large number of Waldegrave girls, from various branches of the family were involved with that particular house, and with other foundations originating from Brussels. For every Waldegrave nun that turns out to have been involved with the Brussels Benedictines, there are as many fresh possibilities as to the identity of the elusive Marie Lairre of Borley Rectory. There were also connections between the Brussels nuns and both Cambrai and Pontoise, both of which figure in the various existing theories about the Borley nun. It also showed that there was a possible source of confusion about Arabella, for it now seems that there were two girls of this name.

Sir Edward Waldegrave's tomb in Borley Church, *opposite above.*
The top-floor extension corridor after the fire, *opposite below.*

King James II and Arabella Churchill had a daughter, Henrietta Fitzjames who in turn married Lord Henry Waldegrave. Henrietta had a sister, whose name was Arabella Fitzjames and she was to be a nun at Pontoise, in which house she bore the name 'Ignatia'. The other Arabella was born to Henry Waldegrave and Henrietta Fitzjames. The Arabella who appears in the Pontoise records was the *daughter* and not the granddaughter of James II. Curiously enough, the archives at Oulton Abbey contained no details of the other Arabella, the King's granddaughter, and it is now apparent that it is this girl of whom all trace has been lost. She also entered the convent of Pontoise, as a child of seven, to be educated, some time between 1693 and 1696, which places her in the period of history suggested by Mary Lycett.

So we have two Arabellas, both of Waldegrave extraction, and both at Pontoise, one as an adult nun and one as a child. The most likely subject for any interest by a young suitor, would of course be the adult, Arabella Fitzjames, or 'Sister Ignatia' as she was called. According to a footnote on Mary Lycett's letter, Arabella Fitzjames became a nun with the English Benedictines on April 16th, 1689, being professed on April 30, 1690. It is now obvious that she was a nun not at Brussels, but at Pontoise in France, and yet, if she had gone on to Brussels, that would have leant some weight to the theory that she was removed from Pontoise when somebody on the outside became too interested in her. The archives, however, tell us that she was clothed at Pontoise, so that deletes her as a candidate as the Borley nun, at least in relation to Brussels.

Attention must now switch to the other Waldegrave girl, Arabella, the daughter of Henrietta. The archives about her are indeed very bare but there is in the records a suggestion that she became a nun with the Paris Benedictines and was professed during the 1700s. Once again, this would be rather in line with Mary Lycett's idea that from Pontoise, she was sent to Paris to be trained as a nun and from where she could also be separated from any possible suitor.

The Paris Benedictine community later settled in Stafford, and so it is to their archives that we must now turn for further clues as to the fate of Arabella Waldegrave. The writer contacted Dame Cecilia Thorpe, OSB, the archivist of St. Mary's Abbey, at Colwich in Staffordshire, and she confirmed only that which Georgina Dawson had suggested many years ago; that after her early teen years all trace of the young Arabella Waldegrave just evaporated, the Colwich community, descendants of the English Paris Benedictines, have no record of such a girl in their chronicles, nor of a girl called Arabella Stuart, her alternative name and neither was there any apparent link with the family of King James II.

So, from the age of, say fifteen, why does Arabella Waldegrave seem to have vanished?

Is it possible that somebody, among the monastic authorities or within the Waldegrave family, decided that for some reason Arabella should 'disappear'? If so, was there a scheme to bury her among the religious communities on the Continent, with no records of her life for prying eyes to find and ask awkward questions about? What better way of removing someone who was a potential obstacle without actually killing them than to make them into a ghost in the metaphorical sense of the word?

If, that *is* what happened to Arabella Waldegrave, then there comes into play a very different way of interpreting the 'ghost nun' of Borley Rectory, fated to appear as a ghost in death, because she was shut away from the world, or literally made into a phantom of the living.

Let us now try to discover where the theory of Joanna of Lier might lead in the light of the foregoing details. I have already mentioned that we have discovered that Joanna Waldegrave did exist but was in fact Sister Theodosia. The chronicles of the Brussels order tell us that Joanna/Theodosia died, not in 1667, but in 1719 and that she was Abbess of the Brussels Benedictines at one time. The same problem arises with the theory of a connection with Lier, because although there was indeed an order of English nuns in Lier, they were not Benedictine, but Carmelite, and the two houses never communicated with each other.

Cottineau, in his monastic directory, describes the Monastere du Chanoines in Lier as being under the diocese of Cambrai, but according to Sister Lucia of the Darlington Carmel, the English nuns of Lier were under the jurisdiction of Antwerp and not Cambrai. So, was the similarity between the names Lairre and Lier or as the French call it, Lierre, purely a coincidence? There is one very tenuous clue in that when the Brussels Benedictine nuns fled Belgium in 1794, they sheltered at an inn outside Antwerp while on their way to Rotterdam and eventually home to England.

Yet another query remains over the Lier monastery listed by Cottineau for, in spite of earnest and persistent enquiries to the archive departments of several communities here and in Europe, nothing has been discovered about the Monastere du Chanoines at Lier.

We now have to consider a fresh possibility. All who have delved into the identity and fate of our elusive 'Sister Marie Lairre' have gone along with the belief that whoever she was, she was the victim of a murder. But was she? The historical records have shown that girls from the Waldegrave family were in many cases nuns on the Continent, both with the Brussels order of Benedictines, the English order at Pontoise in France, and at Cambrai which was itself a filiation from Brussels. There were also Waldegrave nuns at Ghent and another member of the family was a nun with the Poor Clare Sisters at Gravelines. We also know now, that two of these nuns from the Waldegrave family were directly linked with Borley, being the daughters of Sir Nicholas Waldegrave thereof. One of these two, Lady Barbara Waldegrave, or Mary Appolonia as she is often called, died when only in her thirties! The Brussels chronicles list her as 'happily deceased', which may, of course, be quite innocent of any suspicious connotations, but on the other hand, if she died contented, why comment on it in the chronicles? Viewed in another light, the entry 'happily deceased' becomes something of a double edged

remark, by concealing the possibility that in somebody's thoughts she was perhaps 'fortunately deceased'!

In the search for the identity of the nun of Borley Rectory are we dealing, not with the ghost of a murder victim, as has been assumed, but rather with a ghost of conscience? So far, none of the records have given any solid clue as to the disappearance under odd circumstances of a Waldegrave nun, with the notable exception of the young Arabella, and therefore no clear indication of the unnatural death of any Waldegrave nun with the exception of Barbara Appolonia who died strangely young, even for those times. This means that at this stage, we cannot prove that a nun in the shape of a Waldegrave daughter was ever murdered at Borley. But was a Waldegrave daughter 'murdered' in a very different sense of the word, not physically murdered, but spiritually killed? Did Barbara Waldegrave die unfulfilled in her religious life, with some kind of inner burden upon her conscience?

As part of my efforts to resolve the mystery of the nun, I contacted the present day Waldegrave family, to see if they could relate anything about their past history that might have a bearing on the subject, and my enquiries were passed to the Countess Mary Waldegrave.

Unfortunately, the Countess considered the Borley episode to be a fraud, partly on the basis of the 1956 Dingwall, Goldney and Hall allegations, and partly on the basis of her own private investigation of Harry Price's files in the London University.

In spite of her misgivings about the Borley episode, the Countess did relate one very important item relating to the various daughters of the Waldegrave family who became nuns, and for which the writer wishes to express his thanks. The most important point to come out of this correspondence was the apparent fact that the young Arabella Waldegrave, born to Sir Henry Waldegrave and Lady Henrietta and who up until now has been thought to have just vanished without trace, did *not* disappear at all! It was confirmed that Arabella did indeed become a nun in Paris, but more than that, she kept up a correspondence with her mother Henrietta, and also with her brother Lord James Waldegrave when he was Ambassador to the Court in Paris.

What was also apparent from the details kindly provided by the Countess Mary Waldegrave, was that the convental records, as held in this country are probably incomplete because other records are in existence and which are held in Canada.

Of considerable interest is that at least two nuns from the Waldegrave family were in the literal sense of the word 'Borley Nuns', both coming from the Borley arm of the Waldegrave family. Apollonia was one of them, mentioned a little earlier in connection with the Brussels house and born Barbara Waldegrave in 1603, she was the daughter of Sir Nicholas Waldegrave of Borley and his wife Catherine, née Browne, of Wellhall, Essex. She entered the Brussels community in 1622, received the habit on September 12th, 1623 and was professed on November 24th, 1624. The curious thing about Barbara Apollonia was that when she died on April 18th, 1638, she was only thirty six years old. Why did she die so young? The bone fragments found at Borley in 1943 were said to be those of a woman possibly in her thirties.

Barbara Waldegrave had a sister, Jeronima, also from Borley, but she went to the nuns of Ghent rather than to Brussels.

Apart from the many other aspects of this mystery, there are various questions that arise concerning the nun's supposed status and order. One of the queries about the order to which she is traditionally thought to have belonged, can be at least partly answered. The Borley nun, alias Marie Lairre, has many times been described as a Sister of Mercy, but historically the Order of the Sisters of Mercy is neither French nor English in origin. Some time back I had occasion to deal with two members of this order in England, and noting that the sisters were of this order, asked them about their faith and any possible connection with the continent. One of them, Sister Paschal, told me that the Sisters of Mercy had no connection with the continent at all. The

order was founded in Ireland in 1780, by a Sister Macoy, and celebrated its bicentenary in 1980. The main work of the Sisters of Mercy is in education and in ministering to the sick. Its history does not include any involvement in France, where nuns who are engaged in similar duties are sometimes known by the French equivalent of Souers du Compassion.

The Borley nun, be she Marie Lairre or whoever, had nothing therefore to do with the Sisters of Mercy. The order was not even in existence until twenty three years after the date of the supposed death of Marie Lairre.

Another belief that the writer considered should be looked at more closely was that pertaining to the stories about Bures in connection with the nun. It has always been assumed that both the story of the novice of Bures and the details that emerged during table tipping and planchette experiments concerning Marie Lairre had all referred to Bures in Suffolk. This pleasant little place, some six miles south of Borley, actually sits astride the county boundary between Essex and Suffolk, the River Stour passing right through the village. Bures St. Mary with its clerestoried parish church, sits upon the Suffolk side, whilst Bures Hamlet is on the Essex side. About a mile or so out of Bures, hard by the River Stour, stands the massive Smallbridge Hall, seat of the successive Williams and Richards of the Waldegrave clan, who, as at Borley, have a family tomb inside the parish church. But have the chroniclers of Borley documented the wrong Bures?

Examination of a French monastic directory in the Paleography Department at the Middlesex Library, London University, would show that this assumption could well be quite wrong. In the diocese of Rouen in Normandy, there is another Bures, its full name being Bures en Bray. Contained in *Repertoire Topo Bibliographique Des Abbayes et Prieures*, by Dom L. H. Cottinuea O.S.B. (published by Macon), there is an entry for Bures en Bray, recording the existence of the Benedictine Priory of Saint Etienne. Although the existence of this Bures was known about and investigated by a previous researcher, the present writer felt that there would be nothing lost in re-checking this rather interesting possibility.

A footnote in *The End of Borley Rectory* acknowledges the existence of Bures en Bray, referred to therein as Bures Londiniers, but mentions there being no trace of a nunnery in this town. However, from Dom Cottineau's directory, it is now quite plain that Bures en Bray/Bures Londiniers *did* have a monastery. If the monastery incorporated a convent or nunnery within its estate, there might well be a simple reason for a lack of mention of such an establishment.

To conclude this part of the debate however, we come to one final possible solution. This concerns the order of Austin Friars at Clare, some four miles or so beyond Borley, and the site of an order re-established in 1953, after centuries of absence. It is here that we find yet another link between Borley and the monastic world.

One only has to see the name 'Clare' mentioned in connection with Borley and monastic associations, to consider another possible origin of the name of the ghostly nun, because the similarity between 'Lairre' and 'Clare' is close enough for this to be another possibility for a mix up over a place and a person's name. There is also, in the history of Clare Priory, a link with France, and repeatedly France and matters French reappear in connection with stories attached to the site on which Borley Rectory was built in 1863.

Richard de Clare was in France in 1248. He returned during the following year, probably bringing with him, by invitation, members of the Augustininan or Austin order to live under a Royal writ of protection at Clare in Suffolk, of which Richard of Clare was Earl. Over a period of many years, the order established an extensive collection of buildings on the site. For most of its perimeter the estate was bounded by what was then the course of the River Stour. On the third side, the monks created an artificial ditch with flood gates. One is reminded of that curious description from the psychometrist Fred Marion, who at Harry Price's instigation attempted

to obtain some sensation of events from the past from a piece of wood found at Borley Rectory. He spoke of, among other things, a feeling of some sort of collection of buildings, perhaps on an island. Was it Clare Priory that he had picked up from this experiment? The idea could be a possibility relevant to the psychic side of the Borley story at that time, because at that period between the wars, the Clare order was not then in existence at Clare. The Austin friars did not return there until after the Second World War.

Clare Priory in its original form, with various additions, remained a functioning order until November 29th, 1538, having at first been exempt from the compulsory dissolution of all other monastic orders in England under King Henry VIII's edicts, but on that date the monks at Clare Priory were required to surrender the priory to the King's agent, Richard Ingworth. They were not to return to Clare for four hundred years!

But our attention is drawn to one of Clare's now homeles monks, named Stephen Luskin. A year before the final dissolution of Clare Priory, Luskin obtained a dispensation to allow him to continue wearing a monk's habit under the clothes of a priest. The dispensation was granted on the 20th December, 1537, by the then Archbishop of Canterbury, Thomas Cranmer, at a cost of £4.00. Luskin, like many others at that time no doubt, obviously hoped that there would be a reversal of the Dissolution. At that time, it had already become illegal to wear a monk's or nun's habit in public. As the Rev. M. J. Loughran pointed out to me, Luskin could at least claim that the had never stopped wearing his habit, even if unseen under the cloak of a Protestant priest!

The interest in Stephen Luskin arises out of the fact that twenty seven years after the dissolution of Clare Priory, he reappears – as Rector of Borley! In 1565, four years after the death of Sir Edward Waldegrave, Luskin succeeded the Rev. William Cooper as rector, Cooper having been the incumbent at the time of the arrest, for heretical practices, of Sir Edward Waldegrave himself. Some forty years or so after the coming of Luskin to Borley,

149

the wife of Sir Edward's grandson Nicholas bore him a daughter, Barbara Waldegrave, who was to become Sister Appollonia of the Brussels English Benedictine nuns in exile. She was one of the two granddaughters that Sir Edward never lived to see.

One can but wonder what had passed in Stephen Luskin's life in the twenty seven years between his leaving Clare Priory and his appointment to the rectorship of Borley. How came he to Borley? He could just as easily have taken the living of any of the other parishes in the district. During the whole of that time, there had been a Waldegrave at Borley, and these were for long after the Dissolution, Catholic sympathisers who would not have baulked at the task of helping restore a Catholic monarch to the English throne.

Remember, also, that Luskin sought dispensation to continue wearing his monastic robes, and was quite obviously living in the hope of a restoration of the Austin order. What matters of common cause with the Waldegraves could he have been involved with during that time? We can only guess at that! As Rector of Borley, whose living was of course in the gift of the Waldegraves, and as a one time Catholic monk, it seems not impossible that had he been asked to assist in the removal of any members of the Waldegrave family to the safety of France he might well have acceded to such a request. In this respect the reader is reminded of the possible role of the little harbour of Langenhoe in one of the many versions of the nun story.

As to the identity of the Borley nun, it is in my opinion that we are left with two options.

One is that Stephen Luskin, at some time between 1538 and 1565, or even a little later, could have had some close involvement in the affairs of the Waldegrave family, during the course of which it became necessary to send someone from the family to France. Another possible pointer to this, arises from the belief that during the 15th century there was at least one Waldegrave who was a member of the Augustinian order, and that descendants of him may well have followed the same path.

That leaves us with the last choice for the identity of the nun, Barbara Waldegrave. If one is seeking to identify the ghost of a nun seen at Borley, the fact that two daughters of the Waldegrave family, who both became nuns were themselves born there, one must surely be the potential candidate. Of the two sisters, we do know Jeromina died young from consumption and she belonged to the exiled English community of Ghent. That leaves Barbara. She also died young, but all that the chronicles say of her is that she was 'happily deceased'. This leads us to the question that the writer posed earlier. Are we not dealing with a ghost of a nun who died an unnatural death, but rather with the ghost of a nun who failed to find an answer to some deep, internal, possibly spiritual, conflict in her lifetime, and died thus troubled not in her native East Anglia, but in a foreign land?

Is it perhaps the ghost of Barbara Waldegrave that haunted, and perhaps still haunts, that lonely corner of Borley, still waiting after some four hundred years for release from her doubts and misgivings of some long forgotten moment in history?

CHAPTER TWENTY

THE KATIE BOREHAM MYSTERY

I t was in the seance notes compiled by Sidney Glanville in his Locked Book on the Borley hauntings, some of which were incorporated by Harry Price in his two books of 1940 and 1946, that there appeared details which seemed to point to a sad and disturbing episode in the Bull family's life. It was these details that the critics attacked, claiming that they were heavily edited, but Price had a very straightforward reason for editing the results. Relatives of the Bull family were then still alive, and could therefore have been upset by some of the apparent revelations. In consequence, morally at any rate, Harry Price could not really take any other course, and some of the very personal details such as certain names, had to be omitted from the draft, later incorporated into *The Most Haunted House in England* and *The End of Borley Rectory.*

The details of the Bull family's troubles centred upon the results of table tipping experiments and critics have seized upon the whole episode as proof of Price's fabrication of much of the Borley story. According to the results of these experiments, a device which Price himself regarded with some doubt as to its acceptability without other evidence, a fact often ignored by his would-be critics, there had been a maid in the service of the Bull family at Borley Rectory, a girl who, the seance results suggested, was called Katie Boreham. The seance results produced the following sequence of events.

Following an affair, possibly with one of the Bull menfolk, though they were not named as such in the published extracts, the girl became pregnant and in giving birth the resultant child, she died, according to local belief recorded by Glanville, in the arms of Harry Bull in the Rectory kitchen. Surrounding this alleged episode was also a suggestion that not only was the incident hushed up, which of course is what often happened in such cases, but that the unfortunate girl was helped into the next world by a dose of poison administered either by the Rector or his wife.

The date as recorded in the seance results of Katie, was given as Easter 1888 and following the results of the session, the Parish records of Borley were checked, and therein was discovered a record of the death of a Kate Boreham, of Sudbury, on Easter Day, 1888. In the years following Harry Price's death, a number of critics have claimed that no such events ever took place at Borley Rectory. We do know that a similar suggestion that Harry Bull died by poisoning has not been proved, and that he is always recorded as having died from cancer.

If the Katie Boreham allegations prove to have been founded on some element of truth, then it could be said that the image and reputation of the Bull family, held in considerable esteem in Borley even in these days, would suffer a considerable blow in the eyes of many older people. Therefore, it seems only fair to all concerned that the alleged incidents are examined with some care. The whole point of trying to unearth the truth of the Katie episode, lies in its relevance or otherwise to the hauntings at Borley Rectory.

It has been believed by some folk that Harry Bull was involved in the birth of an illegitimate child at Borley, and that the affair was hushed up. To begin with, there is a practical problem with the supposed date of either Katie, or Kate Boreham's death in 1888. If we start with the stories about Harry Bull's involvement in the episode, there is this to consider: Harry Bull was away from Borley Rectory from 1886 to 1889, during which time he was a curate at Westoe in County Durham. In the light of that fact, there are two possibilities. The first is that insofar as any such event was to do with Harry Bull, the whole story is untrue. The alternative is that it might be true, in which case it would surely have had to have arisen out of an affair at a time when Harry could have been home to visit his family at the Rectory during the holidays.

There is another point, no less important. If we suppose, for the moment, that one of the Bull family servants *did* become pregnant, the conception of the child would have been in June or July, 1887. Westoe St. Thomas Baptismal Records, now in Durham Record Office, show that Harry Bull was at Westoe on June 6th, 1887, but could have been home between then and September 9th, 1887.

We also need to know whether the Bull family suffered a loss among its staff at the time alleged, be it a Katie or whoever, and if so, from what cause.

There was indeed a Kate Boreham who died in March 1888. The Kate Boreham who appears in the Death Registers of St. Catherine's House died in Sudbury, not at Borley, from acute cerebritis, and at the same time as the alleged death of Katie Boreham of the Borley Rectory seances. That at least is what the death certificate says. However, given the social position of the Bull family in the community, and the disastrous consequences of any scandal becoming public, can we be sure that what appears on that death certificate is the truth?

Allowing for the reputation of the 'landed gentry', it is not entirely beyond the realms of possibility that the Bull family could have been faced with some serious scandal concerning a member of the family and a maid at the Rectory, an episode that was potentially so damaging to their reputation that they used their position to procure the complicity of a physician in covering up the matter by misrecording the cause of death and the place, or plainly falsifying the death certificate!

One possibility and an associated clue lies in Glanville's Locked Book. While he was at Borley in 1937, Glanville was visited by Harry Bull's brother Walter Bull, who reported the footsteps phenomenon. He also mentioned that of various physicians who visited the Rectory during his father's time, one in particular, Doctor Alexander, said that he would never enter the place again! If that is true, was the good doctor referring to the hauntings and strange happenings in the house or was he referring to some matter concerning the family themselves? Was this doctor called to attend upon the birth of a child or the death of one of the servants? If so, in saying he would never enter the house again, was he inferring that had he been asked he would not serve the Bull family further? The death certificate of Kate Boreham of Sudbury shows not a Doctor Alexander but a certain W. Nigel Mason to have been the attending physician at her death, so it sems that the man mentioned by Walter Bull was not involved in the Katie episode. This does not mean that he was not involved in the medical aspects of another of the Bull household, and we will look later at the events relating to the death of Harry Bull's father, Henry Dawson Bull.

There is another possibility concerning Kate. It is possible that Kate Boreham of Sudbury might have been employed at Borley Rectory and simply have become seriously ill whilst in the Bull's service, and been taken back to her own home in Sudbury, where she died, a perfectly innocent chain of events with no scandalous connotations. If that is what happened, why should she appear in the burial registers of Borley, and not in one of Sudbury's churches? Could the Bull family have provided money for a grave at Borley for Kate because her own family or relatives could not afford to pay for the funeral, or was it that Kate Boreham did in fact become involved in some misfortune within the Bull household, to the extent that they found it expedient to 'manage' the final rites themselves?

It should not be forgotten that there was at least one Katie employed as a maid at the Rectory. She was not, however, one of the Bull's servants but was employed by Lionel and Marianne Foyster, so she belonged to the 1930s and not to 1888. She seems to have been mentioned only once by Price in his account of that period in the Rectory's history, and there is no hint at all that anything untoward happened to her, apart from her being present during the exploding bottle incidents, which resultant mess she was obliged several times to clear up on the evening in question!

In an attempt to make some sense of the Katie Boreham episode, however let me turn my attention to the other end of this business, Priory Walk in Sudbury, where the death certificate says Kate Boreham died in 1888.

The Suffolk County Records Office at Bury St. Edmunds was consulted and the results are somewhat curious. Kate's husband, Walter Boreham, who we know from Borley census records was a farm labourer, would almost certainly *not* have owned the house in Priory Walk, for his wages would not have permitted home ownership.

The odd thing is that in the electoral register for 1888, the *only* person *owning* a house in Priory Walk, Sudbury, was a Jessie Mitchell. According the Suffolk Records Office, there was one person of the name Bull on the electoral register, listed as owning a house in Sudbury, and he was William Henry Bull. Suffolk Records did not state whether or not he was related to the Bulls of Borley or Pentlow, but as the Bull family owned so much property in the Sudbury area, it is not unlikely that W. H. Bull *was* of the same family, especially as his second name is listed as Henry! He is recorded as owning the freehold of a house in Market Hill, Sudbury.

Another odd thing that these enquiries revealed was that at least in 1881, there was no such person as Walter or Kate Boreham residing in Priory Walk, Sudbury. However, the seven years that elapsed up to 1888 were more than enough for that situation to have changed.

If the Katie episode is, or was, indeed a cover up job, how convenient for those involved that the census returns fell due in 1881, when Kate was alive, and next in 1891, when she had been dead for three years.

There remains the query as to why, if Kate died in Sudbury, she was brought back to Borley to be buried, which is not where she was born, especially as a levy would have been charged for each parish through which her body was conveyed. Is that death certificate a pack of lies? If so, those who perpetrated the falsehood must surely have seen the incompleteness of their scheme in recording Kate Boreham's burial at Borley in the parish registers, which if a scandal were being covered up, would surely have been *omitted* from the registers – unless Kate Boreham, in spite of what the register says, was *never buried at Borley at all!* Richard Lee van den Daele, who contributed much information about the late Captain Gregson, visited Borley and mentioned that he could not find Kate's grave in Borley churchyard. In that light, the whole episode becomes, like Alice, curiouser and curiouser!

Was Kate Boreham visiting somebody in Priory Way when she was, perhaps, taken ill? And who was Jessie Mitchell and was she anything to do with either the Bulls or the Borehams?

Let us turn our attention now to Kate Boreham's recorded cause of death, acute cerebritis.

This is listed as inflammation of the brain, and encompasses the condition better known as meningitis.

What can be gleaned from the death of a woman of Kate Boreham's age, 31 years, from this illness, taking into account the living conditions and medical knowledge of the 1880?

The writer again turned to Professor Bernard Knight, who had already given much interesting information on the validity of the bone finds at Borley, and asked for answers to the following questions:

1. What was the nature of cerebritis, how would it be caused in a woman of that age, how would it progress, and what would the end result be?

2. Could cerebritis, or any resemblant disease be connected with childbirth?

3. Could this illness have been induced or brought on by outside factors, such as poisoning?

4. What is sugar of lead, what is or was it used for and what would happen to anyone given it?

The details of Kate's known children's births were given, and also the Professor was informed of the allegation about the finding, in one of the Rectory cupboards, of a half empty bottle of sugar of lead.

The writer was not expecting any great success with this line of enquiry, but the results were better than could have been foreseen, and very suggestive as to the true fate of Kate Boreham!

The basics of Professor Knight's views were as follows:

1. That the cause of death recorded . . . cerebritis . . . is meaningless as such, and was probably speculative.

2. The modern terms for this, denoting inflamation of the brain, would be encephalitis or meningo-encephalitis, an unsual condition, almost always a virus and more common in the tropics than here, though not unknown in England. The prognosis of this illness is made on virological and on some occasions, post mortem evidence, so that unless Kate had a post mortem, the cause of death being described as cerebritis would not be of any validity.

3. At the period of time we are concerned with, the 1880s, most causes of death were speculative, and even post mortems could produce curious results and opinions.

4. As to the true possibilities in this case, either Kate had a febrile illness, attacking the central nervous system, or she could have been suffering fits.

5. The possibilities viz-a-viz childbirth, were also of some validity, because she might have had toxaemia of pregnancy or eclampsia, which can lead to fits, though without her medical history, that in itself has to some extent to be speculative.

6. With regard to the possibilities of poisoning, this could certainly result in signs that could be mistaken for inflammation of the brain, because lead causes an encephalopathy, including fits, tremors or death!

7. The exact nature of sugar of lead was not certain, requiring the consultation of a pharmacist, as it is an old piece of terminology.

The reader will see immediately in these comments the almost unlimited field for concealing a true cause of death in a case where that death was probably *not* natural.

From the professional opinions given, it is of course not possible to *prove* that Kate Boreham met an unnatural end, but one's suspicions are obviously strongly increased by what Professor Knight has outlined.

Sugar of lead turns out to be an old expression for lead acetate, one of the few lead compounds that is soluble, but the most extraordinary point about it in terms of the Katie story is that it was, in former times, sometimes used in diachylon plasters, which could be scraped and swallowed as an abortifacient. One can immediately see the possible course of events that might have surrounded Kate Boreham's last days. It is difficult to ignore the very real possibility that the 'village gossip' stories about a maid's death, and the fathering of illegitimate children by Henry Dawson Bull, have actually been based on fact.

However, another anomaly arises over the matter of Kate's age. The church register gives her age at death as 31, which makes her 19 at the time of her marriage. This tallies with the marriage register, yet her death certificate gives her age at death as 38! It is not impossible for the church register to be incorrect and it is equally possible for the death certificate to be inaccurate. This also shows Walter Boreham being present at his wife's death, and what purports to be his mark, but we know from Suffolk records that there is no evidence that the house in Sudbury where she is said to have died, ever belonged to or was rented by the Borehams. As the cause of death has been shown to be questionable, it seems not all unlikely that the age entry and Walter Boreham's mark could also be spurious or false.

The following circumstances could be one answer to the stories surrounding the role of Katie Boreham in the hauntings.

Consider some of the elements of the story, in particular the coach and horses and the voice that Guy Smith heard pleading 'No Carlos, Don't!'.

Consider also the allegations about the half-empty bottle of sugar of lead, and the long standing local belief that Henry Dawson Bull had relationships with village girls and is said to have fathered three illegitimate children.

It is apparent that the long believed connection between the nun and the horse-drawn carriage is not really tenable. There is some possibility that it could have been connected with events surrounding the Waldegraves in France at the time of the French Revolution, though even that doesn't really answer the query as to the presence of the carriage in the Borley hauntings. But when one recalls the description of the vehicle as resembling an old fashioned cab, then the possibility as to its true place in the saga becomes apparent.

Let us assume that Kate Boreham *was* a maid to the Bull family at Borley Rectory and let us further assume that she did become pregnant during 1887–88 and that the child was not by her husband.

She went into labour whilst going about her duties in the Rectory, and very possibly prematurely, perhaps whilst she was at work in the Rectory kitchen. She was taken up and placed in one of the bedrooms, where the child was born in a very hard premature birth. The infant was either dead at birth or died very shortly after, and Katie herself was now in a very weak state, the birth proving too much. Now the Bulls had a disaster on their hands, Henry's exploits having caught up with him under the worst possible circumstances! What was to be done? If the regular doctor to the family is called, unless he was well in with the family, the game would be up, and the family would suffer a monumental scandal!

The dead child was disposed of, and either because of that or because Katie was now the object of a hastily arranged scheme to get her out of the way before the lid blew off, Katie herself or maybe even Henry's wife protested 'No Carlos, Don't!', obviously to no avail.

The existence of the house in Sudbury was known about. Maybe the William Henry Bull referred to in the Suffolk records was connected with the Borley family and was involved. The Bull's carriage was summoned and a dying Kate placed in it. The coach was now driven away from the Rectory at considerable speed, perhaps after dark, conveying its hapless passenger to the secluded and unimpressive house in Priory Walk. She was taken inside and shortly afterwards died. Now, after a breathing space, a doctor was found to issue a suitable death certificate, perhaps a young doctor who was somewhat inexperienced, and 'cerebritis' was entered as a cause of death. If Katie was given something that was supposed to be a sedative at the Rectory, but which was laced with sugar of lead, then the end would be conveniently hastened, and the stated cause of death in the case of a servant girl would be unlikely to attract any interest from local outsiders.

Now one of two things could happen. The first possibility was that Kate would be quietly buried in an unmarked grave in Sudbury, with nobody else, including Walter Boreham any the wiser; he could even be under the impression that his wife was confined to bed in the Rectory with some illness. In the mean time, a fake entry was made in the parish registers by Henry Bull.

The second and safer option for the Bulls was that Kate was simply reported as having died whilst visiting someone in Sudbury, and her body was then brought back to Borley at the Bull's expense, and buried in an unmarked grave in a seemingly commonplace service conducted by Henry Bull. They had achieved their aim of completely covering up a scandal, or so they thought and for the time being, that was the end of the matter, which was henceforth merely the Bull family's 'misfortune'. That is how it remained, until years later, when a quiet Eurasian cleric was startled by a somewhat disembodied voice pleading "No Carlos, Don't!" . . . and Borley Rectory's grisly secret began to leak like an old mineshaft, the beginnings of Katie Boreham's spirit's struggle to have the truth revealed.

155

The one thing that this suggested course of events does not allow for is the discovery in 1943 of the skull fragments in the ruins of the Rectory. The reader will be aware of the question as to whether or not the bones were those of the nun, or a plague victim, which is mentioned in a chapter about the seances, or whether they were the remains of Kate Boreham.

Kate Boreham could not have been buried in two places at once, so if the skull fragments were those of Kate, then it was *not* she who was buried at the service on Easter Day, 1888. If that is the case, then what *did* happen at that time? The one obvious possibility is that Kate actually died in the Rectory and never left the house again. This means that her death was totally concealed, and that no-one actually died at Priory Walk, or that another unknown person died there and was buried at Borley ostensibly as Kate Boreham. If *that* is what occurred then one is faced with the possibility that Kate was disposed of beneath the Rectory cellar. The one major point that could support this proposition is the view of Dr. David Whittaker, who reassessed the state of teeth in the Borley skull from Dr. Godden's report, and whose views are given in the chapter on the archaeology of Borley Rectory. The relevant point is that the wear on the first and second molar teeth suggested an age close to thirty. Kate Boreham was 31 when she died. One thing that would certainly answer the query as to why one of the wells appeared to have been partly filled and a false bottom put in, would be the alleged disposal of the dead baby, which would mean that what has been village gossip for so long is finally revealed to be only too true! It also means that the remains of the nun have *not* been found, and that the skull fragments buried at Liston are not hers either.

Now, however, in the light of Professor Knight's details, we have a second variation on what could have happened to Kate.

In this version of events, there would have been the same basic background, in that Kate is assumed to have been a maid at the Rectory and during that time was involved in an affair and became pregnant, but in this instance in an attempt to abort the pregnancy, she was either given or took lead acetate in some form. Possibly this occurred too late, and the child was born dead, and Katie herself developed encephalitis from the absorption of the lead. Because of the potentially disastrous consequences for the Bull family, she was hurriedly taken away to the house in Sudbury, where she soon died and was written off as a victim of cerebritis.

There is one final factor in this episode which must be resolved before we can close the book upon Kate Boreham. With the allegation dating back many years that Henry Bull had relationships with village girls, there is also a claim that Henry himself died from what is termed by the current medical world a 'sexually transmitted disease'. In order to discover the truth of this I obtained a copy of Henry Bull's death certificate. At first glance, this death certificate gives no obvious clue to the layman that Henry Dawson Bull might have died as a result of some 'extra-curricular activities', because the stated cause of his death is given as 'Locomota Ataxia', which as its name implies, affects the motor nerve, and causes among other things, failure of leg co-ordination when walking. A medical dictionary describes it as:

'A degenerative disease of the spinal cord; a manifestation of tertiary syphilis allied to general paralysis of the insane.'

and details the symptoms, such as failure of walking co-ordination, lack of reflexes, and so on. It is described as a progressive disease but treatable, or at least controllable by anti-syphilitic treatment. In 1892 however, when Henry Dawson Bull died, it is unlikely that there would have been any treatment for this, but the most important item in terms of the stories about the Rector, is the reference to *tertiary syphilis!*

The dictionary also gives the term 'tabes dorsalis' under the heading *'Locomotor Ataxia'*. When we turn to the heading 'Syphilis' later in the dictionary, we find a cross-link, 'tabes dorsalis'. Being aware of Professor Knight's comments about the accuracy of 19th century cases of death, but assuming that the recorded cause of death was in this case correct, we now appear to have evidence that Henry Dawson Bull *did* indulge in affairs with other women, and paid the price when he was only fifty-nine years old. Also we now have a sound basis for believing that Katie Boreham was one of Henry's 'affairs'.

Whether one could ever make a case that would stand the test of a court action is questionable, but in terms of the causation of the disturbances at Borley Rectory, it seems to me that the case of Henry Bull, Katie Boreham, the dead child and the sugar of lead is only strengthened by what has been discovered from a Professor of Pathology and a modern medical dictionary.

CHAPTER TWENTY-ONE

SOME OTHER POSSIBILITIES

Having made some sense of the Kate Boreham baby episode, I would suggest that in doing so we now also have an answer to the stories about the phantom carriage and the bay horses. When one tries to sort out the link between the carriage and the story of the nun, we keep coming up against the biggest obstacle to any proof between nun and coach, namely that in terms of the story of the nun, the carriage is out of period. In the case of the 13th Century 'Novice of Bures' theory, the idea of the coach is absurd because they didn't exist in those days. In the case of the supposed death of Marie Lairre in 1667, the coach still doesn't really fit in. If the story of the nun was to do with the time of the French Revolution, and the suppression of expatriate English conventual orders on the continent, then the coach becomes just vaguely possible, but when we come to the 19th Century, and the Bull family 'misfortune', the whole idea of a horse-drawn carriage drops readily into place.

Consider one of the descriptions of the coach seen at Borley. It was said, by one witness, to look like 'an old fashioned cab'. The four-wheeled cab belongs firmly to the days of Queen Victoria.

Now let us recall the discarded seance contact, 'Joe Miles', who came to light during the Foyster's tenancy. I earlier suggested the possibility of an Italian migrant worker being involved in the construction of Borley Rectory, who might have been named Joe Miles, for simplicity, when his real name could have been Guiseppi Milo. Remember the Italian fireplace in the dining room.

Now to the 1881 Borley parish census returns, and to the same sheet that carries the information about Maria Rolf. At the bottom of that same document, one finds not a Joe Miles, but Joseph Tyler. In 1881, Joseph Tyler was the Bull family coachman, and in the light of that, a possible sequence of events takes shape regarding the fate of Kate Boreham. It now becomes feasible that Kate Boreham, having become ill as a result of trying to use lead acetate as an abortifacient after being made pregnant by Henry Bull, was placed in the carriage, and Joseph Tyler detailed to drive with all speed to Sudbury and deposit the dying Kate at the house in Priory Walk. This was probably done after dark, when nobody would be about. The Rectory bell might be rung to summon Tyler from the stable cottage, he would be given his orders, and told to keep his own counsel over what he was to do. Possibly, Henry Bull himself rode up on the driver's box to satisfy himself that the plan had succeeded. And there you have the hurtling carriage, and the two men seated on the driver's box, another of Borley Rectory's mysteries that has puzzled the curious for years!

Although the writer thought for some time that Kate Boreham originated from Borley, she was born Catherine Barber in Ballingdon, Sudbury, in 1857, and married to Walter Boreham at Borley Parish Church on February 19th, 1876, aged 19. The wedding was conducted by Henry Dawson Bull, and Catherine signed herself Katherine Barba, no occupation being stated.

Her husband, Walter Boreham, came from Acton, Suffolk, on the other side of the River Stour.

The couple's first child was baptised by the Rev. Bull on June 4th that same year. Mrs M. M. Cook, wife of the present Rector of Foxearth and Borley thought this not necessarily unusual, but she wondered about the 14th Bull child, because the registers only show 13, including Cyril Carwood Bull, who died only a few weeks after he was christened. Mrs Cook was of the opinion that Kate was a maid to the Bull family. Kate also had other children later, and their baptisms are also recorded in Borley's registers. Her burial at Borley on Easter Day, 1888 is also most certainly recorded in Borley's registers, though the writer's doubts about the truth of this have already been noted.

Kate's first child, born so soon after her marriage, may have been by Walter Boreham out of wedlock, but the possibility that it wasn't Walter who was responsible is rather obvious. I would be prepared to lay odds that Kate Boreham *was* employed by the Bulls at Borley Rectory and that her first baby was not her husband's. I would also suggest that she became pregnant again much later, also not by her husband, and that this child was either aborted, died at birth or soon after, and that Kate died as a result of that pregnancy and the possible use of sugar of lead in terminating it.

A Bull child, Cyril Carwood Bull, died on April 9th, 1887, aged only sixteen weeks, but there is no evidence to link Cyril with Kate.

I would now offer the following conclusion:

Kate Boreham, who came from Sud-bury and who married an Acton man, the couple moving to Borley, was at some time between 1881 and 1888 employed at Borley Rectory as a maid to the Bull family.

At some time during 1887, she may have been involved in an affair with Henry Dawson Bull and became pregnant.

Either she took or was given sugar of lead in a vain attempt to induce abortion, and this failed, Kate giving birth to a child that either died at birth or soon after or perhaps being born dead as the result of the lead acetate. Kate herself also died as a result of this episode, and to cover up a possible scandal, she was removed to a house in Sudbury and an inexperienced doctor then gave 'cerebritis' as cause of death.

It is my opinion that the death of Kate Boreham, whilst in the employ of the Bulls, was the root of some of the psychic disturbances at Borley Rectory, and that there was an attempt by Katie's spirit to reveal to the sitters at the seances, during 1937, the truth of what had once happened in the Rectory, but which until now has resisted discovery. Whether this episode can ever be proved beyond any doubt is questionable, but I would submit that the possibilities are strong enough to be seriously considered.

CHAPTER TWENTY-TWO

THE SCREAMING GIRL MYSTERY

We now come to the alleged incident of a young girl seen not long after the building of the Rectory, clinging to the outside sill of an upstairs window and screaming for help, only to lose her grip and fall to her death.

It was explained earlier that for Harry Price, at least, the incident was of dubious feasibility and Price himself showed no further interest in the alleged occurrence, beyond saying that he had found no evidence to validate the story.

However, let me attempt to do so.

Consider the possibility that some kind of incident did, in fact, occur, with unforseen and apparently tragic consequences. Firstly, if a young girl did fall from one of the upstairs windows of the Rectory, who could she have been? It seems, from available records, that the Bull girls can be eliminated, for there is no evidence to suggest that any of them were ever the victim of any such tragedy. That the leaves the following possibilities:

1. A possible visitor to the Rectory killed in an accident.

2. A household servant caught up in similar circumstances.

3. A victim of an assault by a person in the Rectory.

4. A youngster engaged in some stupid prank.

5. A would-be suicide who perhaps panicked and died by default.

One answer may be that it was an incident involving a household maid. The victim was said to have been seen dangling from the window of the Blue Room. If the occurrence did involve a maid, what would she have been doing in the Blue Room in the first place? One simple suggestion was that she had to clean the upstairs rooms of the Rectory, and in the case of the Blue Room, its window, since it was not accessible from outside.

As the writer has already intimated, Harry Price stated quite clearly that he could find no evidence at the time to vindicate the claim, but the alleged incident itself seemed to be of a startling enough nature to me, that its truth or otherwise deserved at least a fresh look.

The writer attempted to locate coroner's records for the Sudbury area, but without success.

I have already suggested the remote possibility of a suicide, but if this is what happened, the obvious question would be who and of course why? Let us just suppose that this incident *did* occur. One could imagine various scenarios. One could suggest that some young woman who had been the subject of another of Henry Bull's affairs might discover his involvement with Kate Boreham, and the possible result, and be driven to suicide, seeing herself as the victim of a betrayal. This produces strange overtones relating to the theory of the supposedly betrayed bride-to-be of Henry Waldegrave, in connection with the many theories of the nun of Borley.

We now could consider another possibility, and this is that such an incident of a woman falling to her death from one of the windows *was* seen, but what the witness saw, was a ghostly re-enactment of a tragedy that occurred in the *old* Rectory that stood there prior to the Herringham house. Remember the figure seen standing at the burned out opening of the Blue Room window not long after the fire, at a spot where no mortal body could be standing because the floor had been burned away?

Was this incident mentioned by Price in passing, a true occurrence, or was it just a local story which would be the most obvious answer to Price being unable to find evidence to vindicate it.

Borley Place. Owned by the Bull family and once used as a rectory, *opposite above.*
The gutted Rectory after the fire of February 1939, *opposite below.*

CHAPTER TWENTY-THREE

THE SEANCES

The subject of seances, as a means of obtaining information from persons who are normally presumed to be dead, remains highly controversial. · Notwithstanding this, the seance has for a very long time been a popular method of obtaining, allegedly posthumous information from other than available sources.

Borley Rectory, during the latter years of its extraordinary existence, was the setting for various seances, and insofar as they relate or appear to relate to some at least of the history of the Rectory and the site upon which it stood, it will no doubt be of interest if some of the results are given here.

Many investigators have warned of the dangers of taking seance material at face value without cross checking it with any available documentary evidence. In my opinion what some of the Borley seance results suggest, is not so much an answer to the mystery as clues to a possible answer to the mystery. These clues are often scattered and sometimes fragmentary, but there is a strange feedback from some of them, as I found during my consultations with several archive establishments, conventual orders, etc.

One of the first seances recorded at Borley Rectory was on the night of June 12th, 1929, under the auspices of Harry Price and in the presence of the Rev. Guy Smith and his wife, both of whom took part. The party assembled in the Blue Room on the first floor.

Some of the questions asked of the planchette were later recorded by Sidney Glanville in the Locked Book, and are reproduced as follows:

Q Is that Harry Bull?
A Yes.

Q Are you happy?

A No.

Q Do you mind Mr and Mrs Smith being here?
A No.

Q Is there money trouble?
A Yes.

Q Were you killed?
A Yes.

That Harry Bull should appear to have responded, post mortem, to such questions is perhaps not altogether unexpected in the light of what we now know about him and his life. The question as to the method of his dying seems to have been a little risky, bordering on 'leading', but on the other hand, there was family talk among the Bull sisters about their brother Harry having been poisoned. Others since have suggested that he might have taken his own life. I have already detailed the upsets that are apparent by reading between the lines of Harry's life, regarding his marriage to Ivy Brackenbury and the departure from the Rectory of his sisters in 1920, as well as the matter of his will.

Another point about this seance is, that according to Mabel Smith, Harry Price surprisingly reported having seen the figure of Harry Bull standing behind Guy Smith during this seance. One possibly relevant point here is that Harry Bull had died in that same room, two years earlier, in June 1927.

Following the answers to the questions, Mr and Mrs Smith found the tone of the proceedings upsetting and asked for it to be stopped. According to Sidney Glanville, the Smiths refused to allow any further seances to be held at the Rectory during the remainder of their time at Borley.

A modern view of Borley hall. On April 20th 1561, Sir Edward Waldegrave was arrested here, charged with heresy, *opposite above*.
Clare Priory, Suffolk: a modern view. After its suppression, one of the former Austin Friars, eventually became a rector of Borley in 1565, *opposite below*.

Probably the most chilling and prophetic seance connected with Borley Rectory was held, not at the Rectory itself, but in the home of Miss Helen Glanville, Sidney's daughter, at Streatham on March 27th, 1938, and revolved around the use of a planchette, or 'psychic aid' that still arouses arguments to this day. It is basically a heart shaped wheeled board, about the size of a beer mat, with a pencil fitted vertically at its apex. When placed upon a sheet of paper or any other flat writing surface, with the sitters' fingers resting lightly upon its surface, it appears to move and write in response to questions put verbally. Many people think that it merely responds to the muscular action on the part of the operators however careful they may be, and others, that it works from the subconscious thoughts of the sitters. On the other hand, there have been occasions upon which the planchette *appears* to have genuinely responded of its own accord.

What is ironic about the session at Streatham, is that it foretold the ultimate fate of the Rectory, but which subsequently came to pass through a normal incident. The planchette produced the information that the Rectory would burn that same night, but it was eleven months to the day, that it burned down. The planchette session, conducted by Helen Glanville and her brother Roger, went as follows:

Q Does anyone want to speak to us?
A Yes.

Q Who are you?
A Sunex Amures and one of the men (indistinct) mean to burn the rectory tonight at 9 o'clock end of haunting go to the rectory and you will be able to see us enter in our own and under the ruins you will find bone of murdered (indistinct) wardens (not clear) under the ruins mean you to have proof of haunting of the rectory at Borley (indistinct) the understanding of which gamenl (large full stop written) game tells the story of murder which happened there.

Q In which room will the fire start?

A Over the hall. Yes yes you must go if you want proof.

Q Why cannot you give us proof here?
A We will.

It is, perhaps, a pity that Helen and Roger did not travel down to Borley that night! For a long time many have believed that the Amures threat was carried out to the letter, but evidence strongly suggests that the Rectory was in fact deliberately set on fire by its then owner, Captain Gregson, to claim 'on the insurance'.

An obvious question would be 'Who *was* Sunex Amures?' One rational suggestion made since, has been that what the planchette may *actually* have written was 'Senex Taurus', which in Latin translates as 'Old man Bull'.

To those with a belief in Spiritualism, it might seem as though either Henry or Harry Bull's life at the Rectory had been so troubled that in death, either one or the other was determined to destroy the scene of events once and for all, and to reveal as a result, the truth of what had occurred. Harry Bull has for long been cited as being at the root of the Rectory's troubles but if the expression from the planchette did mean 'Old man Bull', it might not have referred to Harry at all, but to his father. I would repeat that there are strong indications that the Bull family's life at the Rectory seems to have gone badly wrong viz-a-viz the Katie episode, Harry Bull's will and his disapproved-of marriage to Ivy Brackenbury.

Now to the seances at the Rectory using the tilting-table, for which purpose a very lightweight 12″ square, 2′ 2″ high table was constructed by Sidney Glanville. In this method of operation, the sitters place their hands very lightly on the table surface and, according to an established code, the table tips either one way or the other in response to questions put verbally.

Before going on to detail some of the results of these sessions, there is an important point to be made about the presentation of the details that shortly follow.

The details are drawn from the Harry Price Library's copy of the Locked Book, compiled by the late Sidney Glanville, and the original of which was in the hands of T. H. Hall. In this publication some people's full names were omitted and shown only as initials or by a letter, followed by a blank space, because at the time of its compilation, some of the people referred to were still alive, others not long dead. The apparent results could have been distressing to those living, especially the surviving members of the Bull family.

To carry out some analysis of the seance results, I have inserted the missing full names, in the knowledge that all those originally mentioned are long since dead. Some of the Gregson family and other sitters may still be alive but they are considered as 'operatives' and not 'subjects'.

A table-tipping session was conducted at Borley Rectory on the night of October 23rd, 1937, between 9.55 p.m. and 10.30 p.m. The sitters were Alan Cuthbert, Roger Glanville and Mark Kerr-Pearse, and they established themselves in the kitchen passage on the ground floor, outside the sewing room.

During the sitting, especially when the rocking of the table was most rapid, all present were conscious of an 'ice cold draught' and Roger Glanville felt a sensation of being watched.

The seance ran as follows:

1. Q Is someone there?
   A Yes.

2. Q Who are you, will you spell your name?
   A Tfisme.

3. Q Will you please repeat?
   A Tfismong. (then very indistinct and uncertain).

4. Q Are you a man or a woman?
   A (uncertain).

5. Q Is you name Bull?
   A No.

6. Q Is your name Foyster?
   A No.

7. Q Have you lived here before?
   A Yes.

8. Q What is your age?
   A 91.

9. Q Have you a message for Marianne?
   A No.

10. Q Have you a message for anyone here?
    A No.

11. Q Have you a message?
    A Yes.

12. Q Will you please spell it?
    A If chant mass light erel caedo.

13. Q Is it erel caedo?
    A Yes.

14. Q Is erel an abbreviation?
    A Yes.

15. Q Will you please continue?
    A Blamui.

At this point the sitters stopped, mainly through tiredness, but the sitting was restarted, and continued at the same location:

16. Q Is your message 'If chant mass light erel caedo blamu ipse?'.

17. Q What is 'erel' in full?
    A Erelmno.

18. Q Do you mean 'Erelmno'?
    *See editor's note, page 166.
    A Yes.

19. Q Can you indicate the date you died?
    A an indistinct reply.

20. Q Have you lived in this present house before?
    A Yes.

21. Q Are you Henry Bull?
    A No.

22. Q Harry, Henry Foyster Bull?
    A No.

23. Q Will you spell your name?
    A Car.

24. Q Is it Carlos?
    A Yes.

25. Q Then you are Henry Dawson Bull?
    A Yes.

26. Q Did something unfortunate happen in the kitchen?
    A Yes.

27. Q Did a servant girl die in your presence there?
    A Yes.

28. Q Did she die a natural death?
    A No.

29. Q Was she poisoned?
    A hesitation.

30. Q Was she poisoned?
    A No.

31. Q Was there a baby?
    A Yes.

32. Q Do you mind these questions?
    A No.

33. Q Are you sure you don't mind these questions?
    A Yes.

34. Q Are you angry with us?
    A No.

35. Q Can we help you?
    A Yes.

36. Q Will light, mass etc help you?
    A Yes.

37. Q (asked by Mark Kerr-Pearse) Do you remember me, I've been here before?
    A Yes.

38. Q Do you mind me being in the house alone?
    A No.

39. Q I am staying here this week, is there any danger?
    A No.

40. Q Did you write the messages on the wall?
    A No.

41. Q Can you tell us who did?
    A Yes.

42. Q Who was it, can you spell it out?
    A Oif (then indistinct).

43. Q Is Oif correct?
    A Yes.

44. Q Will you please continue?
    A indecipherable.

45. Q Was it a man?
    A No.

46. Q Was it a child?
    A No.

47. Q Was it a woman?
    A No.

48. Q Is anyone there?
    A no answer.

49. Q Is it Blarnu?
    A Yes.

50. Q Will you please continue?
    A Ip.

51. Q Is it Ipse?
    A Yes.

52. Q Will you please continue?
    A three times through the alphabet very quickly.

53. Q Is that the end of the message?
    A Yes.

54. Q We are feeling very tired, can we continue later?
    A Yes.

*Editor's note: 'caedo' in Latin, can be 'to kill' or 'to beat'; 'blarnu' is untraceable, but 'blandus' means 'flatter, tempt'; 'ipse', of course, is 'self'; 'erel' is untraceable, as is 'erelmno', but would the next letter be 'p'? – as part of the alphabet? The answer could be translatable as 'don't flatter (or kid) yourself', then the rest of the alphabet.

This particular sitting was terminated at that point. Let us now take a look and see what can be gleaned from the results. Fifty four questions were asked, forty eight were answered. The remaining six drew either no response or drew an unintelligible answer.

I would suggest, from a study of the answers, that the sitters at this session were getting feedback from not one, but two entities, and that one of them was the late Henry Dawson Bull. It has to be said that questions numbers 26 to 31 could be criticised as being somewhat leading. However, against that, there is one point that is worthy of consideration.

If the answers recorded as having been received in response to questions about the death of a maid and the matter of a baby were genuine replies, I would suggest that such answers could have come only from Henry Dawson Bull! The reader should not forget about taking seance material at face value without other evidence. Nor should one ignore the possibility of subconscious manipulation through the prior knowledge of details about the Bull family that might have been in the possession of the sitters at the time.

When we come to look at the replies to some of the other questions, some knowledge of general English religious practice will reveal that these could most certainly *not* have come from Henry Bull. Appeals for Mass, chant and similar features, and what is almost certainly broken and fragmentary Latin, e.g. 'caedo blamu ipse', could have very little to do with the Protestant faith, but could relate to matters of a Roman Catholic origin. If we accept the validity of the Catholic origin of the message, then the entity producing those answers could hardly be Henry Dawson Bull. But if not Henry Bull, then who?

There are three possibilities, two of which would be the nun or Miss Brackenbury, Harry Bull's stepdaughter, who was a Catholic, but one candidate is prominent – Sir Edward Waldegrave! Questions and, more particularly, answers numbers 2 and 3, 12 to 15, and 16 to 18 strongly suggest Sir Edward Waldegrave, especially when one remembers the details of his life. That questions 2 and 3, or more precisely the answers thereto, should relate to Sir Edward Waldegrave might at first sight seem ridiculous, the expression 'Tfismong' looking like irrelevant nonsense, but it is not so pointless as it might appear.

I now refer to the standard work of historical reference, *The Calendars of State Papers, Domestic*, 1547 to 1580. In Volume 16, on page 171, folio 13, we find a curious entry which reads as follows:
'Thomas Parker to Sir Edward Waldegrave. Private affairs. Informs him that the wine will cost 10L per tun.

Forster the fishmonger is gone to Lynn mart. Gives an ill character of Goldney a serving man.'

Note the words 'Forster the fishmonger'! Some four hundred years later, three sitters at a seance at Borley Rectory receive the seemingly nonsensical reply 'Tfismong', or to split the message up into its component parts, 'T** fis*mong**', or 'tHE fisHmongER'.

This entry in the *Calendars of State Papers Domestic* dates from 1561, and in April of that year, Sir Edward Waldegrave was arrested upon charges of heresy! Could Forster the fishmonger, have brought about Sir Edward's downfull through careless or even deliberate 'talk' within earshot of or in the presence of Queen Elizabeth's agents? Another ironic coincidence is that the fishmonger's name was Forster, so close to Foyster, long connected with Borley Rectory!

When one puts the 'Tfismong' response together with the Latin appeals and what is known about Sir Edward Waldegrave's own downfall, then it is not unreasonable that of two possible mixed up contacts obtained by the sitters, one was Henry Dawson Bull and the other was Sir Edward himself appealing for redress for his persecution as a Catholic and his ultimate burial in a Protestant grave. At the same time this could lend further weight to the view that the old Rectory almost certainly maintained by the Waldegraves during Elizabeth I's time, stood on the same site as Henry Bull's home, and was very likely frequented by Sir Edward from time to time.

If that is correct, then we can surely suggest that the historical causation of the phenomena is at least three, if not four, hundred years old.

Continuing with this particular seance, there is another aspect of the table-tipping replies which may be of interest. Take another look at questions and answers numbers 40 to 43, which relate to the appearance of the wall-writings that were found in the Rectory between 1930 and 1935. The sitters sought to ascertain who was responsible for the messages on the walls and in answer number 42, the entity replied 'Oif', and confirmed it in answer number 43. May I suggest that what the entity may have been trying to say was 'Foyster', by attempting to spell 'Foister' and managing only the middle piece thus: 'Ois', which was misinterpreted or misproduced as 'Oif'.

In my opinion, we cannot be sure beyond doubt that Marianne Foyster wrote the messages on the walls, as has been claimed. She did, admittedly, quite openly write questions on the walls hoping that whoever was responsible for the wall writings would answer the questions.

On the other hand, Peter Underwood who submitted samples of the writings to a graphologist, tells us that with one exception, the expert opinion was that they all originated with Mrs Foyster. I would repeat the possibility that Marianne was being used as a subconscious 'scribe' by one of the entities in the Rectory, for on their first day in the Rectory, in October 1930, Marianne's name was called by a seemingly remote and disconnected voice somewhere in the building and that pieces of paper with her name on, pleading for help, were seen fluttering about.

It has long been suggested that these appeals for help came from the spirit of the nun, but some of the seance answers could suggest that the call for help could of, course, have come from Kate Boreham.

Now, we move on to the next session at Borley Rectory, which took place between 1.15 a.m. and 1.45 a.m., in the library, on October 24th, 1937. The sitters were again Mark Kerr-Pearse, Roger Glanville and Alan Cuthbert. Apart from the firelight, the sitting was held in darkness.

The numerical sequence of the questions continues from the previous sitting as follows:

55. Q Are you there?
    A in reply, the table tilted at 45 degrees.

56. Q Will you please spell your name.
    A Caldibec.

57. Q Are you a man?
    A Yes.

58. Q Have you lived in this house before?
    A Yes.

59. Q As it is at present?
    A Yes.

60. Q Did you live here before Harry Bull?
    A Yes.

61. Q Did you live here before Henry Dawson Bull?
    A Yes.

62. Q Are you his son?
    A No.

63. Q Are you a relative?
    A No.

64. Q Are you a friend?
    A Yes.

65. Q Are you his wife?
    A Yes.

66. Q Then you are a woman?
    A Yes.

67. Q Is Henry Dawson Bull unhappy?
    A Yes.

68. Q Can we help?
    A Yes.

69. Q By chant, light, Mass and Prayer?
    A Yes.

70. Q Upstairs?
    A No.

71. Q Downstairs?
    A Yes.

72. Q In the kitchen passage?
    A No.

73. Q In the kitchen?
    A Yes.

74. Q Is he unhappy because of what happened in the kitchen?
    A Yes.

75. Q Are you unhappy?
    A Yes.

76. Q Do you also want chant, Mass, light and prayer?
    A Yes.

77. Q Upstairs?

A No.

78. Q In the kitchen passage?
A No.

79. Q In the kitchen?
A Yes.

80. Q Was Henry Dawson Bull connected with the tragedy in the kitchen?
A Yes.

81. Q Was the tragedy connected with the well?
A No.

82. Q Was a baby connected with the tragedy?
A Yes.

83. Q Was the baby connected with the well?
A No.

84. Q Did the baby die?
A No.

85. Q Is it still alive?
A No.

86. Q Was it killed?
A No.

87. Q Then did it die a natural death?
A Yes.

88. Q Was the baby connected with the well?
A No.

89. Q Did the servant die a natural death?
A No.

90. Q Was she shot?
A No.

91. Q Was she poisoned?
A No.

92. Q Did you poison her?
A No.

93. Q Did Henry Dawson Bull poison her?
A Yes.

94. Q Can you give us a sign or a rap?
A No.

95. Q Will you answer some more questions?
A Yes.

96. Q Will you please wait a little as we are tired?
A Yes.

The sitting was halted for a short time, but then recommenced at 2.00 a.m.

97. Q Are you still there?
A Yes.

98. Q Have you a pet name?
A Yes.

99. Q Will you please tell us your Christian name?
A Yes.

100. Q Will you please spell it out?
A Yes.

101. Q Will you please start?
A Jane.

102. Q Is it Jane?
A No.

103. Q Is it Janet?
A No.

104. Q Will you please give us the fifth letter?
A N.

105. Q And the next?
A three times through the alphabet.

106. Q Is your name Janen?
A Yes.

107. Q Will you tell us your maiden surname?
A uncertain

108. Q Will you spell it?
A uncertain.

109. Q Do you remember it?
A No.

110. Q Do you find it difficult to communicate in this room?
A No.

111. Q Would another part of the house be easier?
A No.

112. Q Is there too much light?
A No.

113. Q Is there anything we can do to make it easier?
A No.

114. Q Is the fire too bright?
     A No.

115. Q Do you meet your son Harry
       Bull?
     A Yes.

116. Q Is he happy?
     A No.

117. Q Has he money troubles?
     A uncertain.

118. Q Are there money troubles?
     A uncertain.

119. Q Did he die in this house?
     A Yes.

120. Q Did he die a natural death?
     A No.

121. Q Was he poisoned?
     A Yes.

122. Q Do you know who poisoned
       him?
     A No.

123. Q Are you sure?
     A uncertain.

124. Q Did his wife poison him?
     A No.

125. Q Do you think you know?
     A uncertain.

126. Q Did you rather we did not
       ask these questions?
     A Yes.

127. Q Are you certain you would
       like light, Mass prayer etc in
       the kitchen?
     A Yes (very decided).

128. Q Can we help in any other
       way?
     A No.

129. Q Can we stop now?
     A Yes.

130. Q Can we talk with you
       tomorrow?
     A Yes.

131. Closing comment by the sitters:
     'Good night and thank you'.

Once again, the writer feels that there is a tangle of contacts, of which two are rather interesting. One is very probably

Mrs Caroline Sarah Bull, Henry Dawson Bull's wife, who died in 1914. The other suggests strongly in places, not Henry's nor Harry's wife, but Harry Bull's step-daughter, Miss Brackenbury! Since Miss Brackenbury would presumably have still been alive in 1937, at the time of the Borley seance experiments, one may well wonder why should she respond to questions put to entities in Borley Rectory?

A good many people interested in spiritualist activities think that if such responses are genuine, they can come only from persons who are dead, but I am not at all sure that this assumption is tenable.

Is it not possible, for example, that if something untoward has occurred in one house, an 'atmosphere' built from the lives of occupants who then move elsewhere, remains present in the old abode, along with an ability to respond to, or communicate with, people who come afterwards?

After Harry Bull's death in 1927, Ivy Bull left the Rectory, and her daughter would either have gone with her, or if old enough she might have gone her own separate way. One important link here, between Ivy Bull's daughter and Borley Rectory, is that relations between Harry Bull and his Catholic stepdaughter were said to be so bad that he is alleged to have struck her. Her time at Borley Rectory could not have been at all happy under such circumstances and as the Rectory already had an unpleasant atmosphere, probably as a result of a misfortune in connection with the maid and the child, and not forgetting the details about Harry Bull's will, then the potential unhappiness of Miss Brackenbury would have pervaded the place as well, and very probably remained after she had left.

Once again we come across appeals for Mass, light, etc., which are chiefly Catholic symbols. The matter of a baby and an incident in the Rectory kitchen, crops up again, but if there was an appeal for help from an entity, then it would be unlikely to have been Kate Boreham, for she and her husband Walter, would have been Protestants.

Miss Brackenbury, however, *was* a Catholic. One might well ask whether she could have discovered something about the Rectory kitchen that disturbed her. The reader is reminded that after Harry Bull's death, a half-empty bottle of 'sugar of lead' was discovered in the house. If true, then it is surely possible that Miss Brackenbury might have discovered that same bottle earlier in a cupboard in the kitchen. It doesn't require much thought to picture just such an occurrence, at which point Harry Bull might even have snatched the bottle away and consigned it to the Rectory cellars, locking the access door after him.

That anybody finding such a substance in the kitchen would not query its presence there, is inconceivable, but if Harry Bull had knowledge of what the bottle of 'sugar of lead' meant, then for him to be faced with its discovery by his step-daughter would probably have aroused something akin to panic!

There is, however, another suggestion. Given that relations between Harry Bull and his stepdaughter were bad, there is the possibility, however appalling the idea might be, that she poisoned *him* out of hatred, the instrument of the deed being disposed of in the cellar by her, or discovered by her mother who hid it, realising what her daughter had done, and of course trying to shield her daughter from an accusation of murder.

How can we tie these possibilities in with the answers from the table-tipping sessions.

The writer suggests that answers to questions 65 to 67 probably came from Mrs Caroline Sarah Bull, Henry's wife. Numbers 68 to 69 *suggest* Miss Bracken-bury, though there is a third personality that we will consider.

Numbers 70 to 74 bring us back to Caroline Bull, troubled by some knowledge of the episode of the maid and the baby. Questions and answers 76 to 79 once again suggest Miss Brackenbury, but numbers 80 to 93 must surely revolve around Caroline Sarah Bull, because between herself and Miss Brackenbury, Caroline would surely have been more likely to know the true extent of any such episode than Miss Brackenbury? It should, however, be remembered that there was

an overlap, because Miss Brackenbury would have come to Borley in 1911, when her mother Ivy married Harry Bull. At that time, Harry's mother Caroline Sarah Bull was still alive and indeed she did not pass on until 1914.

It has also been suggested that a Catholic symbol such as a medallion of some sort might have been hidden from her stepfather by Miss Brackenbury, knowing that if he found such an article, its existence in his Rectory could provoke yet another scene of unpleasantness between Harry Bull and his seemingly unwanted stepdaughter.

Whilst recognising the shortcomings of seance material, unless backed up by other evidence, one cannot easily escape the feeling that these table-tipping results, even if only half correct, do little or nothing to counter the impression that Borley Rectory was, by the 1900s at any rate, a rather unfortunate house to say the least.

The next session was held in the Rectory later the same day, October 24th, 1937, in the kitchen with Alan Cuthbert, Sidney Glanville, Roger Glanville and Mark Kerr-Pearse.

They began at 6.50 p.m., the results being as follows:

132. Q Is there anyone there?
     A Yes.

133. Q Is it Henry Dawson Bull?
     A Yes.

134. Q Did you know Marianne Foyster?
     A No.

135. Q Did you wish to speak to her?
     A No.

136. Q Did you die in the room over the library?
     A Yes.

137. Q Did you die naturally?
     A No.

138. Q Were you shot?
     A No.

139. Q Were you poisoned?
     A No.

140. Q Were you killed?
     A Yes.

141. Q Can you spell it?
     A LANVOISEFAIDF.

142. Q Did you son Harry Bull die naturally?
     A No.

143. Q Was he killed?
     A No.

144. Q Was he poisoned?
     A Yes.

At this stage, the sitters failed to obtain any further replies, so they moved to a position outside the adjacent sewing room, and the session continued thus:

145. Q Are you Henry Dawson Bull?
     A No.

146. Q Will you please spell your name?
     A Kat.

147. Q Is it Kate?
     A No.

148. Q Is it Katie?
     A Yes.

149. Q Were you the maid here?
     A Yes.

150. Q Have you a message?
     A Yes.

151. Q Will you please spell it out?
     A Light Mass erslre.

At this point, replies ceased again for a while, but the sitters pressed on once again:

152. Q Are you there?
     A Yes.

153. Q Are you Henry Dawson Bull?
     A No.

154. Q Are you Katie?
     A No.

155. Q Are you Caldibec?
     A Yes.

156. Q Are you Henry Dawson Bull's wife?
     A Yes.

157. Q Have you a message for us?
     A Yes.

158. Q Will you spell it out?
     A Ainrric (then no more).

159. Q Are you there?
     A no answer.

160. Q Are you there?
     A Yes.

There was another break in the replies at this stage, but they then continued:

161. Q Are you tired?
     A Yes.

162. Q Shall we stop?
     A Yes.

163. Q Is your power gone?
     A Yes.

164. Q Do you wish to rest?
     A Yes.

165. Q May we return later?
     A Yes. (weak).

166. Q Had we better go to another part of the house?
     A Yes.

167. Q Upstairs?
     A Yes.

168. Q Landing?
     A No.

169. Q End bedroom?
     A Yes.

170. Q Is Henry Dawson Bull there?
     A Yes (definitely).

171. Q Are you certain you are tired?
     A Yes.

Goodbye and thank you.

This session ended at 9.44 p.m., but they began again at 10.20 p.m. in bedroom number seven, and continued until 2.00 a.m., by which time they had moved to the landing outside the Blue Room. The sitting was held in darkness, and continued as follows:

172. Q Are you there?
     A Yes.

173. Q Will you please spell who you are?
     A reply unintelligible.

174. Q Have you a message?
     A Get . . . (then indistinct).

172

175. Q Have you difficulty in communicating with us?
A Yes.

176. Q Is there too much light?
A Yes. (moon then shining into room).

177. Q Would the passage be easier?
A Yes.

178. Q If we go there, will you give us a message?
A Yes.

179. Q Are you Harry Bull?
A Yes.

The sitters then moved into the 'passage', or more correctly, on to the landing outside the Blue Room, and continued:

180. Q Are you there?
A Yes.

181. Q Is that Harry Bull?
A Yes.

182. Q Have you a message for us?
A Yes.

183. Q Will you please spell it out?
A Mifor ... (then indistinct).

184. Q Do you mean misfortune?
A Yes.

185. Q Will you continue?
A Awife.

186. Q Do you mean your wife?
A Yes.

187. Q Did you die in this house?
A Yes.

188. Q Did you die in the room we left?
A Yes.

The reader will recall that both Henry and Harry Bull died in the Blue Room.

189. Q Did you die naturally?
A No.

190. Q Were you poisoned?
A uncertain answer.

191. Q Were you poisoned?
A Yes.

192. Q Were you poisoned by your wife?
A Yes.

193. Q Was your wife with you when you died?
A No.

194. Q Can we help?
A Yes.

195. Q Have you a message?
A Yes.

196. Q Will you please spell it out?
A Ask ...

197. Q Do you mean Ask?
A Yes.

198. Q Will you please continue?
A Marr.

199. Q Do you mean Marianne?
A Yes.

200. Q Will you please continue?
A Mass.

201. Q The next word please?
A Ligh.

202. Q Do you mean light?
A Yes.

203. Q What sort of light, Candles?
A Yes.

204. Q As in a Roman Catholic church?
A Yes.

205. Q Will you please continue?
A Pr ...

206. Q Do you mean prayer?
A Yes.

207. Q Will you please continue?
A Get ...

208. Q Do you mean get?
A Yes.

209. Q Will you please continue?
A Cha ...

210. Q Do you mean chant?
A Yes.

211. Q Is that all?
A Yes.

212. Q Did you give us a message last night?
A Yes.

213. Q In Latin?
A Yes.

214. Q Was it caedo blamu ipse?
A Yes.

215. Q Was there any more?
     A Yes.

216. Q Will you please continue?
     A Isiaceai . . . (then indistinct).

The sitters broke for a meal in the library base room at this point, so let us now examine what we have.

The tangle of contacts persists through this session, as in the previous ones.

Questions and answers 132 to 139 seem to be fairly straightforward, and can probably be taken to centre upon Henry Dawson Bull.

Question 140 and the answer thereto constitutes something of a puzzle, because it could relate to either Harry or Henry Bull, but the most curious response among this particular group of answers comes in number 141.

'Lanvoisefaidf' seems a ridiculous and irrelevant non-entity, but if one takes another look at it, something interesting reveals itself. The curious response may have been an attempt to produce the simple words 'Lionel Algernon Foyster', a mixed up contact like the word 'Oif' from an earlier session.

But if the words were meant to be 'Lionel Algernon Foyster', then they could hardly be anything to do with Henry Dawson Bull who died in 1892, long before a Foyster had anything to do with Borley Rectory as a resident, but this could be connected with Harry Bull.

Harry Bull lived until 1927 and in 1924, Lionel and Marianne Foyster came to Borley during the course of a short holiday from Canada, a fact very rarely mentioned. That members of the Bull family came to know the Foysters during this visit to Borley is clear from various comments made by the Bull sisters later, including telling Sidney Glanville that they thought Marianne to be a little beast!

Questions and answers 142 to 144, from the tone of the replies, seem to relate once again to Henry Dawson Bull, whilst numbers 145 to 149 obviously relate to Kate, or Katie, Boreham, but in answers 150 and 151 we are back to a Catholic basis again, which means either Sir Edward Waldegrave, the nun or Miss Brac-

kenbury, with the most likely choice being between Miss Brackenbury and Sir Edward.

Numbers 152 to 160 show all the signs of having come from Mrs Caroline Sarah Bull, Henry Bull's wife, but the expression 'Ainrric' in the answer to 158 does not respond to dissection, unless it is again a mix up of part of the name Marianne. If it is, then that tends to cancel out Caroline Sarah Bull. All very confusing, irrespective of whether one accepts the idea of table tipping as a means of communication with the dead or not.

Numbers 161 to 171 can be viewed as probably relating to Henry Dawson Bull, whilst 172 to 199 strongly indicate Harry Bull, with possibly a link with Marianne.

In 200 to 216, a Catholic entity has seemingly broken through again, but this time the contact is very broken and fragmentary. Could this be the nun?

One could suggest that the passage of time might weaken any genuine spiritual contact, especially after three or four hundred years, even after two hundred years, but if that is the case, we could still be dealing with the unfortunate Sir Edward Waldegrave.

But to continue with the seance:

217. Q Are you Henry Dawson Bull?
     A No.

218. Q Are you Harry Bull?
     A Yes.

219. Q Was 'Ceai' correct?
     A Yes.

220. Q Was it Latin?
     A Yes.

221. Q The next letter please?
     A H (T)? K (one only)
       ADSEIHVESAB (indistinct).

222. Q Are you Harry Bull?
     A Yes.

223. Q Was your message a legal one?
     A No.

224. Q Did you write the messages?
     A No.

Then there followed a lot of rather inconsequential and meaningless material, together with repeats of answers given to the earlier questions. This can safely be ignored, and we can continue with the following:

225. Q Has the kitchen anything to do with the misfortune in this house?
     A Yes.

226. Q Was your father the cause of the trouble?
     A ·Yes.

227. Q Has there been any other cause for the trouble?
     A Yes.

228. Q Concerning yourself?
     A Yes.

Questions and answers 225 to 228 echo loudly the Katie story and the later years of Harry Bull's life, reinforcing the belief expressed over the years that an illegitimate child was born to Katie Boreham by a prominent member of the Bull family, often believed to be Harry, but the possiblity that it was his father Henry, keeps coming to the surface.

The next few questions centred upon the story of the nun and whether or not the kitchen had anything to do with her, to which the response was 'No'.

The next stage to be examined starts with:

229. Q Was your wife the cause of the present trouble?
     A No.

230. Q Did it start with your father?
     A No.

231. Q Was it before his time?
     A Yes.

232. Q Was it long before his time?
     A No.

233. Q A previous Rector?
     A Yes.

234. Q In a previous house?
     A No.

235. Q In this house?
     A Yes.

Asssuming that it was still Harry Bull who was producing the contact, the foregoing details are contradictory!

If the problems of the Rectory originated with a previous Rector to the Bulls, they could not have occurred in the Rectory, because prior to the arrival of Henry Bull in 1862, Borley Rectory as we know it did not exist, Borley Place on the opposite side of the road being used as the Rectory.

However, the previous Rector, John Herringham, did have a Rectory on the same site, a house which by all accounts he didn't use. So, was Harry Bull referring to events occurring in Borley Rectory as an establishment rather than specifically his father's own Rectory? Curious indeed, and it suggests that for perhaps the first time, some attention ought to be directed to the time of the Herringham rectorship, with the obvious question; why did he use Borley Place and not the old Rectory?

Readers may recall my hypothetical question raised earlier, as to whether the Herringham rectory could have been haunted in the same way as the Borley Rectory was?

But we must press on:

236. Q Did your father build this house?
     A Yes (faint).

237. Q This house is supposed to be haunted. Was it haunted before your father's time?
     A no reply.

In question 237, the sitters themselves have made the mistake about the existence of the house before Harry's father's time, thereby rendering the question invalid, though as the question was not responded to, it does not really make any difference in this instance. The next question did make sense:

238. Q Was it haunted during his time?
     A Yes.

239. Q Did your father see the nun?
     A Yes.

240. Q Has the nun left now?
     A No.

241. Q Is she happy here?
     A No.

242. Q Can we help her?
A Yes.

243. Q By a service?
A No.

244. Q By a Christian burial?
A Yes.

245. Q Is she in the garden?
A Yes (very definite).

246. Q Shall we see her?
A No.

247. Q Is she near the house?
A Yes.

248. Q Is anyone buried in the garden?
A Yes (definite).

249. Q Has there been a burial in the garden in your time?
A No.

250. Q Has anyone been buried in the garden?
A Yes.

251. Q Only the nun?
A Yes.

252. Q No one else?
A No.

253. Q Is she buried under the house?
A No.

Answer 253 is very odd, because the 1943 excavations *proved* that somebody was most certainly buried underneath the cellar of Borley Rectory, and that some individual's remains now rest in the churchyard at nearby Liston.
But to continue:

254. Q Near the house?
A Yes.

255. Q Could we find her?
A Yes.

256. Q Is she deeply buried?
A No.

257. Q Is she buried near the summer house?
A No.

258. Q On the east of the house?
A No.

259. Q On the north side of the house?
A No.

260. Q On the south of the house?
A Yes.

261. Q On the west of the house?
A Yes.

262. Q On the south west of the house?
A Yes (definite).

263. Q Is she buried under trees?
A Yes.

264. Q Is she buried in a coffin?
A No.

265. Q Is she buried under a stone?
A No.

266. Q Is she buried under a cedar tree?
A No.

267. Q Is she buried near the low brick wall?
A No.

268. Q Is she near the path by the south west of the house?
A Yes.

269. Q Is she buried near the path?
A Yes.

270. Q Has she ever been found?
A No.

271. Q Is she buried within two yards of the path?
A Yes.

272. Q Is she buried near the green house?
A No.

273. Q Is she buried near the stables?
A No.

274. Q Is she buried near the earthen bowl by the lawn?
A No.

275. Q Is she buried near the small pond.
A No.

276. Q Is she buried under a tree within two yards of the path?
A Yes.

277. Q Is she buried under a large tree?
   A Yes.

278. Q Can you spell the name of the tree?
   A Yes (then out of control).

279. Q Do you know the kind of tree?
   A Yes.

280. Q Can you spell its name?
   A Fi.

281. Q Is 'fir' correct?
   A Yes.

282. Q Within two yards of a fir tree?
   A Yes.

283. Q Is the fir tree a large one?
   A Yes.

284. Q Is the fir tree near the vine by the corner of the house?
   A Yes.

285. Q Are you certain?
   A Yes (definite).

286. Q Shall we have difficulty in finding the tree?
   A Yes.

287. Q Has it been cut down?
   A no reply.

288. Q Would she like us to look for her?
   A Yes.

289. Q If we look for her, shall we find her?
   A Yes.

290. Q Is she buried in the garden?
   A Yes (definite).

291. Q Is she buried fairly near the greenhouse?
   A Yes.

292. Q Is she buried more than three feet deep?
   A No.

293. Q Is she buried under a small stone with B on it in the path?
   A Yes.

294. Q Are you certain she is under the stone?
   A Yes (definite).

At that stage, the sitters broke off for supper, and Alan Cuthbert went to bed. The time was 12.20 a.m.

According to the microfilm copy of the Locked Book, this break in the session was recorded by Glanville on page 144, whereupon he informs us that the break lasted until 1.40 a.m., but the next page, 145, picks up the session not at 1.40 a.m. but at 4.15 a.m., a session which is treated as being a new one by Glanville. What, one wonders, has become of the questions and answers that presumably arose during the period from 1.40 a.m. and 4.15 a.m.?

I cannot but wonder whether the Locked Book's contents have been laundered.

A search through *The Most Haunted House in England* reveals no answer, because of course, although Harry Price included a large part of the seance results, he didn't include all of it, for various reasons.

The times indicated by Sidney Glanville strongly suggest that at some time between 1.40 a.m., when they presumably finished their supper, and say about 3.45 a.m. or 4.00 a.m. (allowing for another short break before the 4.15 a.m. session started) they must have picked up on and completed the session that had begun at 10.20 p.m. that night.

However, at the beginning of the typed record of that session, the times are given as from 10.20 p.m. to 2.00 a.m. This partly explains the course of events, so that what we now have is the following:

Start	10.20 p.m.
Break	12.20 a.m.
Continue	1.40 a.m.
Finish	2.00 a.m.

... *but*, the details of the period from 1.40 a.m. to 2.00 a.m. are *still missing!*

The entity replying to 236 could only be Harry Bull, while 237 was an invalid question.

Harry Bull answers again to questions 238 and 239.

From here on, the most obvious subject of the answers is of course Marie Lairre, the supposed Borley Nun. But who is answering questions numbered 240 to 294? As the previous questions seem almost certain to have been answered by

Harry Bull, the natural assumption would be that he is also answering questions about the nun as well. But would the fate of a dead Catholic nun be of any concern to a Protestant rector? But if not Harry Bull, could it be Edward Waldegrave or Miss Brackenbury (Harry's stepdaughter), both of whom were Catholic!

The idea of Edward Waldegrave has certain attractions, but there is a problem. Edward Waldegrave died in 1561. The Borley nun is alleged to have died in 1667. Could the spirit of one dead person be conscious of the fate of another who dies a century *later*? If so, this could suggest that spirits attain a universal and parallel time zone, irrespective of the era of their physical existence as living people, which may concentrate the minds of the thinkers of the spiritualist world.

There is also, in this proposition, another, which is that our whole existence and what comes after is a set of dimensions. There are the three dimensions of every solid object, while the fourth dimension is time, which is of man's invention, so is the afterlife, with its survival of the spirit, the fifth dimension?

If such should prove to be the case, then it might well be suggested that it was Edward Waldegrave who was answering those questions about the nun. If not, then we are left with two main contenders . . . Miss Brackenbury or Harry Bull. There seems to be so little known about Miss Brackenbury that it appears impossible to judge the extent to which she was aware of the stories about the nun, but to Harry Bull the nun and her fate was part of the Bull family culture at Borley.

Assuming, from the answers given to questions about the nun, if it was her, that a holy sister did die at Borley, it seems that we still have no proof that her remains have been discovered at all!

So we must move to the next session. This is dated 25th October, 1937, and lasted from 4.15 a.m. until 4.45 a.m., and the sitters were again Sidney Glanville, Roger Glanville and Mark Kerr-Pearse.

295. Q Are you there?
A Yes.

296. Q Who are you?

A Jane (definite).

297. Q Same as in the library?
A Yes.

298. Q Is anyone else here?
A Yes.

299. Q Do you know Edwin?
A No.

300. Q Do you know Marianne?
A Yes.

301. Q Was she a good influence?
A No.

302. Q Do you know P? . . . (identity of P unknown. IB).
A No.

303. Q Do you know SM? . . . (again identity unknown. IB).
A No.

304. Q Do you spend much time in this room?
A No.

305. Q Did you come here because we are here?
A Yes.

306. Q Has anything important happened in this house?
A Yes.

307. Q Was it a tragedy?
A Yes.

308. Q Was it connected with Katie?
A No.

309. Q Was it connected with Katie, are you sure?
A Yes.

310. Q Do you know who it was?
A Yes.

311. Q Will you please spell the name?
A LIGHT

312. Q Is it the name of a person?
A Yes.

313. Q Is it a message?
A Yes.

314. Q We presume your message is 'light mass prayer' etc.?
A Yes (definite).

178

315. Q Can you tell us the name of the person connected with the tragedy in this room?
A Yes.

316. Q Spell it?
A LUNOLOWTUMNAL.

317. Q Is the word complete yet?
A No.

318. Q Give us the next letters?
A YC.

319. Q Is that still Jane?
A Yes.

320. Q Was the last message in English?
A No.

321. Q Was the last message in Latin?
A No.

322. Q Was the last message in French?
A No.

323. Q Was the last message in German?
A Yes.

324. Q How many words are there?
A the table tipped four times in reply.

325. Q Are there four words?
A Yes.

326. Q Are they in the correct order?
A Yes.

327. Q Did you like the woman who married Harry Bull?
A Yes.

328. Q Do you still like her?
A no reply.

329. Q Will you spell her surname?
A No.

330. Q Will you spell her Christian name?
A J . . . then no reply.

331. Q Are you tired?
A Yes.

332. Q Would you like us to stop?
A Yes.

Goodnight and thank you.

Now let us try to make some sense out of the answers 295 to 332.

The obvious question is who was Jane? The possibilities of Janen have been already discussed earlier, but there remains the identity of Harry Bull's wife Ivy Brackenbury. Was Jane her second name? That this is possible is suggested by questions and answers 299 to 301. The entity claims not to have known Edwin (Dom Richard Whitehouse) but did know Marianne. The point is that if we assume that this is Ivy Brackenbury responding, she would not have known Edwin because he didn't come onto the Borley scene until after the Bulls had ceased to occupy Borley Rectory with the death of Harry Bull in 1927. She would, however, have known about or met Marianne because Lionel and Marianne Foyster are said to have come to Borley for a short holiday in 1924, two years after they married.

The case for Ivy Brackenbury is further strengthened by answer 305, in the idea that the entity 'came to the Rectory' because the sitters were there. Here, for perhaps the first time, there is some definite possibility that Ivy Brackenbury did know something of the past troubles associated with the Rectory and the Bull family.

The next oddity is that seemingly aimless and meaningless expression, 'LUNOLOWTMUNAL'. Further questioning seemed to reveal that the word was supposedly German and was supposedly four words, but a search of a suitable dictionary reveals little that really comes close, but Lügner, which means liar, and the word Lümmel which means lout or ruffian!

It is not hard to imagine aspects of the Borley story where such harsh exhortations as 'liar' and 'ruffian' might come into the picture, but there is another possibility concerning the phrase LUNOLOWTMUNAL, that it refers to something to do with the moon, e.g. LUNO . . . Luna, one suggestion being that the entity was trying to relate that something happened at the time of the 'low moon'. If this is the intended meaning, it could be that either the moon was at its early or its fading stage of visibility, or that it was low in the

179

sky. The only other construction that might be put upon this is that the message was a combination of both suggestions, i.e. that something happened to someone in the Rectory, possibily as a result of physical assault, hence the word 'ruffian' or its German version 'Lümmel', at the time of a certain phase or visibility of the moon.

Now recall the existence of a woman named Maria Rolf (maybe Rolt), resident at Borley Rectory in 1881. Her place of birth is given as Lausanne, Switzerland. The name Rolf, spelt without the E, either Christian or surname, is German. Maria Rolf was therefore almost certainly German Swiss. Here, one can see where the German expression Lümmel might come into play!

The census returns list Maria Rolf as a visitor, and occupation that of governess, so we cannot readily ascertain how long Maria Rolf remained at the Rectory.

There is, however, the very real possibility that Maria Rolf might have been at Borley Rectory in 1888, the year of the real Kate Boreham's death, and might well have been aware of what really happened to Kate.

The next two sessions at Borley Rectory on October 25th, 1937, are out of sequence in the microfilm copy of the Locked Book, even though the pages 146–7 are *in* sequence. As those sessions were unproductive in any positive sense, we will pass on to that which took place between 2.10 a.m. and 3.05 a.m.

This was held in the library, or Base Room in full lamplight, and the three sitters were Sidney and Roger Glanville and Mark Kerr-Pearse.

333. Q What is your name?
A Jane.

334. Q Are you the wife of Henry Dawson Bull?
A Yes.

335. Q Are you happy?
A Yes.

336. Q Do you see your husband?
A Yes.

337. Q Is he happy?
A No.

338. Q Do you have a control?
A No answer.

339. Q Is anyone buried in the garden?
A Yes.

340. Q Who is it?
A FADENOCH.

341. Q Was he a member of the monastery?
A Yes.

342. Q Was he prior?
A No.

343. Q Was he a lay brother?
A No.

344. Q Was he a monk?
A Yes.

345. Q Was he a novice?
A No answer.

346. Q Was he a friend of the nun?
A No answer.

347. Q Had the burial been made before your lifetime?
A Yes.

348. Q Had the burial been made after your lifetime?
A No.

349. Q Is there evil in this house?
A No.

350. Q Was there evil in this house?
A Yes.

351. Q Is there now only good in this house?
A Yes.

352. Q Should the house be destroyed?
A No.

The next few questions related to the sitters themselves, and are of no importance, so the relevant questions and answers continue with:

353. Q Are you Caldibec?
A Yes.

354. Q Is that your pet name?
A Yes.

355. Q Did your husband use it?
A Yes.

356. Q Did you call your husband Carlos?
A Yes.

357. Q Do you know who wrote the messages on the walls?
A Yes.

358. Q Did you?
A No.

359. Q Did Carlos?
A No.

360. Q Did Harry?
A Yes.

361. Q Did Marianne?
A No.

362. Q Did Katie?
A No.

There then followed requests to write more messages on the walls for the sitters to see, and questions as to whether the entity knew about the previous messages. We continue with:

363. Q Do you known Mr Foyster?
A No.

364. Q Do you know Marianne?
A Yes.

365. Q Has Carlos been forgiven?
A No.

366. Q Is Carlos happier now?
A No.

367. Q Is Katie happier now?
A Yes.

368. Q Was Katie a servant here?
A Yes.

369. Q Was Katie your servant here?
A Yes.

370. Q Do you want to stop now?
A Yes.

371. Q Is the light too strong?
A No.

372. Q Then you are feeling tired?
A Yes.

373. Q May we speak to you again later?
A Yes.

Goodnight and thank you.

Let us now look for a moment at question 353. The sitters ask 'Are you Caldibec?' The name Caldibec has variously been thought to be the name of the nun, or the name of place from whence she came, but also a nickname for Henry's wife. It is this latter possibility that should hold our attention for a moment, because what this word Caldibec may actually have been meant to be read as, is a shortened version of Caroline Sarah Bull's name. I would suggest that what the entity was actually saying was not Caldibec, but Carol Beth, short for Caroline Elizabeth. The eldest Bull daughter, who was also called Caroline Sarah, had the name Elizabeth as a third name. She was the girl known in the family as Dodie, and who married the Rev. Hayden and eventually died in 1937. It is quite likely that Mrs Bull also had Elizabeth in her name, though she only seems to have been called Caroline Sarah in most records.

If we accept that the answer to question 353 was from Mrs Caroline Bull, then it would be fairly safe to reckon that results 354 to 362 were also Mrs Bull senior. With the exception of question 364, to which the answer is odd, given the answer to 363, numbers 363 to 373 are also most likely to have come from Mrs Bull.

A fascinating part of the seance arises out of those results obtained by the use of a planchette which were undertaken for a serious purpose.

The first planchette session at Borley Rectory of which a record still survives took place on 25th October, 1937, after a short initial experiment, the writings of which Sidney Glanville reports as being lost, and those listed on page 150 of the Locked Book start in mid-session so to speak, and are of little value.

However, of great value were the results obtained by Helen Glanville at her home in Streatham, using another planchette, and unbeknown to Sidney and Roger Glanville. Helen's results were extraordinary, the more so because her planchette functioned away from Borley, whilst Sidney and Roger's produced nothing *until it was taken to Borley!*

In order to maintain continuity, and to facilitate further analysis of the results, my numbering sequence continues from the end of the table tipping experiments.

PLANCHETTE, HELEN GLANVILLE STREATHAM, OCTOBER 28th, 1937

374. Q Have you a message?
A W . . . (indistinct).

375. Q If the word is 'well', say yes.
A Yes.

376. The planchette wrote Marianne without a question being asked.

377. Q Do you want us to look in the well, yes or no?
A Yes.

378. Q Is the well in the cellar?
A Yes.

379. Q Is there something you want us to find?
A Yes.

380. Q Can you tell us what it is?
A indistinct reply.

381. Q Would you try again? Is it MA?
A no reply.

382. Q Is anything in the well to do with a child?
A Yes.

383. Q Was the child dead when it was born?
A indistinct reply.

384. Q Do you mean yes or no?
A Yes.

385. Q Was it Henry Dawson Bull's child?
A Yes.

386. Q Do you want us to find it?
A Yes.

387. Q Shall we find it in the well in the cellar?
A Yes.

388. Q Do you mean the well that has been filled in?
A Yes.

389. The planchette wrote M, without a question being asked.

390. The planchette wrote . . . Arrianne, without a question being asked.

391. Q Is it someone using this name?
A indistinct reply.

392. Q Could you tell me your own name?
A indistinct reply.

393. Q Are you buried in the garden?
A Yes.

394. Q Can you tell us where?
A Der-re (indistinct).

395. Q Do you mean under the fir tree?
A No.

396. Q Near a tree?
A Yes.

397. Q Is there anything to tell us where?
A Stone.

At this point the reader will doubtless be interested to learn that there was a boundary stone on the far side of the Rectory garden, at a point that is now part of the stable cottage garden belonging to Colonel Dorey. But to continue:

398. Q Can you tell me the rest of your name?
A La . . . (then indistinct).

399. Q Are the first two letters LA?
A . . . irre.

400. Q Do you mean 'Lairre'?
A Yes.

401. Q Can we help? Are you unhappy?
A Yes.

402. Q Can we do anything to help you?
A Mass.

403. The planchette wrote 'Prayers aness' without a question being asked.

404. Q It is Mass isn't it?
A Yes.

405. Q Can you tell me, are you buried in the garden?
A Yes.

406. Q Do you want Mass said in the house?
  A Yes.

The entity replied to the next couple of questions to the effect that it didn't matter where in the house Mass was said. And so to continue:

407. Q If you still want to talk, say yes.
  A Yes.

408. Q Can you tell me the name of your nunnery?
  A Larire.

409. Q Do you mean 'Lar'?
  A ... arre.

410. Q Is it the name of your nunnery you are trying to write?
  A Yes.

411. Q Was it near Bures?
  A Yes.

412. Q Can you tell me how far it was away? Two miles or more?
  A Yes.

413. Q Was it Bures?
  A Yes.

414. Q Do you mean it was Bures?
  A Yes.

415. Q It is your own name you are trying to write, isn't it?
  A Yes.

416. Q Can you tell me the name of the monk?
  A indistinct reply.

417. Q Is he unhappy?
  A Yes.

418. Q Can you tell me when you passed over?
  A 1667.

419. Q The month?
  A May.

420. Q The day?
  A 17.

421. Q Can you tell us why you passed over?
  A Yes.

422. Q Did they hurt you?
  A Yes.

423. Q Was there something you wanted very much before you passed over?
  A Water.

424. Q Do you mean water?
  A Yes.

425. Q Can you try to spell the name of the nunnery?
  A h ... (then indistinct).

426. Q Is the first letter H?
  A Yes.

427. Q The next letter?
  A a.

428. Q The next letter?
  A i.

429. Q The next letter?
  A a.

430. Q Could you do it again?
  A v.

431. Q Haiv, is that right?
  A Yes.

432. Q Is it Haiv?
  A Yes.

433. Q Was it a closed order?
  A Yes.

434. Q Do you want more questions?
  A Yes.

435. Q Has it gone now?
  A Yes.

436. Q Was the monks order O.S.B.? (Order of St. Benedict).
  A Yes.

437. Q Is the monk buried at Borley?
  A Yes.

438. Q Do you know where?
  A Yes.

439. Q In the garden, or under the house?
  A no reply.

Now let us look at questions and answers 374 to 388. These all seem to centre upon Katie Boreham's dead baby. But who is answering the questions about the well? It could be Katie herself, but there is an indefinable something that suggest it isn't Katie at all who is responding, but instead the formerly unknown and ignored Swiss governess, Maria Rolf or Rolt!

This also presents a fresh possibility, that the name Marie Lairre *might* have been intended to read Maria-Lausanne, or part thereof, and thus seemingly nothing to do with the Borley nun at all! Remember that the census returns for 1881 tell us that Maria Rolf was born in Lausanne.

Numbers 389 to 392 suggests Miss Brackenbury, Harry Bull's harassed stepdaughter, because of the link between Harry Bull, and Lionel and Marianne Foyster, through the latter couple having stayed at Borley during 1924, hence the *request*, as I see it, for Marianne!

Number 392 is of little use as the reply was indistinct, but from 393 on, we appear, again, to be dealing with the nun.

There is a mention of Bures. We have already looked at the role of Bures in the story of the nun, and pointed out the exsistence of Bures in Normandy as well as Bures in Suffolk. No evidence has come to light concerning a former convent in or near Bures in Suffolk, but as we know from Cottineau, Bures-en-Bray near Dieppe most certainly had a Benedictine monastery.

Now let's look at the response 'HAIV'. There is nothing like this near Bures in Suffolk, the nearest many miles away being Haverhill which had no monastery or convent. But in the hinterland of Bures-en-Bray is a place called La Haye, and the results of my investigations into that aspect are contained in the chapter on the Borley nun.

The next planchette session we will look at took place at Borley Rectory on October 30th, 1937. The sitters were the Rev. Alfred Clifford Henning, the Rector of Borley and Liston, together with Sidney Glanville.

440. Q Who is there?
    A Jane.

441. Q What date did you live?

    A indistinct reply.

442. Q Was your surname Foyster?
    A no reply.

443. Q How can we help you?
    A Im.

444. Q Will you give us a message?
    A indistinct reply.

445. Q Was there a monastery here?
    A Yes.

446. Q Was there a nunnery here?
    A Yes.

447. Q What happened to you?
    A I died.

448. Q How?
    A Murdered.

449. Q Who by?
    A Henry.

450. Q What is your name?
    A Marr.

451. Q What is your surname?
    A Lairre.

452. Q Were you a nun?
    A Yes.

453. Q Were you buried here?
    A Yes.

454. Q Where?
    A In the garden.

455. Q Do you mean garden?
    A Yes.

456. Q What are you near?
    A Fir.

457. Q Is it near the wall?
    A Yes.

458. Q How can we help you?
    A Light Mass . . . (then indistinct).

459. Q Can the Priest help?
    A Yes.

460. Q Through Mass?
    A Yes.

461. Q Where?
    A indistinct reply.

462. Q In Borley Church?
    A no reply.

463. Q Shall we stop now?
 A Y . . . (then indistinct).

The session ended at 11.50 p.m.

Questions 445 and 446 are of specific interest in connection with the monastery controversy. The entity, when asked whether there was 'a monastery and nunnery here', says 'Yes'. It can be fairly safely assumed that the sitters were asking about a monastery at Borley, but can we be sure that the entity, in replying, did mean Borley, or whether the entity, perhaps confused, was in fact thinking of Bures-en-Bray when it replied?

As we know, there is no evidence to date that there was a monastery *in Borley itself*, although there was one that appeared to have been close to the parish boundary . . . Sudbury Priory! We also know that there was a monastery in Bures-en-Bray in Normandy, but if we go back for a moment, to an earlier question in Helen Glanville's sitting at Streatham, question 437, we will notice something of a complication. In that question, Helen Glanville asked 'Is the monk buried at Borley?' The entity replied 'yes'.

There are two possibilities here. One is that a monk from Sudbury Priory might have been buried at Borley, perhaps a victim of the plague of 1349. If so, assuming that the answers to the Henning/Glanville session *were* coming from the nun, could she possibly know about a monk who died some three hundred years before *her* death in 1667? Again, this throws up the query as to an elimination of any time scale among the spirits.

The second possibility is that at some time in the distant past, there *was* another monastic cell *in Borley*, of which all documentary trace has been lost.

The remaining questions of the Henning/Glanville session, particularly numbers 447 onwards, all seem to relate to the nun, Marie Lairre.

After the experiment at Borley by the Rev. Henning and Sidney Glanville, the next session was held at Helen Glanville's home in Streatham. The sitters this time were Helen Glanville, Mark Kerr-Pearse, Sidney Glanville and Roger Glanville. The sitting was held on October 31st, 1937, and proceeded as follows:

464. Q Who is there?
 A indistinct . . . then Mary.

465. Q What is your name?
 A Lairre.

466. Q How old were you when you passed over?
 A 19.

467. Q Were you a novice?
 A Yes.

468. Q Why did you pass over?
 A no reply.

469. Q Are you under the wall?
 A No.

470. Q Are you at the end of the wall?
 A Yes.

471. Q Where did you hear Mass?
 A indistinct reply.

472. Q Will you spell each letter?
 A B O R L E Y.

473. Q Did you know Father Enoch?
 A indistinct reply.

474. Q Will you repeat your last answer letter by letter?
 A J E S U S.

475. Q Have you a message?
 A Chant light mass.

476. Q Do you want it for yourself?
 A Yes.

477. Q Why?
 A I am unha . . . (two more letters, then indistinct).

478. Q Is it your own fault?
 A No.

479. Q Whose fault?
 A Waldegrave.

480. Q Were you murdered?
 A Yes.

481. Q When?
 A 1667.

482. Q How?
 A Stran . . . (one more letter, indistinct).

483. Q Were your strangled?
 A Yes.

484. Q Will our Mass be sufficient?
     A No.

485. Q What Mass do you want?
     A Requiem.

486. Q Must it be a Roman Catholic
       priest?
     A indistinct reply.

487. Q Will you spell answers letter
       by letter?
     A N A P U P O.

488. Q Are you French?
     A Yes.

489. Q Where did you come from?
     A Havre.

490. Q Is is Havre?
     A Yes.

491. Q What was the name of your
       nunnery or convent?
     A Bure.

492. Q Did Waldegrave take you
       from Bures?
     A Yes.

493. Q Do you want burial as well
       as Mass?
     A Yes.

494. Q Have you ever given us a
       message in Latin?
     A Yes.

495. Q Are we speaking to Mary
       Lairre?
     A Yes.

496. Q Can you tell us the Latin
       message again?
     A L O V U.

497. Q Was the first letter L?
     A no reply.

498. Q Do you want water?
     A Yes.

499. Q What kind of water?
     A Holy.

500. Q What else do you want?
     A Incense.

501. Q And what else?
     A W . . . (indistinct).

502. Q Will you please try again?
     A indistinct.

503. Q Will you please try once
       more?
     A indistinct.

From this point, the replies in the Locked Book (HPL copy) do seem to suggest that contact with the nun was rather abruptly lost, and the next batch of contacts were with another entity, so we will just stop to take a look at what we have in questions 464 to 503.

This whole section shows very clearly the apparent contact with the nun. All the answers seem to revolve around her, and here we now get something of an indication that the nun might very well have come originally from Bures-en-Bray in Normandy, and *not* from Bures in Suffolk. If she *was* brought to England, for some obscure reason, one obvious point of embarkation for the part of Normandy that includes Bures-en-Bray, would have been Le Havre, although as Bures lay not far from Dieppe, anyone embarking for England would surely do so at Dieppe. It will be seen that if any such event involving a nun and a monk *did* take place, they could have embarked from either port, but the answers from the entity all seem to indicate Le Havre.

If this holy sister was brought from France to England, it is quite possible, is it not, that with her on the same boat might well have come a monk?

But for the present we will continue with the seance results, as follows:-

504. Q Are you ever in Borley House?
     A Yes.

505. Q Do you know Jane?
     A No.

506. Q Do you know Caldebec?
     A No.

507. Q Do you know any people
       called Bull?
     A Yes.

508. Q Please spell their names.
     A Henry.

509. Q Can we speak to Henry Bull
       now?
     A Yes.

510. Q What does Henry say?
     A indistinct reply.

511. Q Please spell his name.
     A indistinct reply.

512. Q Mary, are you speaking for Henry?
     A indistinct, possibly 'No'.

513. Q Are you Mary Lairre?
     In answer to question 513, the entity crossed it out, and the planchette wrote ... 'Question me'.

514. Q Who are you?
     A Henry.

515. Q Are you happy?
     A No.

516. Q Who caused your unhappiness?
     A uncertain reply, but apparently 'My wife'.

517. Q Do you mean your wife?
     A Yes.

518. Q Did you know Katie?
     A Yes.

519. Q Please spell her surname.
     A Boreham.

520. Q What year did she die?
     A 18 8 9 0.

521. Q Please try again.
     A 1888.

522. Q Can you tell us the month?
     A April.

523. Q Where did Katie Boreham die?
     A Kitchen.

524. Q From what?
     A Child.

525. Q Was the child's father there?
     A Yes.

In analysing these results, there is nothing really positive until one comes to question and answer 514. Here, the entity is either Henry Dawson Bull or his son Harry. In the light of what we know or suspect about the Bull family, it seems that where unhappiness caused by 'my wife' is concerned, this sounds more like Harry Bull than his father, remembering the possibilities as to friction between Harry

and Ivy Brackenbury, viz-a-viz her daughter, who was a Catholic. So far as Katie Boreham is concerned, Harry would have been just as likely to have known about her as his father, so this could be either of them.

Looking at questions and answers 521 to 525, one can see immediately the links between these results and the known and suspected facts about Katie Boreham's life. The date of death, so far as the year is concerned, is correct, but Kate died in March, not April. The question of her dying in the Rectory kitchen is interesting. We know that her death certificate says she died in Sudbury, but we also know that the lack of evidence for the Borehams having lived in or owned the house in Priory Walk make her death there questionable, and we also know that the stated cause of death as 'cerebritis' is also dubious. But the possibility that she died in childbirth, or through trying to abort is not so doubtful, as Professor Knight shows us, and this relates to answer 524. As to question 525 asking whether the child's father was there, I would suggest that not only was he there, but that 'he' was Henry senior.

The results continue as follows:

526. Q Have you written on the walls?
     A No.

527. Q Who did?
     A Harry.

528. Q Do you know Mary the Nun?
     A Ye or No ... (hesitant).

529. Q Do you know Caldebec?
     A No.

530. Q Do you know Jane?
     A No.

531. Q Do you know Henry?
     A Yes.

532. Q Where are you now?
     A Borley.

533. Q Do you know about the Latin message?
     A Yes.

534. Q Will you write the first word of the Latin message?
     A indistinct.

535. Q Can you spell each letter
     alone in English?
     A indistinct.

536. Q Do you mean you don't
     know what the message is?
     A Yes.

537. Q What is your wife's name?
     A Jane.

538. Q What was her maiden name?
     A Brackenbu . . .

539. Q When were you married, the
     date?
     A 1888 or 1889.

540. Q Where?
     A Borley.

541. Q Will you repeat the date you
     were married. Important?
     A 1889.

542. Q In which month?
     A March.

543. Q Which day of the month?
     A 13.

544. Q Which day of the week?
     A Friday.

545. Q Do you mean Friday?
     A Yes.

546. Q Was it registered at Borley
     Church?
     A No.

547. Q Were you married in the
     church?
     A No.

548. Q Were you married in the
     Rectory Chapel?
     A (Chapel was crossed out) . . .
     Yes.

549. Q Were there any witnesses?
     A Yes.

550. Q Who?
     A Henrie.

551. Q Henrietta.

552. Q Who was she?
     A Nurse.

553. Q Is she alive?
     A Yes.

554. Q Where does she live?
     A Sudbury.

555. Q Can you tell us her surname?
     A indistinct reply.

556. Q Will you please try again?
     A Weller or Meller.

557. Q Can you tell us the road she
     lives in?
     A indistinct . . . possibly
     'avenue'.

558. Q Please repeat the word
     before avenue.
     A Bull e or s.

559. Q The number of the house?
     A 23.

560. Q Who is Jane?
     A Foyster (uncertain).

561. Q Whose wife is she?
     A Henry Bull (very uncertain).

562. Q Did Jane Foyster have
     another name?
     A Marianne.

In trying to sort out these results we
have something of a problem, for many of
the answers are either impossible or
inaccurate!

Some of the replies seem to be coming
from Harry Bull, in particular number 538,
but he didn't marry in 1888 or 1889, but in
1911, and neither was he married in
Borley, but in Holborn, London!

As for the rest of this section, it seems
difficult to assess who is producing the
answers in the first place, quite apart from
the fact that most of them are incorrect.
Harry's wife Ivy was said to have been a
nurse from Sudbury, but her name was
Brackenbury not Weller or Meller.

Henry Bull's wife was Caroline, not
Jane Foyster, and finally, Marianne Foyster's other names were Emily Rebecca,
not Jane.

At this stage, there is no evidence that
anybody in the Bull family was married in
the Rectory itself. It is among these results,
from number 526 to number 562, that one
could find some sympathy with the views
of those that claim that seance results are
the product of subconscious manipulation by the sitters, and yet, within the

overall picture, there are indeed some curious links with what we now know from other sources.

563. Q Who is there?
     A Mari . . . (rest uncertain).

564. Q Can we speak to Harry again please?
     A Yes.

565. Q Is that Harry?
     A Yes.

566. Q Can you tell us Marianne's full name?
     A Jane Marianne Foyster.

567. Q Is she still alive?
     A Yes.

568. Q Where is she living?
     A Ipswi . . . (rest uncertain).

569. Q Will you please repeat?
     A Ipswich.

570. Q Who did she marry?
     A La . . . (rest uncertain).

571. Q Is there another Jane?
     A No.

572. Q Is Marianne in trouble?
     A Yes.

573. Q What kind of trouble? One word please.
     A Love.

574. Q Who?
     A Edwin.

575. Q Do you know Pearless?
     A Yes.

576. Q Was he called by another name?
     A indistinct reply.

Except for the reply to question 563, which appears to come from Marianne, all those from 564 to 576 can be reckoned as apparently coming from Harry Bull.

There are some other interesting points to note. The reply to question 566 is partly wrong. Marianne's full name was Emily Rebecca, first Shaw, then Greenwood, then Foyster, and also possibly Fisher, though her apparent marriage to Fisher, whilst still married to Lionel, would not, of course, be recognised. The name Jane

also cropped up in connection with Ivy Brackenbury, but one thought is that 'Jane' could have been the stepdaughter's name.

The reply stating that Marianne lived in Ipswich is rather curious. Is there some spiritual connection between a then living Marianne Foyster and a dead Harry Bull, perhaps through their having met during the Foysters' visit in 1924, or did one of the sitters know that Lionel and Marianne had moved to Ipswich? Somebody knew D'Arles real name, note the question 575, and the name mentioned . . . Pearless!

577. Q Do you know Santiago Monk?
     A Yes.

578. Q Is he Pearless?
     A No.

579. Q Is 'erel caedo blarnu ipse' correct?
     A no reply.

580. Q Who gave us this (Latin Message)?
     A Henry.

581. Q Do you mean your father?
     A Yes.

So far I have been unable to identify Santiago Monk, unless there was some involvement by a Spanish Catholic monk, perhaps in connection with the nun. There is, however, one other possibility, that this is something to do with Sir Edward Waldegrave, for when he objected to the marriage of Queen Mary to Philip of Spain, he was 'reassured' with a pension of 500 crowns.

In the course of any dialogue between Sir Edward Waldegrave and the Catholic establishment in Queen Mary's time, there may well have been some contact or conversation with those attached to the Spanish establishment.

In this section of questions the curious assumed Latin message appears again. This time, Harry Bull, who appears to be responding to these questions, attributes the Latin message to his father Henry, which seems a trifle odd! But did the message come from Henry Bull, or is the

Henry being referred to Henry Walde-grave? Remember Mary Lycett's theory about Henry and Arabella Waldegrave.

The next few questions and answers had to do with the sitters, not the possible history behind the hauntings, so we will continue at the following stage:

582. Q Is that Henry Dawson Ellis Bull?
     A Yes.

583. Q Did you build Borley Rectory?
     A Yes.

584. Q Do you resent others living there?
     A indistinct reply.

585. Q Will you please try again?
     A indistinct reply.

586. Q Will you write one letter at a time?
     A No o.

587. Q Which part of the Rectory do you like best?
     A Library.

588. Q Did you send us a message in Latin?
     A Yes.

589. Q Will you repeat it so that we can understand?
     A Ad . . . (rest uncertain).

590. Q Is 'ad' the first word?
     A Yes.

591. Q The next word please?
     A indistinct reply.

592. Q Is the message 'erel'?
     A no reply.

593. Q Can you tell us in English?
     A no reply.

594. Q Will you please repeat the whole message?
     A indistinct reply.

595. Q Did you give us a message 'if chant light mass'?
     A No.

596. Q Do you know who did?
     A indistinct reply.

597. Q Do you wish to leave Borley?
     A Yes.

598. Q Are your own past actions the cause of your being unable to leave?
     A Yes.

599. Q What was that action?
     A Death.

600. Q Whose?
     A Katie.

601. Q What shall we do to help?
     A indistinct reply.

602. Q Please repeat, we do not understand?
     A in church.

603. Q What do you want in church?
     A Light mass prayers (one word uncertain).

604. Q Please repeat the last word, we do not understand?
     A Incense.

605. Q Please continue your message.
     A indistinct.

606. Q Please repeat carefully, we do not understand.
     A Get help.

607. Q *Who* do you want to help you?
     A Glan . . . (rest uncertain).

608. Q Will you repeat carefully as we wish to help you?
     A Glanville.

609. Q Which one, spell name?
     A Sidney.

610. Q I am not able to hold a Mass. What can I do for you? Sidney.
     A Get . . . (indistinct).

611. Q I do not understand, please try to tell me more clearly.
     A Get a priest.

612. Q Can Father Henning help you?
     A Yes.

613. Q Did you write the messages on the walls at Borley?
     A Yes.

614. Q Do you want the Mass on any special day, as we wish to help you?
A Yes.

615. Q Which month?
A June.

616. Q Which day?
A 13.

617. Q Is it Henry Dawson Bull still speaking?
A Yes.

618. Q Can you tell us why you want Mass that day?
A indistinct reply.

619. Q Please repeat very carefully.
A My murder.

620. Q Who was murdered?
A indistinct reply.

621. Q Please repeat carefully and name?
A indistinct reply.

622. Q We cannot understand who was murdered, please tell us if you can?
A Glelegln.

623. Q Do you want us to stop?
A yo no.

624. Q Please try to tell us the name of the person who died on 13th June?
A Katie.

625. Q Please tell us the surname?
A Boreham.

626. Q Are you quite sure the date June 13th is the correct one?
A no reply.

627. Q Is there anyone else at Borley who wishes to speak to us?
A Some.

628. Q Who?
A Jane.

This section is also interesting, being very much connected with the death of Katie Boreham, but the whole episode is also rather odd, because assuming that this *is* Henry Dawson Bull, why one won-

ders is he seeking a Catholic Mass when he himself was a Protestant Rector?

Here again the apparent confusion over the date of Kate Boreham's death comes to light, the entity stating June 13th, whereas according to her death certificate she died in March. There is, of course, still the question as to whether Kate Boreham's death certificate can be believed, in the light of correspondence with Professor Bernard Knight. And so to continue:

629. Q Can you tell us your *full* name, please try?
A Jane . . . (uncertain).

630. Q What comes after 'Jane'?
A indistinct reply.

631. Q Will you please try to tell us your surname?
A indistinct reply.

632. Q Please try hard to tell your surname, we are anxious to help you.
A indistinct reply.

633. Q Could you write one letter at a time?
A Jane Foyster.

634. Q Are you married?
A Yes.

635. Q Who did you marry?
A Henry.

636. Q Henry Dawson Bull?
A Yes.

637. Q Were you his only wife?
A Yes.

638. Q Is your name Caroline Sarah?
A Yes.

639. Q Did your husband call you Jane?
A Yes.

640. Q Were you ever called by another name?
A Yes.

641. Q What was it?
A Caldebec.

642. Q Who named you?
A an indistinct reply.

191

643. Q We do not understand,
    please try again?
    A Mother.

644. Q Do you mean your mother?
    A Yes.

645. Q Is it in the Bible?
    A Yes (this referred to
    Caldebec).

646. Q Do you known anything
    about the Latin message?
    A no reply.

647. Q Is Marie Lairre there, will she
    speak to us?

648. Q Do you know anything
    about the Latin message?
    A Yes.

649. Q Can you spell the first word?
    A indistinct reply.

650. Q Can you write each letter
    alone?
    A Ad . . . (uncertain).

The anomalies continue in this section, throwing up a confusing tangle over the actual identity of Henry Dawson Bull's wife, whose real name was, of course, Caroline Sarah Bull. Out of this tangle, answers 634 to 638 are basically right, and one could therefore suggest that two entities are responding, Caroline Sarah Bull being one, but who is the other? Marianne possibly . . . or Miss Bracken-bury?

Numbers 642 to 646 seem to be emanating from Mrs Caroline Bull. From 647 onwards, we seem to be dealing with the Rectory's elusive nun, Marie Lairre, although the results here are vague and non-committal.

We now turn to the last seance session of which a record survices in the micro-film copy of the Locked Book. This took place on the night of November 20th and 21st, 1937,. at the Rectory, and was attended by Dr. H. F. Bellamy, H. G. Harrison, Sidney Glanville and Roger Glanville. The results proceeded as follows:

651. Q Is anyone there? (Marked
    tipping).
    A no reply.

652. Q Who is there?
    A indistinct reply.

653. Q Please try again.
    A no reply.

654. Q Can we speak to Harry Bull?
    A no reply.

655. Q Is Harry there?
    A Yes.

656. Q Please try again.
    A indistinct reply.

657. Q Is it Harry?
    A Yes.

658. Q Will you tap, to show your
    presence, at 10 o'clock on
    your bedroom door?
    A Yes ('Y' reversed, 'es'
    upturned).

659. Q Who ordered that the
    window should be bricked
    up?
    A Henry.

660. Q Why?
    A Nun.

661. Q Do you know of the finding
    of the skull in the library
    cupboard?
    A Yes.

662. Q Whose skull is it, do you know?
    A no reply.

663. Q From where did it come?
    A B . . . (then indistinct).

664. Q Would you write each letter
    separately?
    A B.U.R.E.S. (written upside
    down).

665. Q Do you know that the
    windows here light up?
    A Yes.

666. Q Can you tell us who does it?
    A Ma . . .

667. Q Separate letters please.
    A MarieLa . . .

668. Q Do you mean Marie Lairre?
    A indistinct reply.

669. Q Please try again.
    A Yes.

670. Q Is that the nun?
A Yes.

671. Q Will the windows light
tonight?
A Yes.

672. Q What time?
A 12.

673. Q Which window?
A S.C.H.O.O.L.R.O.O.M.

674. Q Can you use this board? (Dr.
Bellamy's board now in use.)
A Yes.

675. Q Thank you. Shall we see the
window alight?
A Ye . . .

676. Q Who is there?
A Henry.

677. Q Is this room a tragic one for
you? (referring to the
library).
A indistinct reply.

678. Q Will you please try again?
A V.

679. Q Was a woman the cause?
A Yes.

680. Q What was her name?
A Katie . . . (then indistinct).

681. Q We do not understand,
please repeat.
A indistinct reply.

We have now reached the point where
we can stand back from the seances and
assess their role and any possible value in
the overall story of the Rectory and the
many stories and theories about its existence and its past.

Remembering the dictum of not rely-
ing on seance material without other
more credible evidence, it is interesting
to look at the results in the light of information that has come from public records,
which the writer is still convinced goes a
long way towards demonstrating that
there is and was a lot more to the story of
Borley Rectory. Those same public records
to which the writer has just referred, in
many cases reveal that Price was so often
closer to the truth of things than he himself could have known, but it should be
remembered that Price was a psychic researcher, not a historical student.

It is not unreasonable therefore to suggest that had he taken the historical
aspects of the case further, he might well
have been able to assemble more readily
provable material in an addition to his
own work. In reality, perhaps the biggest
tragedy of the story of the Borley investigations was Price's untimely death in
1948. Had he lived to commence his
planned third Borley monograph, he
might have properly capped the story
from a historical point of view.

When we turn to the matter of Katie
Boreham whose possible role in the story
of the Rectory has so often been ignored
by the ciritics, one only has to set the
seance results that seem to relate to her,
against what has been discovered from
public records and from professional
medical opinion, to see that many of the
responses gained by the sitters at Borley
Rectory justify themselves. Nevertheless,
it should be borne in mind that by no
means all of the theories about Katie can
be proved conclusively.

Similarly, there are clear indications in
the seance results of the closeness to what
has been discovered in public archives in
respect of the lives of the two Bull rectors,
Henry and Harry. The evidence of Henry
Bull's death from a syphilis-related disease, and of his son's lack of impact on his
early clerical duties, and the obvious 'atmosphere' in the family over Harry's
marriage and his will, speak for themselves!

The one area where the seance results
tend to remain very much an unsolved
mystery is where they relate to the nun,
and the possibilities as to her true identity
and her ultimate fate.

It is curious that the contact from one
of the supposed entities, should so closely
resemble the name Joanne or Joanna,
curious also that Joanna proves to have
been a Waldegrave, Abbess Theodosia of
Brussels. Not only that but Sister Joanna
belongs to the same period in history as
the young woman supposedly murdered
at Borley in 1667. Only the fact that
Joanna lived after this date, stops her from
being one of the prime candidates for

being the Borley Nun. But when one looks at the association between the persecution of Sir Edward Waldegrave, and the existence of a great grand-daughter he was never to live to see, then one sees where a very likely possibility lies.

The question will probably always remain ... was Barbara Waldegrave, daughter of Sir Nicholas of Borley, the real Borley Nun, and if so, why did she haunt the site of the Rectory for so long?

In the matter of the fire that destroyed the Rectory in 1939, the seances were indeed prophetic, and yet they leave unanswered as many questions as they pose in this particular instance. To this day, it appears impossible to identify the true origin of 'Sunex Amures', with the one exception of the possibility that this could have been either Henry or Harry Bull . . . 'Senex Taurus' . . . Old Man Bull. If so, then the supposed entities that seemed to want someone to be there to see the truth revealed when the Rectory was destroyed, came closer than they knew to the episode of Katie Boreham, at which point

the name Senex Taurus would make sense, whereas Sunex Amures is a riddle! I am firmly of the opinion that the troubles of the Bull family and the fate of Katie Boreham, were part and parcel of the same episode!

It would be too much to expect a series of seances to provide the entire solution to the historical aspects of the Borley hauntings, and indeed not only did Harry Price warn of the dangers of taking seance material at face value, but he also openly stated that several of the Borley seance responses were wide of the mark against known facts.

However, the writer is very much of the opinion that among the clutter and make-weight of a lot of that material, there are indeed several very telling pointers to Borley Rectory's stormy history and that of the site on which it was built. It remains to be seen whether or not that proves to be all that we will ever discover from the spirits of those who occupied this seemingly troubled place in times past.

Borley today: the Rectory corner. The Rectory stood behind the decapitated trees. No trace now remains, *opposite above*.

Borley Parish Church. Disturbances have also been reported here, *opposite below*.

CHAPTER TWENTY-FOUR

SOME VIEWS FROM CONTEMPORARIES

In compiling this work about the enigma of Borley Rectory, I felt that some opinions about the story were worth seeking from some of those people who had were already familiar and knowledgeable with it. One person who has been in direct contact with almost everything pertaining to Borley Rectory for many years was Mr Alan H. Wesencraft, head of the Harry Price Library at the London University, and in whose capable hands has rested the care of Price's books and files since 1956, when he took over from the previous librarian. Oddly enough, Mr Wesencraft's views upon the Borley case have really never been published, except for a brief comment in the Hastings report, and so I asked him for his own thoughts upon the Borley saga. He writes (10th June, 1985):

"I first met Harry Price in 1937 when he was negotiating for the acceptance by the University of his gift of his superb library. He used to come to see Mr Rye, the Librarian, and while waiting in the corridor of the University building at South Kensington, he would often talk to me about his work. I can't remember very much but my impression is that he was sincere, devoted to his work and liked to talk about it to anyone who cared to listen. I do remember that the told me that *Psychic News* was by far the best of the Spiritualist journals.

When World War II came, I was out of touch with the University for seven long years, i.e. two years in full time Civil Defence, five years in the Army. I had heard of his success with the Borley Rectory haunts but unfortunately never met Mr Price after the war, for he died in 1948.

Of course I had read all Price's books

which came out before the war and many of his magazine articles, but it was not until I was appointed Curator of the Harry Price Library in 1956 that I started to read all the rest of his works. Borley Rectory fascinated me (as indeed it does everybody) and I thought the story and Price's presentation of it had a certain ring of truth. On studying the enormous Borley dossier in the H.P.L., I realised that a case could be made against Price on the grounds of exaggeration and possible distortion of evidence. For example, he admits in a letter to a friend that Mrs Foyster was probably faking some of the phenomena, but this is not mentioned in his books. The criticism of Price's books on Borley which was published by the Society for Psychical Research in 1956 is very much a case for the prosecution and needed a suitable rejoinder and this was provided by the excellent study by Mr Hastings some years later also published by the S.P.R.

I met Mr Hastings who worked for a time in the H.P.L. and during the many conversations I had with him I came to realise there was much to be said on Mr Price's behalf. Mr Hastings' report did indeed redress the balance and I realised that the Borley story cannot be dismissed as a journalistic stunt. Many people have reached the same conclusion.

For example, Mr James Turner, who lived for a time in the coachman's cottage adjacent to the ruined rectory assured me there was definitely something very mysterious about the place. I have discussed the matter with him and also with Mr Peter Underwood who is of the same opinion.

I may add I have visited Borley on

Sidney Glanville's locked book of information on Borley, now in the United States, *opposite above.*
Trevor Hall at Glanville's house, Fittleworth. Co-author of the 1956 Critique of Borley, *opposite below.*

many occasions and have succumbed to its charm though I have never experienced any psychic manifestations there, apart from the extraordinary stillness which pervades the location."

That, then is Mr A. H. Wesencraft's view of the Borley story and Price's role in it. There are one or two points the present writer would make by way of addition.

There is evidence to suggest, especially with regard to some of the accusations of exaggeration against Price, that some of these errors occurred through his writing some of the text of his books from memory, and indeed, Robert J. Hastings points out in his report that Price was inclined to a certain carelessness in his writing. It is worth remembering, however, that at one stage Price was also without a secretary who could have checked his files for him.

Mr Wesencraft's point about the Foyster phenomena can really be fairly satisfactorily explained by the change in Price's view of Marianne as a result of the findings of his chief associate, Sidney Glanville. At the time of the wine-into-ink episode, Price felt that Marianne Foyster was indeed faking phenomena. That was in 1931. By 1939 he had received Sidney Glanville's findings which gradually caused him to change his opinion of Marianne and this had, of course, a considerable bearing on the way in which he eventually presented the Foyster period in his later book.

Another view of the Borley story is offered by one of the co-authors of the book on the more recent and well-known Enfield Poltergeist case, Mr Guy Lyon Playfair, who kindly agreed to contribute a précis of his thoughts on the Borley Rectory episode and Harry Price's role therein. Mr Playfair writes:

"The Borley saga is a classic instance of the great difficulty in researching any field of the so-called paranormal. Vigorously defended by Harry Price, equally vigorously attacked by Dingwall, Goldney and Hall, what is the jury member to decide?

For my part, I feel fairly certain that odd things went on in Borley Rectory; that neither Price nor his detractors gave a wholly truthful account of the case; and that the true facts will never be known.

I am perhaps slightly biased against Price, having often discussed him with the late Dr. Dingwall, who knew him well. There can be no doubt that Price was (a) a brilliant writer, whose talent I envy, and (b) far more interested in self-promotion than in serious psychical research. As a member of the S.P.R., I feel that Price let the side down.

On the other hand, I also feel sympathy with him. It has all happened to me. When Maurice Grosse and I spent more than a year in 1977–78 on the Enfield poltergeist case, we felt we were making history by being the first psychical researchers to get in on the start of a case of this kind and stick with it until the finish, as we did.

We did not expect Nobel Prizes, but we thought at least that our work would be received with rather more enthusiasm than it was, to put it politely. We both learned that the sure way to become very unpopular in psychic research circles is to present uncompromisingly positive evidence for the subject we are supposed to be researching.

Borley was, I think, haunted. I only wish I could be sure."

In a way, Mr Playfair is asking the same question as has already been asked so many times before: Did Price fake at Borley, and if so, how much did he invent, and how much was true?

On the strength of the Hastings Report alone, there really is no proof whatsoever that Price ever did commit fraud over the matter of Borley Rectory.

Another interesting point raised by Mr Playfair is that pertaining to Price's thirst for publicity. It was this aspect of Price's long and controversial career that earned him so many brickbats, but as the writer pondered in a letter replying to Mr Playfair, how much of this was really self-centred on Price's part, and how much of it was allied to Price's aim of trying to attract general public interest in psychic research as a principle? There is much evidence to suggest that Price became infuriated with the obstinacy of the psychic research 'establishment' of the day, and judging from the experience of Mr Playfair and his colleague, little has changed since Price's time, so far as 'establishment' attitudes are concerned.

In replying to Mr Playfair I made the following observation: 'That when a man like Price comes along with a case like Borley, or Helen Duncan or Rudi Schneider, there is a great deal of sour grapes on the part of those who profess to be criticising such cases on their merits, when what they are really trying to say is that they wish they could have got there first!'

Price has been posthumously hounded over Borley Rectory for some thirty years, if we take the 1956 attack as a starting point, and the record of the rest of psychic research establishment where Borley is concerned is, with some exceptions, not particularly credible.

During my researches I have come across one item in particular, concerning the 1956 allegations against Price, which to my way of thinking tells very much in Price's favour. Just before the 1956 report was due to be published, a gentleman obviously aware of the line the report was going to take, wrote in a psychic periodical, *Tomorrow Magazine*, concerning the then forthcoming attack on Price. The article was by Nandor Fodor, and in it he denounced the idea that Price's involvement in the Borley episode was fraudulent, on the basis of his own personal knowledge of Price's work and methods. The telling point was that far from being a close friend of Price, and therefore trying to back him up out of a sense of loyalty, Fodor stated quite bluntly that he couldn't stand Price 'as a person'. It is the writer's considered opinion that much of the criticism against Price from various quarters, was made against a background of personalities, and therefore Fodor's contribution to the row seems to have demonstrated the principal that a defence of the work of a person one

disliked was of rather more value than an attack on the work of a person one disliked! Considering the results of the Hastings Report of 1969, which largely cleared Price of most of the allegations against him, Nandor Fodor's defence of Price's handling of Borley Rectory proved to be prophetic.

We pass now to an excellent appraisal of the Borley case and Price's role in it, supplied by Dr. Vernon Harrison, a member of the S.P.R. In my opinion Dr. Harrison encapsulates the very essence of Price at Borley simply and even-handedly. He writes as follows:

"I cannot say that I knew Price. He was 31 years my senior and at the time of the Borley investigations I was still a student. However, I did meet him, speak to him and hear him speak on a number of occasions at pre-war meetings of the Ghost Club from the beginning of 1937 until the 'Blitz' put an end to further meetings. Price was not a good speaker, but he was an enthusiastic chairman who did not attempt to dominate the discussion. He engaged good and often well-known speakers, and the meetings over which he presided were not only socially enjoyable, they were also highly informative. From them I learned a good deal.

Price was not a trained scientist. He was a businessman, journalist and publicist by inclination, and an entrepreneur. He loved a good story; and in the narration of such stories, scientific exactitude could suffer. He could be tetchy and vindictive. He could jump to false conclusions. However, these defects do not, in my experience, make him unique among successful businessmen. On the credit side, his knowledge of psychical research, magic and sleight of hand was formidable, he had collected one of the finest libraries on these subjects to be found anywhere, and he brought to his studies unbounded energy and enthusiasm. He was one of the few doing experimental work on physical mediums with the most up to date techniques available, at a time when most psychical researchers were content to sit back and criticise.

I do not think that Price invented the Borley phenomena for the purpose of publicity. The records show that there were disturbances at Borley long before Price became interested in the case, and they continued after his death. Nor do I find very credible the claim that Price produced some of the phenomena himself. At pre-war meetings of the Ghost Club I had an opportunity of speaking to a few of the observers who had been present at the Borley vigils and they told me from their experience that it was a 'strange place'. Therefore I am of the opinion that Price presented the Borley case in good faith, though his accounts may not be wholly accurate.

Price had Borley under observation for about a year, and looking back now one can point to lost opportunities and questions left unanswered. However, it is important to bear in mind first that Price did more than most of his contemporaries and that without his efforts, it is unlikely that anyone would have heard of Borley, and secondly there are limits to what can be asked of voluntary, unpaid investigators working at their own expense. Criticism is cheap and easy. Investigation is not."

It is interesting to note Dr. Harrison's remark that Price had Borley under observation for about a year, which is of course quite correct in itself, but at the same time, it reminds one that the key to so much of the criticism of Price over the matter of Borley Rectory lies in the fact that so many of his critics forget that the observer team period was only one part of an overall investigation by Harry Price that lasted for some seventeen years or so, and therefore, to judge Price solely by that one year from 1937 to 1938 is to do him a disservice, whatever one thinks of the Borley case as a whole.

From Dr. Vernon Harrison, we pass on now to the view of another member of the S.P.R., Andrew MacKenzie. Mr MacKenzie generally takes the opposing view of Price at Borley, and he writes as follows:

"In my opinion, after carrying out the investigation of literally hundreds of spontaneous cases, including many of hauntings, Borley Rectory provides an example of how an investigation should *not* be carried out. Mr Price issued an invitation to investigators to come to the Rectory and report their findings to him. I have in front of me as I write a copy of his Instructions for Observers with, under the phrase, 'Possible phenomena which may be experienced', a list of such phenomena as bell-ringing, movement of objects, footsteps, forms or apparitions, raps or knocks, perfumes, lights, apports, disappearances, and thermal variations. Such a list could have the effect of suggesting to the visitor that happenings of the kind listed could be expected and, as a result of suggestion, they might well be reported by anyone of a nervous disposition.

It would have been far better, in my opinion, to have asked the investigator to report anything of an unusual nature, without specifying what form it might take. Critics of spontaneous cases are inclined to dismiss accounts of hauntings on the grounds that the sights and sounds experienced are the results of suggestion. As Dr. (now Professor) D. J. West pointed out in *Psychical Research Today* (London, 1954) 'Once a place has achieved a really good reputation for haunting, more and more susceptible persons will see things there, and odd events and coincidences that would in the normal way pass unnoticed will be attributed to ghosts.' Incidentally, Dr. West, a former experimental research officer to The Society for Psychical Research, said in the book from which I have just quoted that Mr Price's books on Borley Rectory were 'highly misleading' (page 123).

For some forty years Professor F. J. M. Stratton, a noted astronomer who was President of the S.P.R. from 1953 to 1955, was keenly interested in stories of alleged happenings at Abbey House, Abbey road, Cambridge. After his death in 1961 his file on Abbey House was passed to the Society with a few small additions by Professor C. D. Broad. Stratton believed that publication of the stories about Abbey House might contaminate the testimony of possible future witnesses and the first reliable report of the haunting, by Dr. Alan Gauld, did not appear until 1972. It is a great pity that Harry Price did not observe Professor Stratton's reticence while the haunting of Borley Rectory, if such it was, was in progress."

Once again, Price is being criticised on the basis of only one period in his overall coverage of the Borley story, whereas he should be judged on the whole case, beginning with his first period of involvement that began in June 1929. The matter of the book of instructions for his team of observers is, and probably always will be, open to question, as the writer explained in an earlier chapter.

Mr MacKenzie's point about pre-suggestion is fair enough, and yet if one asked a team of investigators to simply report 'anything of an unusual nature', one can easily forsee the investigators' response, 'What exactly are we supposed to be looking for?' I would suggest that failure to give the investigator *any* specific information as to what was to be watched or listened for could hamper the effectiveness of the investigation just as much as to give too much prior information. In addition, it does seem that in the case of the rota of observers assigned to Borley Rectory, to give them no specific prior information would be, to some extent, a misjudgement of their potential objectivity. Those who worked at Borley on Price's behalf were not of a particularly gullible or unquestioning disposition, far from it, one needs only to look at the work of men such as Sidney Glanville to see that!

Price's team were not by any means unanimous in a belief in the Rectory's validity as a haunted house. The writer feels he must echo Dr. Harrison's point that Price, whatever one might think of the way in which he administered his investigations, was actually getting on with the job, whilst so many others just sat back and criticised! In the last analysis, surely it must come down to a matter of individual judgement on the part of an organising investigator. It is very easy to be wise after the event!

Another point made by Mr MacKenzie is also open somewhat to debate, and that is the contention that Harry Price's Borley books were very misleading. From a purely academic point of view, one can criticise some aspects of the way Price presented the Borley case in his books, but some may feel in the light of Robert Hastings's assessment of the case, that the charge of there being highly misleading, is perhaps slightly unjust. The writer must reiterate one very important point made by Hastings, namely that the basis for the hauntings at Borley Rectory was not Price's books but his *files!* Those files depended very largely upon others for their content, and in that respect, Price was a collector of data, not the producer of it. What he did produce was his assessment of what that data revealed.

We turn now to an assessment of the Borley Rectory story from the man who has become, in my opinion, Harry Price's natural successor in the long history of Borley investigations, Peter Underwood, who has held a continual interest in the case since the late forties. Mr Underwood has contributed some notes extracted from two of his own publications, *The Ghost Hunters* and *Hauntings*:

"In 1929 Harry Price paid his first visit to Borley Rectory – already famous as 'The most haunted house in England'. The Borley case has fascinated many people, it fascinated Price and he never ceased to be interested in the case for the rest of his life. At one period he organised a rota of investigators, 'responsible, critical and unbiased'; he took reams of notes, wrote hundreds of letters, collected scores of letters, plans and miscellania connected with the haunted rectory and its five successive incumbents and their families, all of whom asserted that they heard, saw and felt things they could not explain. Eight years after his death Price's published findings on the case were attacked by three members of the S.P.R.; subsequently the Society approved a grant to another member who produced a Report that completely vindicated Price, but such is the nature of psychical researchers that the wrangling goes on to this day.

The ghosts of Borley seem to either fascinate or repel most of those who study the case and for every person who seeks to dismiss the ghosts for one reason or another, there are a thousand who avidly read the books, study the evidence, discuss the pros and cons and as likely as not visit the site with notebook and camera, seeking to rebuild in their minds the gloomy, red-brick house on the hill that seems to have been the scene of much human misery and some human happiness and to have housed so many strange people that no one could find peace there.

More than forty years have passed since I first visited Borley, spending a night on the site where the great cellars still gaped at the wide skies and the outline of the vanished rectory was still easily discernible. Since then I have lost count of my visits – to carry out research and investigation, to visit successive owners of the site who had become friends, to call on the various incumbents or local people I had come to know, to make a film or take part in a television or radio programme, to lead a party of Ghost Club members, or simply to enjoy the peace of this pleasant corner of Essex with its delightful church – and always there are the inevitable memories of the past, the intrigue and the ghosts.

Over the years since 1945 I have been fortunate enough to have personally contacted practically every person who has been connected with the Borley hauntings including the suriviving Bulls and Foysters, the Hennings, the Turners, Edwin Whitehouse, the Glanvilles, Mollie Goldney, Eric John Dingwall, Robert Hastings, Trevor Hall, John Pythian Adams, Constance Price, the Paynes, Mrs Mabel Smith, Marianne Foyster (her last letter to me is dated 15th September, 1986) and many more. My extensive files on this strange case (including much confidential material) and the hundreds of photographs in my possession must be unique and thought-provoking for the greatest sceptic.

What is the answer to the mysteries of Borley? Some of the hundreds of reports of curious happenings can certainly be dismissed; perhaps some of the recorded noises have perfectly normal explanations; perhaps some of the alleged sightings of the ghost nun are the result of inaccurate observation, imagination or wishful thinking. But it does seem to me that of all the celebrated cases of haunting that are available for study this remarkable and lengthy story has so many unaswerable problems, innumerable puzzles and strange incidents reported by responsible, independent, unbiased, sane and sensible witnesses that it stands alone in the annals of psychical research as a continuing problem for the materialist and an exciting challenge for the psychical researcher."

Peter Underwood's view of the Borley case echoes many people's thoughts on the subject, and it also confirms Mr A. H. Wesencraft's contention that the story cannot just be written off as a journalistic stunt. Moreover, the reader should note that this view of Borley and its extra-ordinary rectory is put forward by a man who has stated that in his view ninety-eight per cent of the supposedly paranormal phenomena have a mundane origin, and that he has spent much of his life examining the two per cent that do not! Borley Rectory, in spite of all the abuse heaped upon its history by the critics, is in my view very much part of that undismissable two per cent!

Now, to conclude this chapter of contemporaries and their views, we turn finally to Mr Richard Lee van den Daele, of Yorkshire, who is to be thanked for his valuable contributions to the unearthing of the probable truth concerning Captain Gregson and the fire. He has been researching the writings of Harry Price for some time, from a librarian's side of the fence, and like almost all of us who become involved with research into the

Borley story, he has become fascinated by the episode and its many ramifications. He writes as follows:

"In my opinion, Harry Price's years of painstaking work on the haunting of Borley Rectory was undone in a frenzied and shameful free-for-all following his untimely death in 1948.

Critics, too unsure of their facts to tackle Price whilst he was still in a position to sue them, crept out of the woodwork en masse to malign and attempt to discredit his decade of diligent work. From literary rivals to scurrilous journalists, all had their knives out for him and especially for the jewel in his crown – the Haunting of Borley Rectory. But perhaps Price's most ardent supporter over the years, has turned out to be Borley itself. It doesn't seem to matter how much invective critics pour upon the story – it gets right back up and regains its rightful place amongst Britain's truly fascinating hauntings.

Ever since the fire of 1939, and the Rectory's subsequent demolition, the story has never been far from the public's heart. Innumerable people have experienced abnormal happenings in Borley: and that includes my brother and his own intrepid band of investigators.

In July 1984, he and his friends from his university stayed at Borley for two days. They slept, rather courageously, in the church porch and were fascinated by the sibilant whisperings they heard.
1   They arranged to visit again, this time going fully equipped with a professional studio-quality tape deck and multi-directional microphones. The microphone, on the first night, was placed through a broken window (vandals plague Borley) at the rear of the building.

The microphone was bound to a long pole, and this extended reach enabled them to put the mike in close proximity to the altar.

They monitored the recordings through headphones and kept a detailed log of events. Bangs, rustlings, clicks, buzzing and a strange build-up of static almost as if an electrical field were forming – all added to the night's adventure.

The following day they placed the microphone, on a stand, right on the altar itself. The church doors were then locked at dusk (the church being empty) and the recordings were monitored again, this time in the porch. In the early hours of the morning, my brother (who was taking his turn at the headphones) heard an incredible noise. A hissing, semi-audible incantation was being recited! The voice was loud enough to be heard, though not clear enough for the words to become distinct. It was certainly the most frightening event in two very weird nights observation.

Price, however, was not the only person to be maligned following events at the 'Most Haunted House in England'. Captain W. H. Gregson, the last owner of Borley Rectory was condemned by William Crocker and Colonel Cuthbert Buckle as a 'man of straw'. Crocker and Buckle were the lawyer and loss adjuster working for Gregson's insurance company. It is not difficult to see why these two men should be at pains to repudiate any claim for genuine loss.

However, after months of investigative research, I managed to track down Captain Gregson's two livings sons – who inhabited the Rectory cottage with him during his ownership. Alan Gregson, now living on the other side of the world, recalls in astonishing detail the period he spent at Borley. Of the night of the fire, he writes:

'A great deal of furniture was stacked in the entrance hall and stairwell temporarily . . . my father wanted a book or document from the Rectory – apparently he stood a lamp on a table or box while he rummaged about, and then a stack of books suddenly keeled over onto the lamp, overturning it, breaking the glass and spilling kerosene which then caught light and speedily ignited surrounding articles.'

In his letters to me, Alan Gregson comes across as a man of great integrity and also one with an immense memory capable of remembering minute details from over fifty years ago.

He also recalled observing the iron-rimmed tracks of some form of, presumably, horse-drawn conveyance – in a part of the garden that was accessible by nothing larger than a wheelbarrow! The tracks stood out crisply in the freshly fallen snow – and certainly brings to mind the traditional coach and four which come speeding across the Rectory's front lawn.

Borley is now a village without the Rectory that has given it a world-famous reputation. But I and many others, still come to the conclusion that it holds the title of the 'Most Haunted Village in England' . . . and the story goes on."

A particularly interesting feature of Richard Lee van den Daele's assessment of the Borley case, lies in the experiences of his brother's investigation group, whose strange results reveal an apparent continuity in the extraordinary story, these days almost always reported in connection with the church, rather than what is left of the site of the Rectory across the road.

The matter of Gregson and the fire is interesting, but as the reader will recall, it seems that in the very differences between the two sons' versions of what happened that night, there lies a clue as to the probable true course of events. I would broadly agree with Richard's assessment of the veracity of Alan Gregson, because if he was sent off the premises to call the fire brigade, he would probably have little reason then to question his father's version of events. The doubts about the other son are covered in the fire chapter, but when one puts the two versions together, one gets an all too clear image of what almost certainly happened!

CHAPTER TWENTY-FIVE

A RESUMÉ OF SOME 50 YEARS OF BORLEY CHRONICLES

The author feels that the long and curious saga of Borley Rectory and the controversy that has surrounded it, warrants some attention to the various chronicles that have been published over the years, particularly for the benefit of those of the younger generation who today may find it hard to locate copies of relevant books and documents.

It seems only right, I feel, to give the reader some examples of what they will discover if they should choose to investigate on their own accord.

Among early reports of the disturbances at Borley Rectory was that in the *Daily Mirror* for June 10th, 1929, by Mr V. C. Wall, which was indirectly the result of the Rev. Guy Smith's appeal for an investigation of the incidents. The article was, inevitably, embroidered, and it suggested among other things that the Smiths had moved into the Rectory *in spite of warnings* about its reputation.

In 1936 came the publication of Harry Price's book, *Confessions of a Ghost Hunter,* and in it were references to Borley. These reflected Price's then rather unfavourable views of some of the phenomena he had witnessed there during his visit in 1931, a view which he altered after the work of his chief associate Sidney Glanville, and particularly after having learned of the experiences of Sir George and Lady Whitehouse during their visits at the time of the Foyster tenancy. The same book did, however, include a favourable opinion of earlier phenomena.

It was the publication in 1940 of the first full volume about Borley, Harry Price's *The Most Haunted House in England,* that turned the story of Borley Rectory into what was to become a classic among English mysteries. It does, as Mr A. H. Wesencraft explains in his notes about

the case, have a ring of truth about it, in spite of all the ill-judged criticism and abuse that has been heaped upon it since.

Seeming to ignore war-time conditions, Price had hoped that a second edition of it would be published but this did not materialise for a long time. Furthermore, he was more than a little disappointed at the time with the relatively low number of copies that were printed, both in this country and in the United States.

The publication in 1946 of the sequel, *The End of Borley Rectory,* made up for the lack of a second edition, but it was of a rather more technical nature. It did, however, enable Price to bring up to date the story of the Rectory after the fire of 1939, and it also contained the details of the Cambridge Commission's wartime investigations of the ruined Rectory, and also details the excavations carried out mainly by a local man, Mr Jackson, on behalf of Price, in 1943. It was on that occasion of course that they unearthed the jawbone and skull fragments that were to cause such a row in later years. The work also contained several previously unpublished photographs, which generally were of a better quality and giving clearer detail.

Other interesting contents in the *End of Borley Rectory* included the scenario by Canon Pythian Adams concerning the supposed identity of the spectral nun that haunted the grounds of the Rectory, almost from the time it was first occupied. Also in the book in the form of various footnotes, were the remarks by a local historian, Mrs Georgina Dawson, about the one time existence of a priory close by the River Stour, with land that butted onto Borley's parish boundaries, ideas that have since revealed themselves to be basically true.

At the time of his death in 1948, Harry Price had been planning to produce a third book on the subject of Borley Rectory, but the idea was abandoned in the years after his death. When a third book on Borley did appear, in 1956, it resulted in the unleashing of a tide of criticism on the work of Price. *The Haunting of Borley Rectory*, by Eric J. Dingwall, K. M. Goldney and T. H. Hall was published by Duckworths and also appeared in the proceedings of the Society for Psychical Research under whose auspices the investigations were carried out.

In this, the whole fabric of the Borley story and Price's role in it, was attacked as being a fraud, the exposure being penned in such a way as to give the impression that Price was a cheat and the Borley story an exaggerated concoction.

The authors accused Price of duplicity in his relationship with Lionel and Marianne Foyster over his presentation of the Foyster phenomena; of fraud with respect to an incident alleged to have occurred in the presence of a national journalist; of having planted evidence, misled and exaggerated. The evidence upon which these accusations were founded, now shows itself to be invalid because, amongst other things, it relied upon statements from people who were openly hostile to Harry Price, or whose memories on the subject were fallible to say the least. Among those whose views were quoted, or more often, misquoted, in *The Haunting of Borley Rectory*, was the late Lord Charles Hope, who, it was claimed, viewed Price as a rascal. His thoughts, however, carry somewhat less weight when one learns that at the time of the experiments with the young Austrian medium Rudi Schneider, whom Price had brought to London under his auspices, Lord Charles Hope took it upon himself to arrange his own private session with Rudi without consulting Price. In the resulting row between himself and Lord Charles Hope, it was a miracle that the two men did not come to blows. Bad feeling persisted between these two men from then on. Under those circumstances, for the

authors of *The Haunting of Borley Rectory* to have accepted and repeated Lord Charles Hope's opinions of Price without a great deal of caution constituted, I believe, a grave disservice to the late Harry Price himself.

The failings of memories of Borley, insofar as they were reflected in the presentation of *The Haunting of Borley Rectory*, were most graphically illustrated by the evidence of Mrs Mabel Smith, widow of the late Rev. Guy Smith, the Rectory of Borley at the time when Price began his investigation. The three 1956 writers set great store by her post-war dismissals of the Borley saga as being 'superstition and nonsense', and her very unfavourable views then of Harry Price. Her evidence formed a considerable part of the 1956 allegations. However, when one comes to read Hastings on the subject, and also looks more closely at the background to the Smith period, one discovers something more akin to the truth of things. For Mabel Smith, their stay at Borley was a very unpleasant experience, the negative aspects of which were later exacerbated by the loss of her husband in 1940, which seems to have quite broken her spirit.

The point here is that, as with the views of Lord Charles Hope, given Mabel Smith's general emotional state after the war, to have accepted her views at face value was as unwise as accepting the views of Lord Charles Hope or somebody like Marianne Foyster at face value.

The authors of 1956 made other blunders. One of their assertions was that Dom Richard Whitehouse had got most of his evidence for what he reported of the events at Borley Rectory, from Marianne Foyster. Peter Underwood tells us in his contribution to the Hastings report, when interviewed at Ramsgate following publication of the 1956 allegations, Whitehouse dismissed this allegation as rubbish, stating emphatically that he had kept his own notes about what he had witnessed.

Another example of the apparent carelessness in the 1956 allegations came surprisingly from Mrs K. M. Goldney, when it was stated that Dom Richard was suffering from the results of a nervous breakdown during his sojourn at Borley. Whitehouse replied to this by stating that Mrs Goldney obviously did not realise that his illness had occurred several years *before* he became involved in the Borley episode. The writer uses the word 'surprisingly' about this error because Mrs Goldney has long had a reputation for being very thorough and very meticulous in her work on paranormal matters.

Dingwall and Goldney were for many years close colleagues of Harry Price and Mrs Goldney had for some time served on his Council of Psychical Research. Generally opinion would seem to indicate that they had a fairly high regard for Price. Bearing that in mind, it is something of a puzzle as to why they should have been party to such an attack on him after his death.

In my opinion, the answer lies in the contribution of the third member of the 1956 trio, Dr. T. H. Hall, a former member of the Society of Psychical Research.

According to his own version of events, as he related in his book *New Light on Old Ghosts,* Hall wrote four of the chapters on *The Haunting of Borley Rectory.* Consequently, and in the light of what I have been able to discover about his work, Hall must take a large share of the responsibility for the causing of much of the unjust damage to Price's reputation in connection with Borley Rectory.

Trevor Hall, who had a lengthy entry in *Who's Who* and refers to himself as Dr. Hall, was an estate agent who has produced numerous books over the years. Unfortunately, it has to be revealed that at least where Harry Price and Borley Rectory are concerned, his various attacks on Price rest upon a very weak foundation. T. H. Hall was for a time a Perrot student at Cambridge but there have been doubts expressed as to his true academic background. Among other qualifications he applied for a Litt D from Leeds University, but was turned down.

The Search for Harry Price was a solo work by Hall and it appeared in 1978 from Duckworth. It constituted an outright attack on Price and ultimately led to a break between Dr. E. J. Dingwall and Hall and some have described its style as 'malicious'.

Hall apparently came into contact with Dr. E. J. Dingwall through a meeting of the Magic Circle, but so far as his involvement in the 1956 report is concerned I strongly suspect that in what may have been some genuine misgivings about Borley on the part of Dr. Dingwall and Mrs Goldney, Hall saw a shining opportunity for himself in the literary world.

I did in fact contact Dr. Dingwall and requested his present day views on Borley particularly in the light of the Hastings report. His response was that his views had not changed since that report and his colleagues' reply to it.

In the case of T. H. Hall, the reader may feel that I have been unduly hard in dealing with his role in the story, but when one considers the background to his literary work, one realises that his approach is such as to make it difficult to produce an impartial judgement on Harry Price and Borley Rectory. The writer did write to Hall, giving him a chance to defend his views, but his reply showed him more interested in the fact that he couldn't find my name in *Who's Who*, and promoting his book *The Search for Harry Price* as the last word on the subject.

The late Robert J. Hastings was given the brief of re-examining the 1956 report, and on behalf of the S.P.R. a grant was made in aid of expenses. The results of his efforts culminated in an extensive and thoroughgoing dissection of most of the major accusations against Harry Price, but the tragedy of this work was that although it was published by the S.P.R. in their own journals and proceedings, it was never released for general commercial publication.

If ever there *was* a case for the commercial publication of a specialist report, then the 1969 reappraisal of Borley by Hastings would be just such a case. Even at this late stage, I would suggest that some consideration could be given to the possible publication of the Hastings report in book form, to balance the effects of the 1956 report.

Supposedly one of the most damaging accusations against Harry Price at Borley Rectory concerns the claim made by a *Daily Mirror* reporter, Charles Sutton, that

Price had been caught perpetrating fake phenomena at the Rectory, including throwing stones to produce 'poltergeist' effects. This was looked at earlier and the statement made some twenty years after the supposed event by Charles Sutton in the *Inky Way Annual* has also been quoted. As part of the work on the 1956 allegations, Sutton was asked to provide a resumé of his memories of the incident, and this he duly sent to the authors of *The Haunting of Borley Rectory*. Hastings tells us that Sutton's lengthy piece was omitted from *The Haunting of Borley Rectory*, though he *did* include the statement in *his* report, under Appendix A. Another interesting point revealed by Hastings is that in view of the shortcomings in Sutton's evidence, it was decided to re-interview Sutton to see if it could be clarified. Sutton was duly interviewed by Dr. Alan Gauld of the S.P.R., but the only thing that this clarified was that Sutton did *not* see Price throw any stones in Borley Rectory, nor did he or anyone else there at the time, see stones at all, save for the one stone or brick that, as now seems certain, somebody tripped over and sent crashing down the Rectory stairs. So, as Hastings demonstrates in his report, Charles Sutton could not properly substantiate his claim that he had caught Price cheating on the occasion in question. Yet relations between Sutton and Price after the supposed incident continued to be good. Such would not have been the case if Sutton had accused Price of fraud, surely?

Hastings also deals in his report with another of Sutton's allegations, that of hearing noises that he described as sounding like Price using a ventriloquist technique to produce 'ghostly voices'. Dr. Alan Gauld also tackled Sutton on this point, observing that the use of the ventriloquist technique relies on the misdirection of attention. The upshot of the whole episode was that Sutton claimed to have seized hold of Price with the intention of making him turn out his pockets, but as the Hastings report shows, from Gauld's interview of Sutton, the latter's evidence about even this was somewhat weak and contradictory.

Also described by Hastings was the ability of the Rectory to act as an amplifier to voices from people in the stable cottage, that stood behind the Rectory, though I would reiterate my reservations about this given the hefty and complicated structure of the Rectory. Price was unaware of such a phenomenon at the time of his early visits and it was apparently one of his team, Mr Burden, who later reported the Rectory's accoustic properties.

Robert Hastings' report also revealed that both of Price's former secretaries, Miss Kaye and Miss Beenham, gave testimony that was very much at odds with Mr Sutton's allegations, and which was in fact a sound defence of Price's conduct. Miss Kaye's testimony on pages 82 and 83 of the Hastings' report is very interesting and could be considered as essential reading for students of the Borley story.

The report also delves into the contradictory nature of the evidence of Mrs Mabel Smith, the late Guy Smith's widow. The beginnings of Mabel Smith's 'about-face' on Borley is quoted in the form of a letter she submitted to *The Church Times* in 1945.

"Sir,
        I have read with interest your articles and letters on 'Thump Ghosts', and as I was in residence for some time at Borley Rectory, Sussex ('the most haunted house in England'), I would like to state definitely that neither my husband nor myself believed the house haunted by anything else but rats and local superstition.
        We left the Rectory because of its broken-down condition, but certainly found nothing to fear there."

Hastings pointed out the error in placing Borley in Sussex, but did at the same time allow for the possibility of a printer's error.

Also quoted by Hastings was the Rev. Henning's expression of surprise at the contents of Mabel Smith's letter to *The Church Times*, a copy of which he duly forwarded to Harry Price with the following comments:

"I was astounded to read the enclosed

letter from Mrs Smith in *The Church Times*. There are still people in Borley who remember Mrs Smith showing them the mystery light and then taking them into the Rectory and finding no light in the room. It may be true that the Smiths did not leave because of the hauntings, but that they had no strange experiences is something new to me."

Hastings goes into considerable detail over the many variations between Mabel Smith's testimony and that of her husband. It is in this section that Mabel Smith's contrariness is most graphically demonstrated, and the whole section of the Hastings report makes fascinating reading.

Among many other aspects of the allegations re-examined by Hastings, there are the arguments about the medals found at Borley and some very telling points that directly contradict the accusations against Price over the bone fragments found in 1943. In fact, in the light of Hastings' findings, the accusations become rather weak, if not ridiculous.

Also dealt with are the misgivings expressed by Major Douglas Home over the discovery of a roll of cellophane among the contents of Price's ghost-hunting kit, which Home was convinced had been used to create a sound of a swishing garment during a vist to Borley Rectory at which he was present. Hastings argued with some force that there would have been perfectly legitimate reasons for the presence of the cellophane among Price's various bits and pieces. He also expressed the view that if Price had wanted to create fake phenomena by using cellophane, he would have cut off only what he needed before departing for the Rectory, rather than carry the whole roll in his case where it could be, and was, quickly discovered.

We must now press on to the next fully-fledged volume on Borley, *The Ghosts of Borley*, which was penned jointly by Peter Underwood and the late Dr. Paul Tabori, and was published by David and Charles in 1973.

This was a broadly based revisit to the Borley saga and in view of the fact that the 1956 *Haunting of Borley Rectory* shows itself to be somewhat unreliable, it is not unreasonable to view *The Ghosts of Borley* as a natural successor to *The End of Borley Rectory*. Among the most interesting contents of this volume are the details relating to the post war unearthing of the legendary tunnel and also the curious contradictions and oddities surrounding the enigmatic Marianne Foyster, upon which Peter Underwood has commented on various occasions. Also incorporated is a goodly sprinkling of curious events that have occurred on or near the site of Borley Rectory since the publication of *The End of Borley Rectory*, events that have involved people such as James Turner and his wife, who lived in the stable cottage from 1947 to 1950, and the Bacon family who came there afterwards.

It is in *The Ghosts of Borley* that more information comes to light about that odd character Francois d'Arles, or to give him his true name, Frank Charles Pearless, long believed to be French Canadian but revealed by the authors to be nothing of the sort!

After 1948, Dr. Paul Tabori became Price's literary executor and back in 1950, he published a biography of Price, which also contains a lengthy chapter on Borley Rectory. Dr. Paul Tabori is, alas, no longer with us, but Peter Underwood is very much alive and spends much of his time involved in research on mysteries of paranormal phenomena.

Over the years, there have been many newspaper and magazine articles on Borley Rectory, of varying interest and accuracy, ranging from the V. C. Wall article of June 1929 in the *Daily Mirror* to pieces in the *Suffolk Free Press*. Another curio from among those printed in the popular press is an article by Captain Gregson that appeared in *East Anglian Magazine* for 1939, and from which by kind permission of the magazine's owners, the photograph of the Captain has been reproduced in this volume.

Another fairly recent publication (1984) containing references to Borley was *Arthur C. Clarke's World of Strange Powers*, compiled by John Fairley and

Simon Welfare, a publication associated with a popular television series. In this book, published by Collins, the Borley episode is presented as having been exposed by the 1956 allegations. I tackled the writers on the subject of Borley Rectory and Harry Price's role in the episode, but whilst they acknowledged the Hastings report (not even mentioned in the book) in a reply from Simon Welfare, it was obvious that they too have fallen into the same trap as others, in particular by being impressed by the writings of T. H. Hall, the failings of whose work have already been discussed. In a further letter to Simon Welfare, I suggested that to fail to give their readers both sides of the Borley story was in itself a disservice to the late Harry Price, but regrettably it would seem that this may be another instance where a balanced presentation was subordinated to the interests of commercial popularity.

Even the inimitable *Readers' Digest* has had a brief flirtation with the Borley story, in particular in a volume entitled *Strange Stories - Amazing Facts*, in which, on page 410 among some details of the Rectory story, is a lovely photograph of the place, dating from its appearance from somewhere between 1900 and the First World War.

Most of the countless books and articles on Borley can be found in public libraries or the Harry Price Library. Readers of this work could do worse than to track down all these writings on the subject of Borley, and read them through for themselves.

We must now move on to other matters.

CHAPTER TWENTY-SIX

GLANVILLE'S LOCKED BOOK

T revor Hall, author of the strongly critical work *Search for Harry Price,* which seemed to be aimed at destroying Price's reputation and the value of his work at Borley, was at one time head of Leeds Library and, I believe, partly responsible for securing its future. He gained a remarkable record of research achievements yet, at the same time apparently had an unusual lack of ethics.

Compiled by Price's close associate, Sidney Glanville, the Locked Book, consisting of drawings, photos and records of seances at the Rectory, was given to Harry Price, who used much of the contents for his two major works on Borley. In fact, it was of such great value that Price said that if he ever lost all his notes on Borley, he could still have written a complete history of the case solely from the contents of the leather bound volume.

However, the Locked Book was eventually given by Glanville to Trevor Hall 'in appreciation' of his help and encouragement 'when the making of a restatement of the history of Borley Rectory' seemed beyond Glanville's capacity. A point of argument remains though, for Dr. H. P.

Pafford, the then curator of the Harry Price Library implied in 1959, that there was a strong suspicion that the Locked Book was removed from the library 'under debatable circumstances'. This feeling is echoed by Mr. Wesencraft, the current curator, who voiced his doubts to me about Hall's claim to the ownership and his right to eventually sell it to an American for over £1000.

Nevertheless Sidney Glanville's son, Roger, felt that the ownership rested with his father and understood that the gift to Hall was arranged during a lengthy meeting at his home. It must be remembered though that Dr. Pafford claimed that Sidney Glanville asked him if he could borrow the book from the library, implying that he, Glanville, felt the work was owned not by him but by the library, and was therefore, not his property to give to Hall.

The real ownership of the valuable record at the time it was sold, is a mute point, but it is certainly another example of conflict of interests, of possible theft and a further mystery to add to the Enigma of Borley.

CHAPTER TWENTY-SEVEN

IN CONCLUSION

The writer now has the none too easy task of summing up the story of Borley Rectory, as he sees it, through the eyes of a layman.

The writer has sought to retell the existing story of Borley Rectory for the benefit of newcomers to the episode, to tell the reader something of the many characters involved, and to reveal some of the contents of the lengthy report on the case by the late Robert J. Hastings, because it directly contradicted a view of the inaccurate story that had become fashionable.

Another major part of the present writer's aims in writing this book has been to take a fresh look at some of the fascinating stories that came to light about the Rectory, its past history and the site upon which it stood.

Borley Rectory was constructed for the Rev. Henry Dawson Ellis Bull in 1862-3 and was occupied by various members of the Bull family until 1927. The Rectory, built on the remains of at least two older buildings, stood on that site for some seventy six years as an intact structure, before being damaged beyond repair by the fire of February 1939. During that time, Borley Rectory, against a background of controversy that has rumbled on ever since, attained the reputation of being the most haunted house in England, and was ultimately viewed as being so by its chief investigator, the late Harry Price.

To simplify the matter of reaching a conclusion on Borley, the best way of dealing with this is to split the story up into the various elements that go to make up the whole. If we put all the elements of the episode into chronological order, they run more or less as follows:

1. The historical possibilities attached to stories about the past history of the Rectory site, including the matter of the monastery involvement, the story of Sir Edward Waldegrave, the matter of the nun, and role of each of these points in the possible historical causation of the hauntings at Borley Rectory.

2. The era of the Bull family, and aspects of their lives that seem to relate to additional possible causes of the hauntings at Borley Rectory.

3. The role of the Smiths and the Foysters in the overall picture.

4. The role of Harry Price in the investigations into Borley.

5. The role of Captain Gregson leading up to the fire of 1939.

We began with the popular belief that Borley Rectory stood on the site of an old monastery. This is not provable from historical records, but what is provable from historical records is that Sudbury Priory lay on the opposite bank of the River Stour, in sight of the parish of Borley, and it appears to have had access to woodland in Borley. We also know that this little Priory was in existence during the plague epidemics of the late 1340s, and that some monks may therefore have died there. It has long been suggested that the knoll upon which Borley Rectory was later built, was originally a plague burial pit, though there is no evidence to prove this. We also have clear evidence that part of Borley once belonged to Barking Monastery, and that the manor of Borley belonged to the monastery of Christchurch, Canterbury.

There remains the possibility that there may have been another monastic cell actually on the Rectory site, of which no remains or records have survived the centuries. Without documentary proof thereof, only very extensive excavation would provide an answer to that possiblity, but unless fresh information comes to hand, Sudbury Priory will remain the most likely origin of stories about a Borley monastery.

The next episode in Borley's history that the writer feels does suggest a cause for the hauntings at Borley Rectory is that connected with the life and downfall of Sir Edward Waldegrave because of the following points. Firstly, there is archaeological evidence that there was a brick building on the site during Tudor times. Secondly, Sir Edward Waldegrave was Lord of the Manor of Borley during the time of Henry VIII, and was, during that period, responsible for the provision and upkeep of a Rectory at Borley. Thirdly, Sir Edward was a Catholic, and this brought him into direct conflict with the Protestant church that was vigorously maintained under Elizabeth I. Sir Edward Waldegrave was arrested in 1561 on charges of heresy, but the writer has also discovered from public archives that against the background to his arrest, were plots to oust Queen Elizabeth I from the throne. Furthermore, Sir Edward now appears to have been betrayed by a fellow Catholic, himself a priest, and who in turn may well have been betrayed by a manservant in Sir Edward's employ. Following upon this, Waldegrave, still a devout Catholic, was ultimately buried in a Protestant grave. Some four centuries later, in Henry Bull's huge Victorian rectory, one of his daughters was disturbed by the figure of a man sitting on her bed. The figure was dressed in what she described as old fashioned costume and a tall hat! That suggests the sort of clothing commonplace during the time of Elizabeth I. It is on the basis of these facts that the writer suggests that the fate of Sir Edward Waldegrave constitutes a possible historical cause for hauntings at Borley Rectory.

From Sir Edward Waldegrave, we move on now to the story of the nun, which is probably the most elusive of all the characters linked to Borley Rectory. There are stories that she came from France, or that she tried to elope from Borley in a horsedrawn carriage during the 13th Century, but most of these stories when checked against known history, show themselves to be fascinating but fallacious. The long standing belief that the nun was connected with the Waldegraves is by no means so ridiculous. Historical archives, show that numerous daughters of the Waldegrave family were nuns, almost all of them with expatriate English orders in exile on the continent, at a time when such religious houses were banned from England. Furthermore, records show that two Waldegrave nuns came from Borley, being the daughters of Sir Nicholas Waldegrave of Borley. One of them, Barbara Appallonia Waldegrave, died in Brussels when only in her thirties.

There is a further source of interest in that a monk from the dissolved Clare Priory turns up twenty seven years later as Rector of Borley and that his former order, the Austin Friars, included at least one Waldegrave from a previous generation. One factor in all of this brings us back to the Waldegraves who came from Borley anyway and any candidate for the identity of the nun, must have a high probability of having come from Borley in the first place. Whatever the merits of the various theories about France or elsewhere, none of those answer the question as to why the figure of a nun should appear at Borley at all. When you have two Waldegrave nuns who were both born in that branch of the family, and when it is known for certain the cause of death of one of them (Jeronima . . . who died from consumption), the one who is left must surely be the most likely candidate. Although it may never be possible to prove that Barbara Waldegrave is the sad figure so often seen drifting about the grounds of Borley Rectory, is it not in the adventure of The Bruce Partington Plans that Holmes says to Watson, "When you have eliminated all other possibilities, what remains, however unlikely, must be the answer"?

Now we come to the Bull era at Borley Rectory, and it is here that, in my opinion, there lies the bulk of the historical causation of the hauntings, and it is this, coupled with the documentary evidence that ironically seems to vindicate the suggested background to the hauntings, that the late Harry Price *didn't* investigate.

Had he done so it is not unlikely that his critics would have had little with which to attack him over the Borley story. Only in his recording of the seance results did Price tough vaguely on the fringes of the role of the Bull family as a possible basis for the hauntings. For example, though he detailed the seance sessions at which the character of Kate Boreham came to light, and stated that her existence was proved by the parish records, he failed to attach much importance to the necessity for delving deeper into the matter. Over the years various things have come into the limelight concerning the Bull family, and these have appeared to be a mixture of fact and village gossip. It has been suggested that Henry Dawson Bull indulged in relationships with village girls, and that he died from syphilis. That the suggestion of an affair or series of affairs is certainly not impossible is supported by documents in public archives, indicating that Henry Dawson Bull died from an illness directly related with syphilis, *Locomotor Ataxia*, which is associated with tertiary syphilis. Also on record is the fact that he died at no great age even for those days. He was 59.

Another fact in this episode is that Kate Boreham certainly gave birth to at least one child whose date of baptism indicates it to have been born out of wedlock and though that doesn't prove that Henry Bull was the father, the suspicion is hard to avoid. The census returns for the parish of Borley fail to prove beyond doubt that Kate Boreham was employed as a maid at Borley Rectory, but between the census for 1881 and 1888, when she died, there is a period of her life and the records of the rectory, that cannot be definitely accounted for, during which time she could well have taken up a post at the Rectory. At the time of the 1871 census she was too young to be a maid, whilst by the time of the 1891 census she was dead! When we come to the matter of her death, there are two very telling points. Firstly, she is recorded as dying in Sudbury in a house that is not listed in any public records as ever having belonged to or been rented to the Boreham family and secondly, she is recorded as having died from cerebritis, but this is shown to be unreliable as a cause of death. The medical opinion does suggest that death from lead poisoning, incurred whilst trying to abort an unwanted pregnancy, might very well lead have been the true state of affairs. In addition to this, the recording of Kate Boreham as being buried in the churchyard at Borley at Easter 1888, which is what was entered by the Rev. Bull in the parish records, is not as it appears. The writer also suggests that what really happened to Kate was known to the Swiss governess, Maria Rolf, who was with the family in 1881, and who was very likely still there in 1888. A final point as to the truth of the Katie story lies in the reported finding of a part-used bottle of sugar of lead, which is a soluble substance, in a cupboard in the Rectory. I strongly suggest that the Kate Boreham episode is at the root of psychic disturbances at the Rectory, and that this matter came to light during the seance sittings of 1937, without the sitters realising the significance of the results.

Apart from the episode of the screaming girl, which remains impossible to substantiate, the final element of the Bull family's role in the Rectory disturbances is connected with the life of Harry Bull. The writer strongly suspects that Harry Bull was a disillusioned and troubled man, and that the final years of his life, from the time of his marriage to Ivy Brackenbury, was overshadowed by domestic conflict, and that this left an entrenched atmosphere in the Rectory, which only added to the essence of what had gone before.

The next element revolves around the Smiths and the Foysters and their part in the overall picture. From comments in the Hastings report, it is quite clear that both Guy and Mabel Smith believed the Rectory to be haunted, and that they both still held this view for a long time after moving away. Guy Smith remained convinced that the place was haunted from 1929 until his death in 1940, but not so Mabel Smith. After the war, she turned completely against the belief that Borley Rectory was haunted, and the critics have presented a case that with Price dead, Mabel Smith could, as they saw it, now tell the truth about the Rectory. The Hastings report, coupled with the effect on Mabel

Smith of her husband's death, reveals the real reason for her sudden about face. Far from having to do with telling the truth, it had to do with Mabel Smith trying to obliterate from her mind the whole Borley period of her life, because for her, their stay there had been very unpleasant. Taken in that context, Mabel Smith's feelings towards the reputation of the Rectory cannot be taken at face value, and it is by failing to allow for this that some of the main critics of the case have rendered their submissions invalid, especially in attempting to attack Harry Price's role in the Smith era.

It is over the tenancy of the Foysters that some of the most heated rows have blown up in connection with Borley. Many have tried to suggest that Lionel Foyster invented much of what went into his diary of incidents in the Rectory, whilst during the early stages of his involvement with the Foysters, before he wrote his first Borley book, Price thought that Marianne Foyster was to blame for some of the phenomena. He formed a different view after seeing the results of Sidney Glanville's investigations, and the evidences of the Whitehouse family. The claim that Lionel Foyster invented much of his diary entries is not by any means sufficient to accuse him of so doing with any surety, whilst Marianne's evidence since the war has been so contradictory that it cannot be accepted as proof one way or the other. Probably the fairest assessment one can give the Foyster period, and Price's coverage of it, is that the foundation of the reports are probably true and that Price presented what he believed to be the facts in good faith. The writer feels that even if one disregards the Foyster's own evidence, one cannot easily dismiss the evidence of other people who witnessed phenomena there during that same period, if for no other reason than for the number of witnesses and not all of them knew the Foysters or Harry Price.

We now come to Harry Price himself, Borley's pioneer investigator, an extraordinary man, either lauded as presenter of one of the greatest cases of haunting in modern times or despised as the biggest fraud the psychic world has ever known!

Price began his investigations into the hauntings at Borley Rectory in June 1929, and was still busy with correspondence on the case a few days before his death in 1948. To the public who read his two classic books on the story of Borley Rectory, there must have seemed little doubt that the hefty Victorian monstrosity built for the Rev. Bull was indeed the most haunted house in England. It is quite obvious, from both the books and, perhaps more importantly, from his files, that Price believed the Rectory to be haunted and presented it as such in good faith. As will be apparent from the view expressed by Guy Lyon Playfair, there is a body of opinion that thinks that Borley Rectory *was* haunted, but that Price's role in reportintg it was questionable. That is fair enough, but the general public, since 1956, has been led to believe that both the story of Borley Rectory and Harry Price's role in it amounted to nothing more nor less than a giant concoction and fraud. In the report of 1956, by Dingwall, Goldney and Hall, evidence was presented that purported to prove beyond doubt that Price, in his work on the Borley case, was guilty of fraud, duplicity, manufacturing evidence and misrepresentation on a grand scale. It now seems quite likely that Dingwall and Goldney started out with some genuine doubts and misgivings about Borley. It also appears likely that they took at face value the inclusion in their project the work of inimitable Mr Trevor Hall, having no idea at that time of how Hall would approach his share of the investigation. I believe that Hastings proved that the claim that the Borley story and Harry Price's role in it was a proven fraud can no longer be sustained, and that the allegations against Price over Borley are completely discredited.

All those attacks on Price over the haunting of Borley Rectory, if not disproved by the late Mr Hastings, must surely founder on the rocks of a defence of Price's work by a man who could not stand Price as a person, namely Nandor Fodor. Here was a man who was prepared to defend Price's integrity over Borley in spite of disliking him, and the writer submits that in the end, it will be those such as Fodor, Hastings and Underwood, whose work on Price's role at Borley will carry the banner for Borley Rectory, and not the attacks of his critics, though doubtless there will be those who will violently disagree with that opinion, and go on arguing about Borley for many years to come. Where Price did fail at Borley was in not carrying out enough scientific quantification of the phenomena, and in failing to investigate in sufficient depth, the possible historical background to the hauntings.

I only hope that in my own small way and humble efforts some of the gaps in Price's epic but controversial narratives have been filled, but obviously I must leave that judgement to my readers.

Now it is time to deal finally with the last drama and this concerns the fire itself!

For many years, the suggestion that the fire that gutted Borley Rectory happened under mysterious circumstances was almost taken for granted by the enthusiasts of the story. Certainly the 'Amures' threat of 1938, to burn the Rectory, proved to be prophetic, but in the memoirs of Sir William Crocker there appeared the first hints in print that the fire of February 1939 occured through other than paranormal causes, and yet there is in a way a curious sort of inevitability in the fire, almost as though it was a means to an end initiated by the spirits of those dead and gone, utilising the human weakness of a living occupier for whom the fire was also a means to an end!

But for the tracing of the two Gregson sons, it is very likely that the full story of the fire would yet be untold, but armed with the evidence of the two seemingly conflicting versions of the fire by the two sons, I would suggest that we now have the most likely facts behind the fire that destroyed the most haunted house in England. Whilst the two Gregson sons give conflicting accounts of how the fire occurred, the observant reader will no doubt realise that the two men have unwittingly revealed the likely truth by their very contradictions. The evidence in favour of Captain Gregson having set fire to the Rectory for the insurance money is quite strong, and the writer submits that Gregson did just that, sending both of his sons to call the fire brigade, probably believing that with both of them safely off the premises for some twenty minutes or so, whilst they went to the public telephone at Borley Green, he could make sure that the Rectory was burning like a torch before the brigade got there. And yet, at the same time, there is an undercurrent to the fire, and the writer suggests that, unwittingly, the Captain and his dubious intention was being used as an instrument of exposure of the truth of events long past! There will be those readers who will consider such an idea to be nonsense, and yet let us just remember one thing. Whoever the entity really was who produced the 'Amures' threat to destroy the Rectory, stated in that contact that the fire would signify the end of the hauntings at Borley Rectory and reveal the story of a murder that happened there, but the fire *did not* stop the disturbances! Could it be that the entity or entities that seemed to have preordained the fire intended that after it, someone should publicly reveal the evidence that the fire was supposed to reveal? If so, then one could suggest that perhaps the disturbances continued because this final part of the strange pageant of Borley Rectory was not enacted, and that the entities are still waiting for their task to be completed?

Over the past thirty years or so, this extraordinary story has alternated between scorn and high praise, and in spite of the frequent attempts to destroy the credibility of the haunting, each time when the dust settles, there it stands still, like the dome of St. Paul's, above war torn London, and overseen by the beleagured but obstinately resolute image of Harry Price! May I venture to conclude that in times far ahead, when the truth of the story of Borley Rectory has ceased to be of much concern, the substance of it will pass imperishably into English lore when the Prices, Halls, Dingwalls and the author have already been, for long, little more than crumbled dust in the ground.

SELECT BIBLIOGRAPHY

The volume of material that has been produced on the Borley Rectory case since 1929, is so enormous that it would take a work of this size to list it. However, the following selection constitutes some of the key sources of information about this extraordinary episode. There are great many essays of varying length in editions of the *Journal of the Society for Psychical Research,* also in the *Proceedings* thereof. Most of this material can be examined by the bona-fide researcher at the Harry Price Library of the London University and of course in the S.P.R.'s own library, by serious students.

Arthur C. Clarke's World of Strange Powers, Ed. Simon Welfare & John Fairley . . . Putnam 1984
An Examination of the Borley Report, Robert J. Hastings . . . . . . *Proceedings* SPR, Vol. 55, Mar 1969
Christmas Ghosts, Harry Price . . . . St. Hugh's Press (nd 1948?)
Confessions of a Ghost Hunter, Harry Price . . . . Longman Green 1936
Daily Mirror, article by V. C. Wall . . . . June 10th, 1929
East Anglian Magazine, article by Capt. W. H. Gregson, RE retd. . . . . Autumn 1939
English Mediaeval Monasteries 1066–1540, Roy Midmer . . . . Heinemann 1979
Far from Humdrum: A Lawyer's Life, Sir William Crocker . . . . Hutchinson 1967
Ghosts in the South West, James Turner . . . . David & Charles 1973
Ghosts and Hauntings, Dennis Bardens . . . . Zeus Press 1965
Hauntings, Peter Underwood . . . . Dent 1977
Haunted Borley, A. C. Henning . . . . Privately published 1949
Haunted East Anglia, Joan Forman . . . . Robert Hale 1974
History of Essex 1768, Joan Morant . . . . E.P. Publishing edn. 1978
Harry Price, The Biography of a Ghost Hunter, Paul Tabori . . . . Athenaeum Press 1950
Most Haunted House in England, Harry Price . . . . Longman Green 1940
My Life with Borley Rectory, James Turner . . . . The Bodley Head 1950
New Lights on Old Ghosts, Trevor H. Hall . . . . Duckworth 1959
Poltergeists, Hauntings and the Haunted, David C. Knight . . . . Dent 1977
Readers' Digest Strange Stories, Amazing Facts, p140 . . . . . Readers' Digest Assoc. Incorp. 1989
Search for Truth, Harry Price . . . . Longman Green 1940
Some Unseen Power, Philip Paul . . . . Robert Hale 1985
Sometimes Into England, James Turner . . . . Cassell 1970
The End of Borley Rectory, Harry Price . . . . Longman Green 1946
The Haunting of Borley Rectory (A Critical Survey of the Evidence),
   Dingwall, Goldney & Hall . . . . Duckworth 1956
The Ghosts of Borley, Peter Underwood & Paul Tabori . . . . David & Charles 1973
The Search for Harry Price, Trevor H. Hall . . . . Duckworth 1978

In addition to the above, there is also an enormous amount of often rather fragmented material dealing with Borley among the archives of such places as the Public Record Office, British Museum, Cathedral of Canterbury and elsewhere. Particularly interesting items are the following:

Calendars of State Papers Domestic, 1547 to 1580, Vol 16 and Vol 17.
Canterbury Charter, mss, Register. B. f176 and f178; Register K f253, Canterbury Cathedral Library.
Patent Rolls, 38, ed. 111.
Lambeth Court Rolls, 71A and 74.
Feudal Aids, Vol 2, pp 144 and 168.
Morant's History of Essex, Vol. 2, p 317.

INDEX